INTERNATIONAL
ORGANIZATIONS
AND DEMOCRACY

INTERNATIONAL ORGANIZATIONS AND DEMOCRACY

Accountability, Politics, and Power

Thomas D. Zweifel

LYNNE
RIENNER
PUBLISHERS

BOULDER
LONDON

Published in the United States of America in 2006 by
Lynne Rienner Publishers, Inc.
1800 30th Street, Boulder, Colorado 80301
www.rienner.com

and in the United Kingdom by
Lynne Rienner Publishers, Inc.
3 Henrietta Street, Covent Garden, London WC2E 8LU

Library of Congress Cataloging-in-Publication Data
Zweifel, Thomas D., 1962–
    International organizations and democracy : accountability, politics, and power /
Thomas D. Zweifel.
        p. cm.
    Includes bibliographical references (p.   ) and index.
    ISBN 978-1-58826-367-4 (hardcover : alk. paper)
    ISBN 978-1-58826-392-6 (pbk. : alk. paper)
    1. International agencies—Political aspects—Case studies.
    2. International agencies—Management—Case studies. 3. Democracy. I. Title.
JZ4839.Z86 2005
341.2—dc22

                                                                2005021178

British Cataloguing in Publication Data
A Cataloguing in Publication record for this book
is available from the British Library.

Printed and bound in the United States of America

       The paper used in this publication meets the requirements
 ∞   of the American National Standard for Permanence of
       Paper for Printed Library Materials Z39.48-1992.

       5   4

For Karin B. Zweifel
1965–1983

Contents

Tables and Figures

Tables

Figures

Acknowledgments

To acknowledge all my intellectual debts would take a whole book by itself, so I can mention only the highlights. I greatly benefited from early discussions with Valentin Zellweger on the International Criminal Court, and with Robert Weissman on multilateral economic institutions. Both helped me put my thinking in perspective, and continue to do so through their important work.

William Phelan and other participants at the 2002 annual meeting of the American Political Science Association critically reviewed my bureaucratic democracy indicators. My former students of international organization at New York University in the fall of 2001, immediately following the September 11, 2001, terrorist attacks, dealt directly with the topic of this book and generated case studies and heated discussions that helped both stimulate and challenge my ideas.

Special thanks go to Jillian Cohen and Johannes van de Ven for coauthoring the chapters on the World Bank, the International Monetary Fund, and the World Trade Organization. I am indebted to Yoram Wurmser and Elliott Bernstein, who did significant research for the chapters on global and regional organizations. Annis Steiner, Endre Boksay, and Liubov Grechen deserve thanks for additional research, and Jolie Carey, Lea Kilraine, and Nick Wolfson gave valuable feedback for the final manuscript. I thank two anonymous reviewers for their constructive criticisms and useful comments on earlier versions of the book. Of course, any mistakes are mine.

For almost half a decade, Lynne Rienner inspired the book with her original vision and unflappable guidance. Sally Glover and Lisa Tulchin saw the manuscript through to production; Karen Williams shepherded it through the production process; Jason Cook did a superb editing job; and Deborah Knox helped promote the book to the many audiences for whom it might be relevant. Their commitment to this long-standing project and their confidence in me are much appreciated.

I am grateful to my Swiss Consulting Group partners and colleagues in our global network for watching my back during the extensive research and writing of this book. It is their leadership and willingness to keep pushing beyond intellectual boundaries that created the fertile breeding ground on which this book could grow.

Above all, I thank my parents, Dr. Eva Wicki-Schoenberg and Dr. Heinz Wicki-Schoenberg, for introducing me to international affairs and for being my role models as global citizens.

INTERNATIONAL ORGANIZATIONS AND DEMOCRACY

Introduction

When the morning of September 11, 2001, came, I'd been working on this book for several months. The sky was deep blue and I was sitting on the Promenade at 8:46 A.M.—alone except for a few runners and dog walkers. Then the first plane hit the World Trade Center. Smoke and millions of tiny metallic glitters were in the air; a light wind drove them toward me. The glitters turned out to be white papers, documents flying across the East River. One of them was a FedEx envelope with a contract that someone had just signed when the first plane hit.

At 9:03 A.M. I saw another plane—so close to me that I thought it would fly up the East River—but it banked like a fighter, suddenly ducked behind a skyscraper, and a moment later disappeared into the South Tower. By this time I and about a dozen others were watching from the Promenade, speechless. We stood there immobilized. I called as many people as I could on my cell phone, but got through only to my parents in Sydney. I saw one tower collapse, then the other, and I sat down and wept. It was hard to breathe.

That morning changed my relationship with this book. The suicide attacks on the World Trade Center and the Pentagon made a glaring case for the need for global cooperation. To deal with terrorism and its root causes—and a host of other problems, from AIDS to the environment to trade and tsunamis—we need a global, multilateral response. Can international organizations represent the interests of humanity as a whole, rather than just those of a few? If they suffer from a democratic deficit,[1] how can they become more democratic? These are the questions this book asks.

Democracy is on the rise as a core value and the dominant governance principle worldwide. During the past generation, a "third wave" of democracy washed over many countries.[2] But international institutions have not necessarily followed suit; as states transfer more and more rulemaking powers to them, they suffer from a growing crisis of legitimacy. Surely, if a

1

national government gave its worst-off citizens no effective influence in its policies and laws but still ordered them to obey, we would call that government illegitimate.[3] The debate about the lack of democracy of international organizations will only get louder as they integrate more deeply and gain more power. But virtually no scholars or practitioners have systematically analyzed transnational democracy, let alone offered solutions.

Neither traditional international relations theory nor traditional democratic theory alone is capable of providing answers to the complex issue of a transnational democratic deficit. The two subfields of political science have existed largely in splendid isolation,[4] and have long ignored each other. Democratic theory has been concerned with making state power more accountable, while international relations has focused on interactions between states in a global system of anarchy and thus outside the reaches of political theory. In order to think about democracy at the international level, we must marry the two theoretical frameworks.

Students of the rational design of international institutions have begun this work of theoretical integration and asked why international institutions vary in their design. Other scholars have focused on international legalization to show how international law and politics are intertwined across a wide range of international institutions.[5] But perhaps as a result of their theoretical lenses, students of international organization have focused on the bargains states strike to create or change them, and have paid very little attention to their day-to-day operations.[6] This book aims to build on both literatures by exploring what I see as the missing link between institutional design and institutional performance: transnational democracy.

This book is *not* about the effects of international institutions on democracy *in* countries. It does not compare democracy, throughout the world or in any state now, to democracy before the founding of, say, the United Nations. Although questions about such issues as whether or not the World Bank has a democratizing effect on member states are no doubt worthy of further research, the book will not explain whether NATO helps democracy in Romania, nor whether the IMF does or does not alleviate poverty. In short, the book is not about the effectiveness of international organizations per se. But the core assumption of this book is that democracy is better for performance—that it leads to better policy outcomes than does dictatorship. For example, empirical studies, leaving everything else equal, have shown that democracies clearly outperform dictatorships in improving the quality of life.[7] The legitimacy and performance of organizations are linked: institutions that lack legitimacy are seldom effective over the long run.[8]

The book's focus is to scrutinize the democracy of international organizations themselves: the extent to which they and their policymaking are governed by democratic rules, formal or informal. In the twenty-first century, international institutions make more and more rules that affect our lives—from banking to the Internet, from trade to labor standards, from airline regulation to the environment—so this focus is of ever-increasing importance. The book is driven by another, unabashedly normative assumption: that institutions are not purely the result of path-dependence—they do not depend entirely on prior outcomes. Conscious design (and redesign) is not only possible, but also key in the development and change of international institutions.[9] I hope that this book will make a contribution to building global, regional, and functional organizations that are truly democratic—in other words, organizations that represent the interests and aspirations of the peoples they have been founded to serve.

Overview

Chapter 1 asks how transnational democracy can be enhanced in a global society. In a case study of *Yahoo! Inc. v. France,* it examines regulation of the Internet as the quintessential global space. The chapter builds on theories of democracy and delegation to develop a methodology, including seven dimensions of transnational democracy, for assessing and rating international organizations systematically. Chapter 2 gives a brief history of international law and organization.

The remainder of the book applies this theory and history to three types of international organizations: global, functional, and regional. Chapter 3 examines the democracy of global organizations, above all the United Nations. It evaluates the UN's transnational democracy and reviews the oldest international organization still active (the International Labour Organization) and the newest (the International Criminal Court) as case studies. The topic of Chapters 4 to 6 is the democracy of functional organizations. Chapter 4 covers the World Bank, Chapter 5 the International Monetary Fund, and Chapter 6 the World Trade Organization.

Chapters 7 to 9 discuss the democracy of regional organizations. Chapter 7 covers the European Union, the most prominent regional bloc that has moved from an international organization to a "regulatory state."[10] Chapter 8 covers the Organization of African Unity and its successor, the African Union, in a bold experiment to adopt for Africa the lessons from the EU. Chapter 9 deals with other regional organizations; some have a single focus on economics (e.g., NAFTA) or defense (NATO), while others are multipurpose organizations aspiring to emulate the EU (e.g., ASEAN).

Chapter 10 concludes the book, draws together the main findings, offers recommendations for improving transnational democracy, and gives stories that point to a new, elusive concept: global citizenship.

Notes

1. Williams 1991.
2. Huntington 1991. The wave started in southern Europe (Greece, Portugal, and Spain) in the 1970s and continued in the 1980s to Latin America (Brazil, Ecuador, Peru, Bolivia, Honduras, Argentina, Uruguay, El Salvador, Nicaragua, and Guatemala), Asia (Turkey, the Philippines, Korea, and Pakistan), and Africa (Uganda and Sudan, which later reverted to dictatorship). By the end of the decade, democracy had taken hold in much of eastern Europe (Poland, Hungary, Russia, East Germany, Czechoslovakia, Romania, and Bulgaria), Asia (Mongolia and Taiwan), Latin America (Panama and Chile), and Africa (Benin, Cape Verde, Zambia, Congo, Mali, Central African Republic, Madagascar, Niger, Malawi, South Africa, Sierra Leone). Of course, this statement is a sweeping generalization. To call some of these regimes democratic is a stretch; others, such as Sudan, Congo, or Pakistan, have since reverted to dictatorship.
3. Bohman 1999.
4. Wendt 1994.
5. See the special issues of *International Organization* 55(4) (Autumn 2001), on the rational design of international institutions, and 54(3) (Summer 2000), on international legalization.
6. Barnett and Finnemore 1999.
7. Zweifel and Navia 2000; Navia and Zweifel 2003.
8. Commission on Global Governance 1995: 66.
9. Koremenos, Lipson, and Snidal 2001.
10. Majone 1996.

1

Transnational Democracy: A New Framework

C onsider the big issues: international terrorism and violence in the Middle East; the threat of nuclear war between India and Pakistan and between North Korea and its neighbors; the spread of HIV/AIDS, mad cow disease, and SARS; global warming, the harvesting of rain forests, and the threat of tsunamis; pressures of overpopulation and migration; child labor, child prostitution, and child pornography; hunger and poverty; unstable financial markets and third world debt; national security and international arms trading; drug smuggling, white-collar crime, and Internet crime.

What do all of these challenges have in common? Each transcends national boundaries. Emissions of greenhouse gases by factories in the US Midwest compound global warming everywhere on the planet. Poverty and AIDS in Africa lead to mass migration into Europe. Child pornography spreads from eastern Europe or southeastern Asia via the Internet. So does online fraud: a twenty-five-year-old college dropout in Pakistan allegedly stole some $3 million in computer equipment from US companies without ever setting foot in the United States.[1] Transnational issues confront multiple nations and sometimes humanity as a whole. They present challenges that no individual nation-state can confront alone. With globalization, national governments are increasingly forced to delegate rulemaking and adjudicative powers to international institutions.

Some international bodies, like the International Atomic Energy Agency (IAEA), the Universal Postal Union (UPU), and the World Intellectual Property Organization (WIPO), are global and open to all states; others are regional or functional, like the North Atlantic Treaty Organization (NATO) and the World Trade Organization (WTO), with restricted memberships. Some give each state an equal vote, like the UN General Assembly; others, like the UN Security Council and the EU Council of Ministers, have weighted voting. Some are strongly centralized with large-scale operations and budgets (e.g., the World Bank and its thou-

5

sands of staff and billions of dollars in lending each year); others are little more than forums for consultation, like Asia Pacific Economic Cooperation (APEC), with small secretariats and tiny initial budgets. All are international governmental organizations (IGOs); together with international nongovernmental organizations (INGOs), whether large or small—like Amnesty International, Greenpeace, or The Hunger Project—they make up the system of international governance, which, simply put, is the process whereby an organization or society steers itself.

Since governance processes at the global level are inherently more fragile and uneven than in most national political systems, one characteristic of global politics is governance without a government.[2] Perhaps the last well-known person to seriously advocate a global government in the twentieth century was physicist and Nobel laureate Albert Einstein. Horrified by the atomic bomb and its destructive use in World War II, Einstein spoke out in favor of world government, mostly in order to prevent a world nuclear conflict—though he granted that it might mean global tyranny. "But I fear still more the coming of another war or wars."[3]

World government is unlikely to become a reality anytime soon. In its absence, international regimes create sets of rules, norms, and decision-making procedures to shape the expectations, interests, and behaviors of actors.[4] An institution is usually seen as international if it comprises at least three nations as contracting parties[5]—an explicit arrangement, negotiated among international actors, for prescribing, proscribing, and authorizing behavior.[6] International organization (singular sense) is a framework of trilateral or multilateral governance in which parties subject themselves, and their negotiation, to an institutional authority, a third party acting as arbitrator.[7] International organizations (plural sense) are the physical institutions—entities with names, offices, letterheads, rules, and procedures—that together constitute the practice of international organization.

One trend that set the twentieth century apart from previous centuries was the growth of such international organizations, particularly over the past fifty years, in virtually all fields of policymaking, from nuclear arms to human rights, from the environment to child labor, from biodiversity to trade. As we will see in the next chapter, on their history, international institutions used to be mere treatied entities among independent states. The terms "League of Nations" or "United Nations" show that at least initially, they were simply the sum of their parts: they had either no independent powers of their own, or only those that member states were willing to grant them. But that has changed in the past generation: many organizations have acquired supranational competencies. The General Agreement on Tariffs and Trade (GATT) and its successor, the WTO, tore down trade barriers around the world and helped boost world trade from $308 billion in 1950 to $9.1 trillion in 2003.[8] The World Bank and the International Monetary

Fund (IMF) can impose economic policies in Turkey, Tajikistan, and Togo. The EU is rapidly becoming a regulatory superstate with its own currency and central bank, courts and legislature, flag, and even armed forces—with the power to affect people's lives from Sweden to Sicily.

International regimes can gain (or lend) legitimacy when those who are addressed by a rule or a rulemaking institution see that rule or institution as being in accordance with generally accepted principles of "right" process; regimes prize such validation as evidence of their legitimacy.[9] But their legitimacy is under attack. Millions of end-users of multilateral institutions are speaking up and withdrawing legitimacy from them, reasserting their basic property rights over local resources, and demanding greater public accountability from transnational institutions and corporations.[10] Critics, from the far right to the far left and almost everything in between, couch their criticisms of globalization in the rhetoric of democracy and charge that international organizations are not democratic enough.[11] Some call the behavior of international organizations dysfunctional, even "pathological."[12]

Antiglobalization groups like "50 Years Is Enough!" go even further. They have given up hope that the multilateral economic institutions created at Bretton Woods in World War II can be democratized, and are working to abolish the World Bank, the IMF, and the WTO altogether. Seeing themselves as the global underdog against laissez-faire global capitalism and Coca-Cola monoculture, such groups tend to work without a sole leader or a hierarchy; they are led from the bottom up. They harness the technological power of globalization itself—from the Internet to virtual teams—to make known their grievances and organize with a speed unprecedented in history. They launched their first massive demonstration in the streets of Seattle in November 1999, when as many as 40,000 protesters marched to shut down the ministerial meetings of the WTO. The following year, they repeated their protests during the millennial meetings of the IMF and World Bank in Prague. In 2001, they held yet another protest in Genoa; swelling to more than 100,000 people, it was the biggest antiglobalization demonstration anyone had ever seen.

The movement is remarkably diverse: trade unionists and priests, communists and ecologists. Yet its credibility has suffered because its protests have often been accompanied by violence. A few hundred masked anarchists, who called themselves the "Black Block," clashed with security forces in a ruthless exchange of Molotov cocktails and rubber bullets. On July 20, 2001, a protester was killed for the first time in Genoa. While his blood made front-page headlines and helped publicize the antiglobalization movement further, it also allowed the movement's critics to paint the protesters into a corner of extremism.

But instead of talking about the protesters' tactics, we should ask the more important question: Are their complaints valid? If international organ-

Case 1.1 *Yahoo! Inc. v. France:* The Internet Versus the State

The Internet is the metaphor par excellence for the powers of globalization. Are nation-states still in charge in the current era of cyberspace? In a 2001 "Declaration of the Independence of Cyberspace," issued one month before September 11, 2001, Internet activist John Perry Barlow declared: "Governments of the industrial world, on behalf of the future, I ask you of the past to leave us alone. You are not welcome among us. You have no sovereignty where we gather. You have no moral right to rule us nor do you possess any methods of enforcement we have true reason to fear. Cyberspace does not lie within your borders."[a]

Despite such glorious declarations of independence, the Internet is not universally accepted as a global—let alone a lawless—space. In April 2000 the International League Against Racism and Anti-Semitism, together with the French Union of Jewish Students, sued Yahoo! Inc. over its sale of Nazi-related memorabilia on its auction sites. (Already in 1999, so many Germans had ordered *Mein Kampf* from Amazon.com that Hitler's book had made the top-ten bestseller list on Amazon's German site.[b]) The items were not auctioned on Yahoo!'s French site, where French law prohibits the sale of items that incite racism—but then the suit against Yahoo! was expanded to include its French subsidiary because it provided hypertext links to its US owner, Yahoo! Inc. In May 2001 the Paris Tribunal de Grande Instance ruled that the US site was in violation of French law, and that Yahoo! was to block French users from accessing its auction sites and specifically its Nazi insignia, which the court deemed an "offense to the collective memory of the French people."[c] Yahoo! France had to eliminate any navigational links to its parent company, and both companies were ordered to pay the equivalent of $1,371 in penalties to the plaintiffs. Yahoo! was given three months to adopt a technology that would block French users from its auction sites. The company faced fines of some $13,000 for every day it failed to comply.

It was nearly impossible to stop French users from viewing Nazi-related items sold on a US site, and their sale was permitted by the First Amendment of the US Constitution. But Yahoo! did comply. By January 2001 it had banned Nazi memorabilia from all its auction sites, less because of the French lawsuit than as a result of societal pressures and reputation costs. At the same time, Yahoo! filed a motion with a US district court to overrule the French ruling, arguing that French law was unenforceable because the company was based

(continues)

on US soil and protected by the First Amendment. In November 2001 the US court indeed refused to enforce the French ruling, since it would violate the free speech guarantees in the US Constitution.

Yahoo! Inc. v. France illustrates the clash of jurisdictions and the lack of a regulator or overarching legal regime to govern cyberspace commerce. The French ruling, although based on understandable and rational principles, established a precedent by allowing one state to interfere with the process of lawmaking and rights allocation for citizens and firms in another state. Yahoo! is a US-based company, and US law regulates the company's activities. But the company also has a subsidiary in France, which operates for French citizens under French law.

How sovereign are states in the cyber age? Is the Internet the vanguard of a new arrangement in which sovereign territorial entities are no longer at the top of the food chain? Policymaking has been national, rule-oriented, and issue-specific; the Internet marketplace is global, technologically dynamic, information-rich, and network-driven.

The lack of global, enforceable standards creates huge transaction costs—"anything that impedes the specification, monitoring, or enforcement of an economic transaction"[d] or simply put, the costs of negotiating, policing, and enforcing contracts. Actions in virtual space produce externalities (social costs) for people in real space. If cybercrime is not outlawed, people's identities can be stolen, and so can their money. When transaction costs are high, government can ensure an efficient allocation of resources by inducing private actors to internalize externalities or by making them liable for any harmful effects. The French ruling attempted this—by shifting the transaction costs onto Yahoo! But internalizing externalities is seldom feasible.[e] According to transaction-cost economics, an international organization or a multilateral agreement harmonizing cyberspace laws could greatly lower transaction costs, but would also ask states to give up more sovereignty.

A December 2003 UN conference organized by the International Telecommunications Union (ITU) resulted in the establishment of a UN working group devoted to more international oversight of the Internet's semiformal administrative bodies.[f] The WTO, another plausible candidate, does not seem to see itself as being in charge. According to one official there, "The WTO is totally unrelated to Internet issues."[g] This is not entirely true: WTO members face the challenge of building a predictable space for electronic commerce so that all consumers in all countries can benefit. The stakes are enormous: the information technology sector contributes to some 8

(continues)

Case 1.1   continued

percent of the US economy alone. In the final four years of the twentieth century, it yielded more than one-third of real output growth in the United States. Keeping electronic commerce outside the scope of the WTO would undermine trade liberalization and hinder innovation.[h]

In the absence of a global regime, regional or national bodies have stepped in. The Council of Europe held a convention on cybercrime in 2001. In a 1996 background paper, the European Commission had already granted that "each country may reach its own conclusion in defining the borderline between what is permissible and not permissible."[i] Individual states have imposed local Internet regulations and have shouldered the burden and costs of the technology and laws needed to "control" the boundless World Wide Web. China has installed firewalls against overseas sites and monitors strictly what users post online. In Iran, Internet service providers are required to prevent access to "immoral or anti-Iranian material."[j] Singapore and Saudi Arabia both filter and censor Internet content. South Korea has outlawed gambling websites.

But can nation-states stem the global tide? At the peak of their power over society, states claimed and exercised the right to control the substance of information and the means by which information was communicated.[k] This is no longer the case. States find themselves being challenged in their sole exercise of power over their populace. And as long as no international regime regulates the Internet, there will be a vacuum of authority.

Notes: Laura Azze, Endre Boksay, Annis Steiner, and George Tsinias provided research for this case study.

a. *The Economist,* August 11, 2001: 9.

b. Friedman 2000: 37.

c. *New York Times,* November 9, 2001: C5.

d. Dixit 1996: 38. See also Williamson 1985. The term "transaction cost politics" was first used in North 1990.

e. Conybeare 1980.

f. *New York Times,* December 15, 2003: A1.

g. Email message, November 2001.

h. Mann and Cleeland Knight 2000: 265.

i. European Commission Communication to the European Parliament, the Council, the Economic and Social Committee, and the Committee of the Regions, *Illegal and Harmful Content on the Internet,* Com (96) 487, Brussels, October 16, 1996.

j. *The Economist,* August 11, 2001: 9.

k. Strange 1996: 100.

izations are accountable only to the states that created them (as the name "international" implies), why should we care about their direct accountability to the public? This question brings up another: Under globalization, are nation-states still the primary actors in world politics, or have other actors emerged as their rivals?

Toward an International State

Realist observers of international affairs disagree that international institutions play an independent role in international politics. They see organizations like the UN as epiphenomenal (Greek for "showing up after the fact"); nation-states are and remain the principal actors in international relations. If we take government revenue as an indicator of state power, they have a point: in most of the world's richest countries, far from declining, government spending has actually risen since 1980.[13] The number of separate nation-states grew steadily during the twentieth century: from 62 in 1914, to 74 in 1946, to 193 at the turn of the century. Despite technological revolutions that have made the borders between states porous, and despite a global push toward free markets, at least two key competencies of the nation-state remain intact: its power to tax its citizens and spend some of their money (even in the most integrated of all international organizations, the EU, member states pay only 2.4 percent of their public sector spending to the Union),[14] and its monopoly on the legitimate use of violence, permitting it to punish its citizens for crimes and to send them into battle. The once-popular idea that the United Nations or some other international body should have a standing army of its own—and perhaps even a nuclear armory, with an international committee of several hundred people to decide whether and when it should be used—predictably failed to win approval. The monopoly of organized killing power is still the sole domain of the state and its main characteristic. And that monopoly is largely intact today, even as the EU is now building an armed "Eurocorps" of its own.

But realists might be wrong. The two major military engagements of the 1990s, the wars in Kosovo and the Gulf, demonstrated that international organizations are central features of modern international relations—even in the realm of security.[15] Institutionalist scholars agree with realists that anarchy prevails and that states are the primary actors in international relations. But in contrast to realists, institutionalists say that anarchy is conducive to the emergence of international organization, since states need to cooperate—in their own interest. Adherents of transaction-cost economics would add that because there is no world government, states have an incentive to create order and cooperation, if only to lower the costs of their transactions with one another.[16]

No matter their differences, these theories take two things for granted: that states are the primary actors under international anarchy and that their preferences do not change. But in a globalizing world where Microsoft has the ninth largest economy, this dual assumption has been under attack. For constructivists, anarchy among states is not inevitable, but "constructed" by the history of their interactions. States are embedded in networks of transnational and international social relations that shape their perceptions and roles; they are "socialized" to want certain things by the international society in which they and the people in them live.[17] Why did US decision-makers refrain from using nuclear weapons in the Vietnam War, even if, on grounds of anarchy and self-interest, dropping an atom bomb would have been a viable option to win that war (much like a generation earlier, when the United States dropped the bomb on Hiroshima and Nagasaki)? Constructivists have suggested that successive US governments held back on normative grounds: states follow norms not because it is in their self-interest, but because it is the right thing to do.[18]

The good news, according to constructivists, is that just as states can create a system of anarchy and self-help, they can create an alternative. As their ability to meet their needs unilaterally declines, so does their incentive to hang on to egoistic identities that give rise to such policies; and as their common fate grows, so does their incentive to identify with others. National interests can converge across borders through interdependence, and domestic values can converge in certain issue areas, as has already happened with the spread of global consumerism, technical standards, human rights, and standards of democracy.[19] Take NATO for example: even if the organization's original design reflected its members' self-interests, over time they arguably have come to identify with NATO and now see themselves as a collective identity.[20] This remodeling of national interests happened in countries around the Mediterranean: many states may not have wished to make the environment a priority, but a transnational coalition of experts (an "epistemic community") compelled them to change their minds and clean up the polluted waters.[21] We will see in the final chapter of this book that networks of activists motivated by principled ideas and values ("transnational advocacy networks")[22] can change the minds and policies of states. In the first grassroots campaign I ever witnessed, as a teenager in Switzerland—the 1970s global campaign to stop the promotion of infant formula to women in poverty—activists pressured governments to regulate Nestlé, the largest producer of infant formula and a transnational economic actor that warranted transnational networking.

Saying that structures are constructed is of course not the same as saying that they can be changed easily. Even social conventions confront actors as hard social facts—structures that cannot be altered within a given historical context. But states can form collective identities and interests, which in turn can transform systemic anarchy into an "international state":

a transnational structure of political authority that lacks a single head. This internationalization of authority has long been the case with NATO in the defense arena, but also in the arena of global capital flows.[23]

And constructivists are not alone. "World polity theory" proponents have shown that world cultural forces play a key causal role in constituting state characteristics and action.[24] Some have come up with a model of political community more unified than a loose confederation of states, but less centralized than a federal state, to build what they call "cosmopolitan democracy."[25] Others have argued for a "transnational civil society in which certain groups emerge and are legitimized (by governments, institutions, and other groups)."[26] In such a global civil society, shared understandings of state authority, and even sovereignty, can change. The expansion of human rights law is only one example of a conscious, collective effort to transform state sovereignty.[27]

Why is the idea of an "international state" important for this book? To apply the concept of democracy to the global realm, we need to think—in theory at least—of a global polity and a global population. An international state allows us to make that leap. If there is such an international state, it matters a great deal to know whether its institutions are democratic or dictatorial, and whether or not they represent the global citizenry.

Democratic Deficit

The rise of an international state brings up entirely new problems. As prominent democracy scholar Robert Dahl wrote, the boundaries of any nation-state are "now much smaller than the boundaries of the decisions that significantly affect the interests of its citizens";[28] in other words, decisions that your government had nothing to do with can now dictate much of your life, including, in the case of the EU, even your interest rates and what you eat. This erodes the autonomy of states and hence democratic control of their decisions. Michael Hardt and Antonio Negri, the authors of *Empire,* assert that "no national power is in control of the present global order. . . . If it is not national but supranational powers that rule today's globalization, however, we must recognize that this new order has no democratic institutional mechanisms for representation, as nation-states do: no elections, no public forum for debate."[29]

Few would disagree that international organizations suffer from a "democratic deficit" or an "accountability deficit."[30] It is generally acknowledged that all international institutions lack democratic procedures and compare badly with democratic nation-states in this regard (except perhaps the EU, whose democracy comes close to that of the world's most democratic federal polities, as we will see in Chapter 7).[31] Ten years after his first assessment, Dahl drew an even more sweeping conclusion, that international organizations are not and are not likely to be democratic:

> My argument is simple and straightforward. In democratic countries . . . it is notoriously difficult for citizens to exercise direct control over many key decisions on foreign affairs. What grounds do we have for thinking, then, that citizens in different countries engaged in international systems can ever attain the degree of influence and control over decisions that they now exercise within their own countries?[32]

There are three possible reactions to this democratic deficit of international institutions.[33] First, we can decry how undemocratic institutions are and urge caution in their use. Second, we can reject international organizations on the grounds that democracy and international relations are two incompatible concepts in two different domains, and that each concept is invalid in the other domain—much like "breathing" and "water," which are both valid terms, but "breathing under water" is deadly. Some proponents of these two views, especially among antiglobalization activists, have taken them to their logical conclusion and have urged the abolition of international organizations, above all the World Bank, the IMF, and the WTO. The problem with both responses is of course that they get us off the hook. If international organizations are just pawns of corporate or great power politics, then there is no accountability, nor can there be. Hence the third response: we can decry the lack of democracy of international institutions, but push for their reform and democratization. Instead of chiming in with the chorus of generalizations that puts all international organizations in the same box, it might be worthwhile to look systematically at *where, to what extent,* and *which* international organizations are undemocratic, with the aim to derive a nuanced assessment of their level of democracy and recommendations for improvements. The simple reason is that globalization cannot be stopped, and that international organizations are here to stay. In the words of *New York Times* columnist Thomas Friedman:

> The [antiglobalization] protesters fall into two broad categories: those who think the issue is *whether we globalize* and want to stop globalization in its tracks, and those who understand, as I would argue, that globalization is largely driven by technology—from the Internet to satellites to cell phones to PCs—which is shrinking the world from a size medium to a size small, whether we like it or not, and therefore the issue is *how we globalize.*[34]

Democracy Without Elections: Outsourcing, Delegation, and Control

Usually, definitions of democracy require elections as a key criterion.[35] "Democracy is a system in which parties lose elections. . . . [O]ne elementary feature—contestation open to participation[36]—is sufficient to identify a political system as democratic."[37] Such definitions don't help us much here, since most international bureaucrats wield power without being elected, without even being directly accountable to elected officials.[38]

But there are definitions of democracy without elections. One says: "Democracy is a system in which the demos can expect to play at least some causal role, sooner or later, in the activity by which changes in their leaders are engineered."[39] Another defines "a political system [as] democratic if it operates in such a way as to ensure that makers of law and policy are responsible to the people."[40] Even Dahl does not insist on elections as a prerequisite for democracy, because they imply "processes by which ordinary citizens exert a relatively high degree of control over leaders."[41] Indeed, changes in leadership can come about without elections, through the force of public opinion, for example. (The only case so far where the head of an international organization was ousted by public opinion involved the European Commission of Jacques Santer. The EU executive and its president were forced out of office in March 1999 after widely alleged corruption charges.)

It is not clear anyway whether elections ensure representation. Utilitarians like Jeremy Bentham argued long ago that legislative representation is impossible, since each person is the best judge of their own interests: "There is no one who knows what is for your interest, so well as yourself."[42] Jean-Jacques Rousseau wrote that legislative representation is impossible for the same reason, because it means "willing for others," and nobody can will for another.[43] Only the wearer can tell if the shoe pinches. But this does not mean that the wearer knows in advance whether the shoe will pinch him or her; in fact it is more likely that a shoe specialist will know.[44]

As at the national level, member states of international organizations delegate a great deal of lawmaking to specialists—agencies charged with developing international law, regulations, and policies. In short, delegation makes the difference between authority and raw power.[45] Why would states agree to "outsource" rulemaking to international organizations? Commonly accepted reasons for delegation are the complexity of decisions, the quality of decisions, and the expertise needed for decisions.[46] The modern administrative state requires highly complex and specialized expertise for many policy areas. Delegation to agencies is rational: it reduces decisionmaking costs that rise as legislation becomes more detailed and complex. States have limited resources (time, money, and relationships), so they must leverage them by delegating the details. Regulating and adjudicating are inappropriate for government departments. Precisely because they are not elected, agencies are more committed to policy continuity than politicians, who may care more about reelection; they are more flexible in policy formulation and execution; and they can handle controversial issues and enrich public debate.[47]

In short, delegation yields gains in efficiency. Just as a company's managers must ask themselves whether it is better for their firm to perform an activity (from manufacturing to billing to research) itself or to buy that activity on the market, we can say that members of a parliament, for example the US Congress or the German Bundestag, face a "make-or-buy" decision when they weigh the internal policy production costs of the committee system against the costs of delegation to an agency.

Take the regulation of airlines: policymakers get little credit as long as things go smoothly—but if a plane crashes, they face intense public scrutiny. Failures tend to be spectacular and well publicized. So airline regulation (like other information-intense policy areas) is an issue with only a political downside, and legislators whose chief interest is reelection will be only too happy to delegate it to an agency. By contrast, legislators will be loath to delegate tax policy (or other distributive issue areas like social policy, where there are winners and losers), but will write detailed laws that leave little or no discretion for agencies, to keep them in line. They will choose between "make" and "buy" depending on their political benefits relative to political costs.

In short, specialized agencies exist to lower transaction costs. In the words of Oliver Williamson, if consumers are poorly organized vis-à-vis a firm, lack the relevant information, and are unknown to one another, then "a bilateral governance structure between firm and consumers may fail to materialize. An agency equipped to receive complaints and screen products for health hazards could serve to infuse confidence in such markets."[48] This can happen at the national or international level. Just as national legislators delegate policymaking to national agencies, so national governments delegate it to international agencies when the political benefits outweigh the political costs, for example in reputation or credibility. Politicians in democracies have few incentives to develop policies whose results voters might not see until the next election; and since one legislature or majority cannot bind a subsequent one, public policies lack full credibility because they can always be overturned. Hence the move to independent agencies not subject to election cycles.[49] Similarly, national officials might delegate policymaking to multilateral agencies (for example, the IMF) to bolster the belief in their policies (IMF finance ministers can always protest to voters in their own countries that "our hands are tied—the Fund is forcing this tough policy on us").

To be sure, "delegation" need not be a dirty word—it can be compatible with representation. Based on theories of business management, the performance of an organization is determined not by *how much* authority is delegated, but by *how well*.[50] Delegation does carry risks though. If contracts and laws are analogous, agency losses from delegation are tantamount to transaction costs[51]—for example, when an EU member like France farms out the regulation of corporate mergers to the European

Commission, which then makes rules that have unwanted side effects for French firms. While delegation lowers some transaction costs, it does raise others, both before delegation (costs of selecting the right agents or rigging incentives for their performance) and after (costs of monitoring their performance, of punishing them when they shirk, or of their defecting from a ratified policy).[52]

If delegation is so risky, then why do policymakers outsource policy-making so often? Put less kindly, to shirk blame.[53] The blame-shirking model assumes that both benefits and costs of government programs are not perfectly perceived. Legislators work hard to improve perceived program benefits or to disguise responsibility for failure in the eyes of voters. (Ironically, the very act of shirking blame also weakens these legislators' claim to fame whenever success does happen.) Such blame-shirking may happen even more at the transnational level: the governments of member states have an incentive to delegate the authority—and pass the buck—for unpopular policies to multilateral agencies.

But even without blame-shirking, transnational dealings would still be highly uncertain. All too often, international contracts are incomplete, ambiguous, or insufficiently specific; power relations are unequal; and international bureaucrats know more than states do about global issues. The output of transnational bureaucrats is often undefined and hard to measure, and political institutions are missing that could benefit from controlling them.[54] As Max Weber had found already in the nineteenth century, bureaucrats can maintain their power because they make themselves the real experts, and keep and control virtually all information.[55]

The more uncertainty, the less likely is representation; the more ignorant citizens are about issues, the more officials can switch policies with impunity.[56] Uncertainty is bound to be greater around issues that transcend the borders of a citizen's own country—for example, CO_2 emission ceilings, cross-border mergers, or the ingredients of imported food (see Chapter 7, which discusses EU regulation of genetically modified organisms in foods). Uncertainty permits officials to incur rents: benefits from holding office other than total representation in the best interest of the public. Rents can range from receiving the perks of holding office, to preventing the success of rivals, to simply shirking rather than working. The more hidden their actions from public view, the more officials can get away with these rents—the infamous principal-agent problem.[57]

Principal-agent problems arise from relationships with conflicting interests and asymmetric information: the agent knows something the principal does not know, with the risk that the agent will exploit this edge strategically. Without information asymmetries between firms and regulators, there would be no rents for captured agencies to distribute, and without asymmetries between regulators and the public, it would be much easier to ensure that regulators fulfill their mandates (though the public might still incur organizing costs to enforce compliance).[58] Moral hazard and adverse selection[59] result because firms and regulators share private information that neither legislators nor consumers know, and because regulators are not always benevolent either.[60] Organized interest groups influence policymaking because they can provide politicians with information about regulatory performance. If they have sufficient resources, multinational firms, but also big nongovernmental organizations (NGOs), often have access to expertise and information rivaling those of the agency.[61]

Now that we have sketched out the principal-agent relationship in the abstract, we can explore a concrete example to see how knotty the dilemma is. Together, international organizations and their officials, from the UN Secretary-General to the UN staff to the World Bank's board of governors and so forth, are the agents. But in this case, who are the principals? We have already seen above that member states, even if they cofounded these organizations, are no longer their only principals. The World Bank is accountable not only to the US secretary of the treasury, but also to resource-poor people in developing countries. The IMF is accountable to those states whose money it is lending, but also to those whose lives it affects.[62] The next chapter will show that in the past generation, individuals have attained legal standing under international law, which makes the global citizenry an important principal whom international organizations must serve as agents. Not only that, but international treaties like the Kyoto Protocol or the UN's Agenda 21, a comprehensive blueprint for the planet's survival that came out of the 1992 Rio Summit, imply that ultimately international organizations should be accountable not only to humanity today, but also to future generations, and should override nation-states in the interest of the planet as a whole and all species living on it.[63]

Seven Dimensions of Transnational Democracy

Based on these delegation and agency theories,[64] we can now build an analytical framework for systematically evaluating transnational democracy. Such an approach would have to be based on multiple dimensions, since the term "democratic deficit" refers to multiple defects of public policymaking: lack of transparency, insufficient public participation, insufficient reason-giving, excessive technical and administrative discretion, and inadequate mechanisms of control and accountability.[65]

Appointment

A key mechanism of checking bureaucratic discretion (and indiscretion) is appointment and removal power.[66] How are key officials appointed or elected, and what is the agency's governance structure (single-headed agency, multi-headed commission, self-regulatory organization, etc.)? Are key prospective agency officials vetted by a directly elected legislature? Do principals (member states and ultimately their citizens, or an elected parliament) have a "club behind the door" to throw the agents out if they don't perform?[67]

Another facet of the appointment dimension is membership. Who can belong to the institution—only states, or also nongovernmental actors? What are the membership requirements? (NATO will not accept a new member state until it has secured democracy and civilian control of the military.[68] In 2001 the Organization of American States [OAS] adopted its Inter-American Democratic Charter, which suspends a member state that has "an unconstitutional alteration of the constitutional regime that seriously impairs the democratic order." In 2000 the Organization of African Unity [OAU] adopted its Response to Unconstitutional Changes of Government, which would trigger condemnation by members and provisional suspension from OAU policy bodies.[69]) And what are the voting rules? Is every vote equal, as in the UN General Assembly, or do some states have more voting power than others, as in the UN Security Council or in the EU Council of Ministers? The voice of rising powers is likely underweighted and the voice of former powers exaggerated in long-standing institutions, compared to how brand-new institutions would weigh them.[70]

Note that the unequal power of states need not be codified in official voting rules and can still be real. In the International Commission for the Protection of the Rhine Against Pollution (or Rhine Commission), several states share the river. Each state pollutes it but uses it for drinking water too. Even if all Rhine Commission states have equal weight, the states upstream (for example, France or Germany) have more de facto power than the ones downstream (for example, the Netherlands), since upstream states cause more of the pollution problem but have less interest in solving it, while downstream states cause less of the problem but have more of an interest in a solution. Regime designers have to be cognizant of such informal power differences.[71]

A final aspect of appointment is funding. With appropriate transfers, principals can prevent collusion by agents.[72] At the same time, states that contribute more than others to an institution (as the United States does in the UN and the World Bank, for example) often demand more sway. Membership and voting rules typically formalize this control, as in the weighted voting of the UN Security Council and the IMF.[73]

Participation

Already in the nineteenth century John Stuart Mill had demanded participation in government by all: "It is important that everyone of the governed have a voice in the government, because it can hardly be expected that those who have no voice will not be unjustly postponed to those who have."[74] In 1948 the Universal Declaration of Human Rights followed Mill's principle: Article 21 provided for the right of all persons to take part in government. A generation later, in 1976, the Civil and Political Covenant entered into force. Its Article 25 extends to every citizen the rights to take part in the conduct of public affairs, directly or through freely chosen representatives; and to vote in and to be elected at genuine periodic elections that shall be held by universal and equal suffrage and by secret ballot, guaranteeing the free expression of the will of the electors.

What are the requirements for public participation in an institution's decisionmaking? Is it designed to amplify signals from the electorate?[75] For example, must the institution hold public hearings, and does it encourage and/or financially sponsor the participation of diffuse, weakly organized interests? Can people like you and me—and ultimately the worst-off members of the global community—influence public decisions that will affect our lives? "Without such accessibility, there can be no basis for accountability to transnational publics."[76] Effective democracy must help enfranchise underrepresented interests such as shareholders, consumers, and employees, and must ally with groups excluded from the alliance of managers and politicians in the modern polity. The task of public policy is *not* to prevent special interest group pressures from affecting regulation (this would be virtually impossible anyway), but rather to ensure that the pressures to which regulators respond are reasonably representative of society at large.

Nongovernmental actors, for example multinational corporations, industry associations, or transnational NGOs, can impact decisions in policy areas over which they have influence.[77] At least once, as Thomas Friedman illustrates in his discussion of General Electric and other companies in India, corporations brought India back from the brink of war—acting purely in their own self-interest—by threatening to look for other countries where they might move their outsourcing if India went to war.[78] (Of course corporations can be a less benign influence too.) NGOs can exert pressures that are in some respects functional equivalents of checks and balances.[79] INGOs like Greenpeace can push for changes in the regulation of genetically modified foods. And transnational advocacy networks of diverse actors can move issues up on the international agenda, and influence positions, policies, and behaviors of states, multinationals, and international organizations.[80] For example, groups fighting exploitative child labor entered alliances with UNICEF and obtained funding they needed to be effective against entrenched interests.[81] Broad-based civic participation does not guarantee wise policymaking, but it does give a voice to those who must live with the results of policies.

Another facet of the participation dimension is decentralization, which can reduce the likelihood of agencies being captured by particular interest groups.[82] Decentralization means diffusion of power, which is "a functional equivalent to democracy."[83] Is the power to decide on a policy devolved to some mechanism of local public choice?[84] How much ultimate authority and sovereignty do principals (in this case member states) keep when they delegate tasks to international organizations as agents? For example, under the WTO the retaliation of states against other states must be centrally authorized, while the Organization for Economic Cooperation and Development's 1998 Anti-Bribery Convention leaves enforcement to domestic lawmakers and courts. The International Labour Organization (ILO) is a hybrid: highly formalized, but quite decentralized.[85]

Transparency

How can the public observe agency behavior when information is incomplete?[86] Are the decisionmaking procedures clear and accessible to the public? Do affected interests have access to information? For example, does the agency hold votes on its decisions, and is it required to make these votes public? In its first thirty years, the Antarctic Treaty operated under unanimity rule for changing the treaty, making it impossible for outsiders to see how it made its decisions; now member states can press for changes under the more transparent majority rule.[87]

Transparency is necessary for the agency's credibility; its aim is not to banish the influence of political pressures, but to make those pressures visible.[88] The organization can strengthen its "output legitimation" by granting individual rights and access to information on policy implementation. If the US president delegates to the US trade representative authority for negotiations in the WTO, transparency is crucial. The public has a right to know what the agent did.

Reason-Giving

Public accountability requires reason-giving.[89] The representative must not only do what is right, but also tell constituents why it is right.[90] This requirement is centuries old: already Jeremy Bentham had written that the representative "must enlighten the people, he must address himself to the public reason; he must give time for error to be unmasked."[91] Officials make better decisions if they must give reasons for them. "Giving reasons is a device for enhancing democratic influences on administration. . . . The reasons-giving administrator is likely to make more reasonable decisions than he or she otherwise might and is more subject to general public surveillance."[92] Is the agency required to publish reasons for its decisions, and are these reasons widely and easily accessible, for example in the mass media and on the Internet? Paradoxically, an agency committed to objective analysis has an interest in its own potential embarrassment by making its procedures as clear as possible: this signals to firms its refusal to be manipulated.

Reason-giving is linked to what Giandomenico Majone calls "accountability by results," another important standard of substantive legitimacy. A key condition for accountability by results is that "objectives must be clearly specified: ambiguous or multiple objectives make it difficult to assign precise responsibilities."[93] While some leaders of international organizations, for example James Wolfensohn, the former president of the World Bank, practiced reason-giving informally, others have made it law. Reason-giving was ensconced already in the 1951 Treaty of Paris, establishing the EU's predecessor, the European Coal and Steel Community (ECSC). Article 5 provided that "the Community shall . . . publish the reasons for its actions," Article 15 that "decisions, recommendations, and opinions of the High Authority shall state the reasons on which they are based."[94]

Overrule

James Madison wrote in the eighteenth century that diversity is important for fair democracy, because the variety of parties and interests in a large republic makes it less likely that factions "will have a common motive to invade the rights of the other citizens; . . . where there is consciousness of unjust or dishonorable purposes, communication is always checked by distrust in proportion to the number of whose concurrence is necessary."[95] But the assumption that diverse factions will naturally check and balance each other is a leap of faith. A crucial feature of checks and balances is the capacity to overrule,[96] which needs to be granted by law. What are the procedures for agency decisions being overruled by principals or by judges in a court?[97] Are political decisions to overrule the agency taken transparently and according to clearly defined and generally known rules? For example, can democratic NATO member states veto NATO decisions? (The short answer is yes.) Can independent judges overrule World Bank policies? (The answer is no.)

Monitoring

Since specialists are usually better informed than principals, a key agency problem is monitoring. The intensity of monitoring is the probability that a directly elected legislature, an interest group, or another affected party discovers that the agency has not carried out its mandate.[98] What is the extent of monitoring through ongoing legislative or executive oversight,[99] the budgetary process, citizens' complaints, or peer review?[100] Is there an elected legislature, and if so, how directly can it monitor the agency? For example, are there regular, institutionalized meetings and reports in which the agency must account for its work to its principals?

States may set up a central monitoring institution or empower a quasi-legislative institution to keep moral hazard problems in check.[101] Monitoring can theoretically be improved by two options: either by creating a supranational legislature, or by giving national legislatures direct oversight over international institutions. In the EU, both options exist: there is a parliament and, for example, Denmark's legislature monitors EU decisionmaking—but only the parliament's European Committee, not all lawmakers, exercises oversight, and it does not receive timely information.[102]

Independence

The above six criteria by themselves are all necessary, but not enough for bureaucratic democracy. First, accountability is not the same as democratic accountability. The influence of a powerful member state like China or the United States may deepen the bureaucratic accountability of an international organization—but to whom? The answer is, to that member state and not to broad interests. One hegemonic member state might single-handedly exert influence on the hiring or firing of key international organization officials, as happened when the United States opposed, and denied, a second term for Boutros Boutros-Ghali as Secretary-General of the UN, and instead pushed through Kofi Annan's appointment. Such influence increases accountability but reduces transnational democracy. Neither was it democratic when the inept Senegalese head of the United Nations Educational, Scientific, and Cultural Organization (UNESCO) was kept in office by a one-state, one-vote majority of undemocratic African states, leading the United States and some other democracies to withdraw from the organization.[103]

Second is the issue of the perfect accountability relationship. John Stuart Mill wrote that in such a relationship, "the rulers should be identified with the people, their interest and will should be the interest and will of the nation."[104] But is this sort of perfect accountability desirable? Madison countered that a complete, one-to-one congruence between the popular will and policy decisions by rulers is not in the best interests of the people, since public opinion can be uninformed and fickle. (Imagine what would happen if, on a whim, most citizens of a country voted to abolish taxes altogether, which would benefit them short-term, but with disastrous consequences.) If representatives are 100 percent accountable in Mill's sense, then the exact same passions and transient interests that affect the people will be transmitted to their delegates, the representatives.[105] The US framers created both the Senate and judicial review as checks against too much accountability; and, as Alexander Hamilton argued, "the courts were designed to be an intermediate body between the people and the legislature in order, among other things, to keep the latter within the limits assigned to their authority."[106]

If too much accountability of elected politicians can be bad for democracy, it is even worse for agency officials with special expertise. In the United States, congressional delegation has been decried as abdication of the responsibility to govern: legislators surrender their powers to unelected bureaucrats, and special interests cozy up to the very bureaucrats supposed to regulate them while legislators look the other way. Policy reflects the demands of these special interests—at the expense of consumers and the public at large.[107] This view is not new: already Karl Marx, and before him Baron Charles de Montesquieu and the American Federalists in their own words, had warned that governments are merely executive committees of the bourgeoisie and big business. For this reason we must add to the six criteria of bureaucratic accountability a seventh, as a sort of counterweight to them: independence.

How independent is the agency from political processes? To what extent has the principal delegated decisions to the independent agent?[108] For example, on whom does it depend for funding? How independent is it in personnel matters?[109] How limited or expansive is the scope of regulation the agency enjoys?[110] Much like in a large corporation, where shareholders grant authority to corporate officers, but (at least on paper) supervise them through shareholder meetings and a board of directors, states give some autonomy to international institutions, which enhances their efficiency and effectiveness in implementing international agreements. This independence gives international organizations vital agenda-setting powers and the opportunity to lead. The UN Secretary-General may put in front of the UN Security Council any matter that in his opinion threatens international peace and security. The UN Environment Programme kept ozone protection alive when interstate negotiations deadlocked, and built support for the Montreal Protocol to prevent global warming. Not only this, but independence also means impartiality and neutrality. States can give resources to multilateral agencies—from funds to information to peacekeeping troops—without the impression of doing so for selfish reasons.[111] Independence is crucial for enforcement and performance.

We can distinguish between legal/formal and actual independence. Since actual independence is hard to see, research has stressed legal independence: clear rules on the appointment, dismissal, and terms in office of top officials; clear mandates and objectives; clear final authority for decisions; clear conflict resolution rules between governments and agencies; and clear freedom from government influence.[112] Agencies also need to be independent of undue influence by special interests: independence is the opposite of capture by private interest groups,[113] whose lobbying power likely increases more than proportionately with the resources spent on lobbying, thereby disadvantaging other interest groups.[114] Agency officials can be captured by a regulated industry, but also by government and even by other bureaucrats.[115]

*   *   *

What about an eighth dimension: To what degree does an institution carry out its mandate and produce the results it should? This dimension is about "output-oriented" legitimacy (effectiveness and performance) as opposed to "input-oriented" legitimacy (the seven indicators detailed above).[116] But output accountability is not a separate dimension for our purposes. Institutions cannot be accountable to the people they are sworn to represent without serving them.[117] As we will see when examining the World Bank, for example, there is a direct link between input and output accountability; wherever the Bank lacks input legitimacy, its outputs will reflect this. Like in John Rawls's view that procedural justice (or fairness) and substantive justice (or fairness) are connected,[118] greater accountability and independence at the input stage enhances greater output accountability; inputs and outputs are directly linked. That is why we don't need a separate output accountability indicator.

We could of course take the position that output legitimacy by itself is enough to legitimize international organizations. If the United Nations Children's Fund (UNICEF) helps children all around the world, who cares whether UNICEF's head is selected in democratic procedures or appointed by the powers that be? If the UN makes a difference in combating AIDS, does it matter whether the UN Secretary-General was democratically elected or whether his appointment was pushed through by the United States? If output legitimacy were sufficient for transnational democracy, we could simply measure certain quality-of-life indicators (e.g., life expectancy or literacy or infant mortality) before the existence of an international organization charged with improving those indicators, such as the World Health Organization (WHO), and compare the same indicators after that organization's inception. But this would be dangerous: unless there are democratic controls today, there is no guarantee that international organizations will not suddenly stop delivering the goods tomorrow or that their leaders will not suddenly turn corrupt. It is a basic premise of this book that greater democracy produces better outputs, as research has shown at the national level in 138 countries.[119]

In sum, there are seven dimensions for evaluating transnational democracy: appointment, participation, transparency, reason-giving, overrule, monitoring, and independence. In concluding this chapter, a quick word about mechanics is in order. How do we match these seven indicators against actually existing organizations? I have built a crude system that rates an institution in each dimension: a rating of +1 where its transnational democracy is strong, 0 where it is medium, and –1 where it is weak. Of course I could be accused of oversimplifying the complexities of international organizations with this "one size fits all" approach. We know that a legal body like the International Criminal Court is vastly different from an alliance like NATO or a regulatory body like the EU Commission. But the advantage of applying the same seven dimensions to the institutions across the board is that we can compare them and perhaps begin to develop reliable standards of transnational democracy for any type of institution (multinational firms or nongovernmental organizations or religious groups). The ratings are admittedly subjective (I based them on each organization's stated rules, other key documents, the literature about it, and interviews with informed observers). Each indicator carries equal weight, while in the real world, some dimensions may matter more than others. For example, one might argue that the appointment dimension should carry double weight, since an institution's officials, once selected, make rules that shape other dimensions, such as overrule or independence.[120] But the final chapter will show that a double weight for appointment would not change the transnational democracy ranking—at least of the eleven organizations reviewed here—at all.

Notes

1. *New York Times,* January 20, 2003: A3.
2. Rosenau and Czempiel 1992; Rosenau 1998.
3. *New York Times,* May 7, 2002: F1. Another Nobel laureate, eccentric mathematician John Nash, renounced his US citizenship and insisted on being recognized as a global citizen—but in vain.
4. Goldstein et al. 2000: 385. See also Krasner 1983: 1; and Keohane 1984. Following Mitchell and Keilbach 2001, I use the terms "regime," "institution," and "organization" interchangeably.
5. Slomanson 1995: 99–100. Agreement on this definition is not universal, by the way. One standard work on international organization defines even bilateral institutions as international as long as they have "participants from more than one state." Jacobson 1979: 4.
6. Koremenos, Lipson, and Snidal 2001. Koremenos and colleagues also include "well-defined (and explicit) arrangements like 'diplomatic immunity' that have no formal bureaucracy or enforcement mechanisms but are fundamental to the conduct of international affairs" (Koremenos, Lipson, and Snidal 2001: 76). Given the focus of this book on the democracy of institutions, I do not include such arrangements.
7. Williamson 1985: 71–78.
8. WTO press release, October 25, 2004.

9. Franck 1990, 1992b.

10. Korten, Perlas, and Shiva 2002: 19.

11. Moravcsik 2004.

12. Barnett and Finnemore 1999.

13. "Survey: The New Geopolitics," *The Economist,* July 31, 1999: 8. Both tax revenue and government spending, as a percentage of gross domestic product, increased after 1980 in Australia, Canada, France, Italy, Japan, Spain, Sweden, and the United States. In Britain, tax revenue increased as well, but spending decreased from 43.0 to 40.2 percent. In Germany, both declined slightly (tax revenue from 38.2 to 37.5 percent, government spending from 47.9 to 46.9 percent).

14. Majone 1997a: 14.

15. Koremenos, Lipson, and Snidal 2001.

16. It is not sure, by the way, that institutions universally lower transaction costs for participating states. According to Barbara Koremenos and colleagues, "Establishing and participating in international institutions is costly." But they also argue that with increasing numbers of members, an organizational structure replaces a large number of bilateral negotiations or even a cumbersome multilateral one. Koremenos, Lipson, and Snidal 2001: 782–788. See also Keohane 1984 or Martin 1992. Note that transaction costs can be uneven and can give wealthy countries an advantage. For Bangladesh, sending even one attorney to Geneva for a WTO dispute panel is a significant cost. For the United States, sending a legal team of twenty attorneys to the same panel comes at a much lesser cost relative to the US government budget.

17. Finnemore 1996: 2.

18. Tannenwald 1999; Wendt 2001.

19. Wendt 1994.

20. Wendt 2001.

21. Haas 1989.

22. Keck and Sikkink 1998: 1–14.

23. Wendt 1994; see also Cox 1987: 253–265; and Hurrell 1990. Also, Martin Shaw talks about a global state to describe what he sees as the reestablishment of the monopoly on legitimate organized violence under the tutelage of the United States. Shaw 1997.

24. Meyer and Hannan 1979; Thomas et al. 1987.

25. "Cosmopolitan democracy is a project to build a world order capable of promoting democracy on three different but mutually supporting levels: (1) democracy inside nations; (2) democracy among states; (3) global democracy." Archibugi 1998: 209.

26. Hurrell and Woods 1995: 464.

27. Sieghart 1985: 67–68.

28. Dahl 1989: 2, 318–320.

29. *New York Times,* July 20, 2001: 21.

30. Aksu and Camilleri 2002; Stephan 1999: 1562.

31. Zweifel 2002b.

32. Dahl 1999: 32.

33. Keohane and Nye 2001a: 1–2.

34. *New York Times,* July 20, 2001: 21, emphasis in original.

35. For an overview, see, for example, Schumpeter 1976 [1942]: 269; Downs 1957: 23; Lipset 1960: 71; Huntington 1991: 7; or Inkeles 1990: 3–6.

36. Dahl 1971: 20.

37. Przeworski 1991: 10.

38. This need not mean that bureaucracies are out of control. B. Dan Wood and Richard Waterman found that the bureaucracy and its expertise can be a corrective that produces policy more consistent with the public good, and stands as a check on the abuse of power by politicians. Wood and Waterman 1994: 144.

39. Dunn 1999: 343.

40. Plamenatz 1973: 69.

41. Dahl 1956: 3.

42. Bentham 1843, vol. 3: 33.

43. Rousseau 1905–1912, vol. 3: 318.

44. Pitkin 1967: 204.

45. Grant and Keohane 2005: 4.

46. Fiorina 1985.

47. Majone 1996: 63.

48. Williamson 1985: 309.

49. Majone 1998: 3–4; 1997.

50. Kiewiet and McCubbins 1991: 19.

51. Epstein and O'Halloran 1999: 45–48.

52. Horn 1995.

53. Fiorina 1985: 176.

54. Frey 1984: 221.

55. Warren 1991: 51.

56. Stokes 1990.

57. The "prototypical principal-agent problem analyzes the difficulty that one actor (the principal) will have getting another actor (the agent) to work on her behalf in the presence of incomplete information." Epstein and O'Halloran 1999: 39. See also Wildavsky 1964; and Schultze 1968. The terms *principal* and *agent* come from information economics: "Assume a bilateral relationship in which one party contracts another to carry out some type of action or to take some type of decision. We will refer to the contractor as the *principal,* and the contractee as the *agent.*" Macho-Stadler and Pérez-Castrillo 2001: 4.

58. Neven et al. 1993: 170.

59. Put simply, moral hazard is the risk that the presence of a contract will affect the behavior of one or more parties. Moral hazard stems from the fact that under asymmetric information, once the principal has accepted a contract with the agent, the agent will choose the level of effort that maximizes his utility, but the principal cannot verify whether the agent puts in low or high effort. The classic example is in the insurance industry, where coverage against loss can increase the risk-taking behavior of the insured: somebody who is insured might smoke more—a behavior that is difficult for the insurance provider to monitor—and increase the financial risk to the insurance provider. "In moral hazard situations, the principal cannot observe the agent's behaviour (actions or decisions). . . . An adverse selection situation appears when, previous to the signing of the contract, the agent is aware of some relevant information of which the principal is ignorant." Macho-Stadler and Pérez-Castrillo 2001: 6–7. Adverse selection in a political context is the difficulty voters have distinguishing between "good" and "bad" regulators, which leads to the prevalence of low-quality regulators.

60. Laffont and Tirole 1993: 35–45.

61. Banks and Weingast 1992.

62. Grant and Keohane 2005: 5.

63. I owe these potentially far-reaching thoughts to an anonymous reviewer.

64. See Zweifel 2002a: 65–73 for a review of the so-called congressional con-

trol literature on whether or not the US Congress—and by extension the directly elected European Parliament—can control regulatory agencies.

65. Majone 1996.

66. Moe 1985.

67. Note that the agent's accountability does not have to mean that the principal is happy with the agent's performance. It does mean that the principal, having the means to replace the agent with a feasible alternative, has no inclination to do so. Laver and Shepsle 1997.

68. Kydd 2001.

69. Clark 2002: 114–115.

70. Koremenos, Lipson, and Snidal 2001: 1076.

71. Mitchell and Keilbach 2001.

72. Laffont and Tirole 1993: 630. Koremenos and colleagues call this dimension "control." Koremenos, Lipson, and Snidal 2001: 772. But sometimes it is the other way around: a multilateral organization like the World Bank has the power to withhold resources from states, which gives the Bank significant leverage over weaker states.

73. Koremenos, Lipson, and Snidal 2001: 790–792.

74. Mill 1879: 21.

75. Sutherland 1993.

76. Bohman 1999: 507.

77. Keohane and Nye 2001a.

78. Friedman 2002.

79. Rosenau 1998: 42.

80. Keck and Sikkink 1998: 25.

81. Beetham 1998: 67.

82. Neven et al. 1993: 3, 11, 166. However, decentralization need not enhance accountability. It may instead compound information asymmetries, and member states may leverage the threat of autonomous decisionmaking to extract political concessions from the central authority. Neven et al. 1993: 181.

83. Rosenau 1998: 40.

84. Seabright 1996.

85. Koremenos, Lipson, and Snidal 2001: 761–799, 1058–1060. Koremenos and colleagues are ambivalent on centralization: "Will resources be squandered in bureaucratic excess? Even more important, will international agencies expand their authority over time? Consequently, states view centralization warily, and its overall baseline level may remain quite low" (p. 791). On the other hand, "contrary to the common presumption that centralized institutions are more effective, more centralization is not always better. States design international institutions to meet specific needs, and decentralized arrangements often serve this purpose more effectively" (p. 1060).

86. Minford 1995. Incomplete information means that not all information relevant to a particular situation is available to the participants. The assumption of incomplete information is more realistic than the perfect information assumed by orthodox economics, wherein all actors make perfectly rational decisions based on having all the relevant information—for example, about prices or quality.

87. Koremenos, Lipson, and Snidal 2001: 794.

88. Neven et al. 1993: 219.

89. Majone 1998: 13–14.

90. Pitkin 1967: 206.

91. Bentham 1930: 77.

92. Shapiro 1992: 183.

93. Majone 1998: 19. But note that in the context of reason-giving, accountability by results is not to be confused with output accountability, which is really about the performance and efficiency of an institution. See Chapter 4 in this volume, on the World Bank, for the relationship between output and input accountability.

94. Incidentally, these reason-giving requirements were—and to some extent still are—not only different from, but also more advanced, than national laws. Hartley 1988.

95. Madison 1981 [1787]: 22.

96. Bulmer 1994.

97. Sutherland 1993.

98. Bendor 1988.

99. Finer 1940–1941.

100. Shapiro 1997.

101. Koremenos, Lipson, and Snidal 2001: 795.

102. Hegeland and Mattson 1996.

103. Keohane and Nye 2001a.

104. Mill 1874: 24.

105. Sanchez de Cuenca 1997.

106. *Federalist Papers* nos. 63, 78.

107. Lowi 1969.

108. Persson et al. 1993.

109. Eijffinger and de Hahn 1996: 2.

110. Laffont and Tirole 1993: 4–5.

111. Abbott and Snidal 1998.

112. Eijffinger and de Haan 1996: 5–7.

113. McConnell 1966.

114. Krueger 1974.

115. Noll 1989.

116. Scharpf 1999.

117. Fox 2000.

118. Rawls 1993: 421.

119. Zweifel and Navia 2000; Navia and Zweifel 2003.

120. I owe this suggestion to an anonymous reviewer.

2

A Brief History of
International Organization

B efore we analyze the democracy of international institutions, we should
first understand their historical evolution, including the evolution of
international law, which is their underpinning and foundation: international
organizations are the products of international law.[1] Somewhat analogous
to the domestic level, where law aims to ensure order and rightful behavior
of the members of a national community, international law is a code of
behavior designed to guide, as much as possible in a relatively anarchic
international system, the behaviors of members of the international community. This brief historical journey will give us an appreciation of the
forces acting on transnational democracy today.

Precursors of International Organization

How did states come to create international organizations? Probably the
earliest historical prototype of the modern international organization had
been the Delian League, an off-and-on association of Greek city-states
dominated by Athens with the purpose of facilitating military cooperation
against common enemies in the fifth and fourth centuries B.C.E. Another
early precursor, one and a half millennia after the Delian League, was the
Hanseatic League, a trade association of northern German towns that lasted
from the eleventh through the seventeenth centuries.[2] But much before the
Hanseatic League came another forerunner of international organization:
the Christian Roman Empire after the conversion of Constantine to
Christianity until the end of the Middle Ages. Certain elements during this
long period made Western Christendom a political and legal unit. The
popes had emerged as the heads of the Western church and claimed the
power to influence politics throughout Western Christendom.[3] Going
beyond mere spiritual authority, the church undertook certain governmental

31

functions such as education and care for the poor. It felt the right to intervene for the defense of those who were treated unjustly by secular authorities. It could render judgment on whether a ruler's cause for war was just. It could even force depositions of secular rulers through excommunication and interdict.

But the church of the Middle Ages was not a regular state comparable to today's nation-state. Rather, it has been called an "international state"[4] (the same term used in Chapter 1). The plurality of temporal rulers within the Christian world, united in the church—the Respublica Christiana, as the popes liked to call it—gave the Christian community a character that could be called "universal federalism."[5] Its international structure kept this community from becoming a theocracy, that is, a government by priests in a unified state, where laws are dictated by something higher than human will. But the spiritual sphere did regulate the relations among the temporal rulers of the Christian world, who did not recognize any common temporal authority. Against this background emerged some other precursors of the modern transnational organization.

A Legal World Community

With the rise of territorial states after the 1648 Peace of Westphalia, the church as a transnational organization vanished. What did not vanish was Roman law, the positive law of the ancient Roman Empire. After the decay of imperial Rome, Roman law survived, but had lost its connection to actual authority and become a system of ideal rules. Although originally established by the emperor Justinian for private individuals, Roman law also applied to relationships between princes, that is, to international relations. This made it possible, after the breakup of medieval unity, in a world of states recognizing no common superior, for Roman legal principles to serve as the highest standards of conduct, governance, and mutual relations. These standards were seen not merely as moral rules but also as legal rules, which made the world appear as a legal community despite the absence of a worldwide central organization.[6]

Seventeenth-century Dutch scholar Hugo Grotius went further and argued that the law of nature was binding for all human beings. International law did not merely regulate relationships among states. It was universal law, the law of the human community, including all reasonable beings, meaning all members of the human race.[7] To be sure, Grotius's legal community of humankind, in which no common authority above the various political units decides what is just or unjust, is not a world state. At that time, the world legal community had no organization of its own; the only force binding all members of the human race was its legal order.

Case 2.1   Merchant Guilds:
Prototypes of the Transnational Organization

In Boston, England, in or shortly before 1241, a Flemish merchant accused an English trader of not repaying a commercial loan. This resulted in "an uproar on all sides and the English merchants assembled to attack the Flemings, who retired to their lodging in the churchyard. . . . The English threw down the pailings, broke the doors and windows and dragged out Peter Balg [the Flemish lender] and five others whom they foully beat and wounded and then set in the stocks. All the other Flemings they beat, ill-treated and robbed, and pierced their cloths with swords and knives. . . . Their silver cups were carried off as they sat at table, their purses cut and the money in them stolen, [and] their chests broken open and money and goods, to an unknown extent, taken away."[a]

English-Flemish trade was only one example of how insecurity jeopardized medieval transnational commerce. In 1162 the Pisans attacked the Genoese quarter in Constantinople; at least one merchant was killed, and the Genoese merchants had to escape to their ship, leaving all their valuables behind. In 1171 the Venetians attacked and destroyed the same Genoese quarter. In 1182 a mob destroyed the Italian quarters in Constantinople during the so-called Latin Massacre.[b] A document dated 1280 reports that "it is unfortunately only too well known that merchants travelling to Flanders have been the objects of all kinds of maltreatment in the town of Bruges and have not been able to protect themselves from this."[c]

Rulers often failed to protect traders from such violence and robbery, or reneged on agreements in other ways. A city could confiscate the belongings of some traders or deny them legal protection without directly harming other alien merchants. For example, in 1050 the Muslim ruler of Sicily imposed a 10 percent tariff (instead of the 5 percent specified by Islamic law) only on goods imported by Jewish traders. Three centuries later, in 1340, the ruler of Tabriz, a vital trade center on the route to the Persian Gulf and the Far East, confiscated the goods of many Genoese traders. Genoa responded with a *devetum*, or commercial embargo, against Tabriz. To patch things up, Tabriz's ruler sent ambassadors to Genoa in 1344, promising an indemnity for everything that had been taken and protection of the Genoese in the future. Genoa promptly removed the *devetum* and

(continues)

Case 2.1   continued

Genoese traders flocked again to Persia. But the ruler of Tabriz broke his promise to protect their rights: the Genoese merchants were robbed and many of them killed; the material damage reached the immense sum of 200,000 lire, the ancient equivalent of many millions of euros or dollars. When the ruler later invited the Venetians and Genoese to trade, he "could not give them the guarantees they required. . . . [Hence] the Italian merchants, eager as they were to recover their prosperous trade in Persia and to reopen the routes to India and China, felt it was unsafe to trust a mere promise."[d]

After 1648 and before the rise of the nation-state, trade took place in a highly complex and uncertain environment of frequent surprises and misunderstandings. Alien merchants had little or no protection when doing business far from home. Rulers of foreign lands might suddenly stop protecting visiting merchants or impose higher tariffs. It was basically a commitment problem: Could merchants count on rulers to honor their agreements? If merchants mistrusted a land's ruler, or if the risk was too high, they stopped trading, often at a huge cost to both themselves and the rulers. Christian merchants, for example, did not dare trade in the Muslim world unless they received appropriate securities.[e]

In the late medieval period, merchant guilds arose to fill this vacuum—to compel rulers of trade centers to guarantee the security of alien merchants. Ruler-merchant relations were governed by administrative bodies outside the ruler's territory, which regulated their member merchants in their own territory and supervised their operations in foreign lands. The guilds secured merchants' property rights, lowered transaction costs for both sides—rulers and merchants—and contributed to a significant expansion of world trade during the late Middle Ages. What was the rulers' incentive to support merchant guilds? The guilds enforced agreements with their own members and so lowered the transaction costs of rulers,[f] who understood that they stood to profit from increased trade volumes.

Just like in the trade war between Tabriz and Genoa, an effective tool of these early transnational organizations was the embargo. When in 1284 a German trading ship was attacked and pillaged by the Norwegians, the German towns forbid the export of grain, flower, vegetables, and beer to Norway. According to the chronicler Detmar,

(continues)

"there broke out a famine so great that [the Norwegians] were forced to make atonement."[g] In the case of the tariff hike by Sicily's Muslim ruler, the Jewish traders also responded with an embargo and, what is more, sent their goods to the rival trade center Tunisia. The sanction was effective: after one year the ruler relented and removed the tariff.[h] The benefits to trade were obvious: for example, when in 1161 the Genoese legate in northern Africa, Otobonus d'Albericis, and the local ruler, Abd al-Mumin, signed a fifteen-year agreement securing the property rights of the Genoese, trade more than doubled and stayed at this higher level throughout the term of the agreement.[i]

Notes: This case study borrows heavily from Greif, Milgrom, and Weingast 1994.

a. Curia Regis, 121, m. 6; cited in Greif, Milgrom, and Weingast 1994: 750.

b. Day 1988.

c. *Urkundenbuch der Stadt Lübeck* [Document Book of the City of Lübeck], vol. 1: 156, 371, translated in Dollinger 1970: 383.

d. Lopez 1943: 181–184.

e. See, for example, De Roover 1948: 13; De Roover 1966; and Dollinger 1970.

f. Greif, Milgrom, and Weingast 1994.

g. Dollinger 1970: 49.

h. Greif, Milgrom, and Weingast 1994: 752.

i. Krueger 1932: 81–82; Krueger 1933: 379–380.

Grotius recognized that without a world government, the law of nations could never be binding like municipal law within a state. Instead he created a legal science designed to regulate the worst interstate interaction—warfare. "When judicial settlement fails, war begins."[8] Since there was no central organization, law enforcement could result only from the reaction by other members of the global community against unlawful acts of an individual member. That spontaneous reaction was war in the interest of universal justice; it was law enforcement through war. And the state against which war was waged for a just cause had no right to defend itself.[9]

Grotius's principle of course begs the question of who decides who is right and who is wrong. What happens if not all states in the community agree that international law has been violated (as happened in 2003 when the United States and its allies waged war against Iraq, but other great powers like France, Germany, and Russia refused on the grounds that Iraq was not in breach of UN Resolution 1441)? Grotius wryly admitted that "certainty is not to be found in moral questions in the same degree as in mathematical science."[10] The ultimate guarantee of lawful conduct is that fickle quantity, fear of divine power: "those who sin against the law of nations are everywhere said to transgress international law."[11] But in today's world, religious fear no longer guarantees moral action.

Grotius's chief contribution was his idea that nations had an alternative to living either in an anarchic and unpredictable state of nature or under the dictatorial thumb of an empire. That alternative was to form an international community.[12] It marked the beginning of a development that centuries later would lead to the League of Nations, the United Nations, and collective security arrangements such as NATO.

Free and Equal Nations

Grotius's German contemporary Samuel Pufendorf built on the Dutch scholar's theories and designed a system of jurisprudence to govern relations between states. But Grotius had sought to base natural law on the general agreement of all humans and nations (or at least the more civilized among them). Grotius's *jus gentium,* the law of peoples, is derived not from reason, but from the will of peoples expressed by custom. (This idea resembles customary law, as we will see below.) It depends on rulers' knowledge of the rules and on their willingness to obey them.[13] In contrast, Pufendorf declared that if a customary law of nations were derived from states' actual practice, then such a law would sanction complete license in their mutual relations: "waging of wars for mere ambition, or with the prospect of making gain, than which nothing is more frequent among most nations."[14] For Pufendorf, treaties between states were temporary and fragile, and should "no more form a part of law than do agreements between individual citizens belong to the body of their civil law."[15]

Still, Pufendorf laid important groundwork for the modern international organization. He conceived of the state as "a single person with intelligence and will, performing other actions peculiar to itself and separate from those of individuals."[16] This notion of the state as a legal person allowed for the sovereignty of states and for their global community. The state of nature, or the international sphere, is a state of natural liberty, where self-love is reconciled with social life and its duties and where peace is the natural condition of humankind—unlike for Pufendorf's British contemporary Thomas Hobbes, who famously held that war is natural and that life is solitary, poor, nasty, brutish, and short.[17] In natural liberty, no human is beneath another's authority. The same is true for states: they coexist in the state of nature and enjoy equality, regardless of their size or wealth or power. This equal natural liberty of states was to become an important feature of international law.[18]

In Pufendorf's doctrine, in contrast to Grotius's, war is no longer a legal action sanctioned by law, but simply one of self-help. When a person in the state of nature helps him- or herself, that person is not a judge, and his or her decisions may not be valid for the other party or any other person. Grotius's concept that rulers act as agents of the human community for the maintenance of law has disappeared. Pufendorf suggested another method for the preservation of peace: mediation. Third states can mediate between two states engaged in or preparing for war. Centuries later, certain clauses in the Covenant of the League of Nations provided for just that: joint mediation.

A Global State

Writing a century after Grotius and Pufendorf, Michael Wolff created a new idea: the global citizenry. Like Pufendorf, Wolff saw states as free and equal persons coexisting in the state of nature, their conduct governed by natural law. States had neither rights nor duties. From Pufendorf's idea of their natural liberty in the state of nature, Wolff deduced their freedom from outside interference—and their right to noninterference. For Wolff, in stark contrast to Grotius, even if a ruler oppresses his subjects, no other ruler has any right to use force for the defense of the oppressed people. According to Wolff, the United States today would have no right to interfere in the affairs of Iraq, Iran, or China to redress oppression by autocrats ruling those states. (Nor would US law—based on a measure passed by Congress in 2003—allow US federal officials to prosecute American pedophiles who sexually molest children in Cambodia or Thailand.[19]) Instead, nature itself has united all nations in a supreme state, the *civitas maxima,* a global body analogous to the national community that governs the conduct of individuals. In such a world community, peace would be permanent. Wolff knew, of course, that this expectation was overly optimistic, since states do not always follow the dictates of reason. Wolff's *civitas maxima* is a legal fiction, and lawmaking in the global state has a somewhat imaginary character; the world state, composed of free and equal bodies, has a kind of popular regime that deliberates with majority decisions. But since "all the nations scattered throughout the whole world cannot assemble together," the will of nations is apparent "if following the leadership of nature they use right reason."[20]

Popular Sovereignty and a "Common Congress"

The Swiss jurist Emerich de Vattel closely followed Wolff, but disagreed with him on several notions. One is the concept of the supreme state:

Vattel opposed a world government. But since Wolff's world state was not real but fictional, Vattel's and Wolff's ideas are quite compatible.[21] Another departure from Wolff is Vattel's attitude: it is more humanitarian, more cosmopolitan, and more democratic. Very much a citizen of Switzerland, Vattel rejected the idea of kingdoms based on monarchical ownership, and instead advocated popular sovereignty—even before his fellow countryman Jean-Jacques Rousseau published his epochal works. This puts Vattel among the writers who contributed to the ideas of the French Revolution, and whose ideas are consistent with the US Declaration of Independence.[22]

Vattel also differed with Grotius and Pufendorf, for whom "nature" had meant the ideal nature of a creature in its fullest development. To Vattel, nature meant what it had meant to Hobbes—the "actual" rather than the "ideal" nature of the creature. Key for Vattel as for Hobbes was "the state of nature": men in their presocial isolation, each self-dependent for survival.[23] (Given the countless wars ever since Vattel's writing, his assumption seems not entirely unrealistic.)

Vattel's British contemporary Jeremy Bentham was the political philosopher who coined the term "international law"—in 1789, the year of the French Revolution. In a footnote that seems prophetic today, Bentham wrote:

> The word international, it must be acknowledged, is a new one; though, it is hoped, sufficiently analogous and intelligible. It is calculated to express, in a more significant way, the branch of the law which goes commonly under the name of the law of nations: an appellation so uncharacteristic that, were it not for the force of custom, it would seem rather to refer to internal jurisprudence. . . . Now as to any transactions which may take place between individuals who are subjects of different states, these are regulated by the internal laws, and decided upon by the internal tribunals, of the one or the other of these states: the case is the same where the sovereign of the one has any immediate transactions with a private member of the other.[24]

In short, Bentham assumed that international law was about rights and obligations of states, not individuals. He knew that disputes between nations about their rights under international law would still arise; his solution was "a common court of adjudicature" to settle such disputes.[25] Bentham's vision of this international tribunal was a "congress" or "diet" of representatives from each country. This was prescient: Bentham anticipated the League of Nations and the UN, which were still over a century away. In the meantime, the great powers in Europe extricated themselves from the throes of a chronic war and built the first modern international organization.

Case 2.2   The Concert of Europe

The Congress of Vienna convened in 1814, after the Napoleonic War had cost some 2 million lives—a staggering number before the advent of modern mechanized warfare. The consensus was that the cataclysm had been brought on by one predominant power—Napoleon's France. The victors permitted France to return to the world stage, but Congress participants had learned their lesson: they agreed that no power should ever become too dominant again, that the cost of war had been too high, and that war should be prevented, even if the long-term benefits of peace meant short-term sacrifices. To avoid future wars, the Congress of Vienna established what might be regarded as the first international organization in the modern era of nation-states: the Concert of Europe, a treaty among the great powers of the day, designed to maintain a delicate balance of power.

The Concert heralded a long period of relative peace, from 1815 until 1870, when Germany and France went to war with each other; up to that point its values, norms, rules, and procedures were a major cause of stability. Another result of the Congress was the precious neutrality it granted to smaller states, for example Belgium and Switzerland. What made the Concert work were the shared values of its members, the relative transparency of its dealings, compared to opaque bilateral backroom deals before it, and the fact that its members were few. These factors allowed for a state-change in international organization: in the second half of the nineteenth century, a number of public international unions, such as the Universal Postal Union (UPU) and the International Committee of the Red Cross (ICRC) sprang up. These public unions were quite open and not simply beholden to the states that created them. One study shows that 71 percent of all their decisions were taken by majority rule or weighted voting. In fact these organizations made 13 percent of their decisions without official oversight by the member states.[a] A transformation had taken place: the multilateral organization was born, and with it came a shift from bilateral to multilateral diplomacy and summits.[b]

But the Concert of Europe was not without disadvantages. The great powers either oppressed some small states, eliminated them altogether, or used them (Baden-Württemberg, the Netherlands, Rhineland-Palatinate, Sardinia, and Switzerland) as buffer states against others; and except in the United Kingdom, reactionary gov-

(continues)

Case 2.2   continued

ernments ruled. Another price of the relative peace was colonialism: the great powers simply aimed their greed elsewhere and took possession of much of the world. The greatest among them, the British Empire, at one point covered one-quarter of the world's entire landmass.

Are the principles underlying the Concert of Europe applicable to our world today? Somewhat. Compared to the world of 1815, there are many more states now (some 200 worldwide); their sheer number gives rise to countless problems of collective action; their shared values are questionable; and it is quite possible that the Concert of Europe was epiphenomenal, meaning that it was the effect, not the cause, of stability in the nineteenth century. There are other possible explanations for nineteenth-century stability—for example, that British hegemony acted as a stabilizer that shouldered the burden of maintaining stability;[c] that the great powers satisfied their appetite for expansion and power by acquiring colonial possessions elsewhere instead of going at each other's throats directly; or that the rising bourgeoisie used industrialization and capitalism, rather than having to resort to arms and war, to dominate.[d]

Notes: a. Murphy 1994: 108–109.
     b. Reinalda 2001: 4; Couloumbis and Wolfe 1990: 276–277.
     c. Kindleberger 1973.
     d. Hilferding 1981.

World Organization and the Representation of All Peoples

The next quantum leap in international law came more than a century after the Vienna Congress, when international jurist Lassa Oppenheim wrote after World War I that "with the Final Act of the Congress of Vienna, the quasi-legislative activity of international conventions asserted itself for the first time."[26] Already before the Great War, Oppenheim's thought had become a typical example of the positive law doctrine. Wolff's law had been based on the *presumed* consent of the members of the international community to what is natural behavior. But the positivists sought to create an international legal order derived from the *actual* consent of states. They derived the legal order not from a desired ideal, but from real existing conditions. Oppenheim defined law as "a body of rules for human conduct within a community which, by common consent of this community, shall be enforced by external power."[27] Internationally, law enforcement through external power happens because "in the Law of Nations, the States have to take the law into their own hands. Self-help and intervention on the part of other States which sympathise with the wronged one are the means by which the rules of the Law of Nations can be and actually are enforced."[28] In this way, Oppenheim stood in the realist tradition of Hobbes and Vattel, but also in the communitarian footsteps of Grotius.

Oppenheim insisted that international law "lacks absolutely the power of altering or creating rules of Municipal Law."[29] It differs from municipal law in four respects. First, "whereas Municipal Law is a law of a Sovereign over individuals subjected to his sway, the Law of Nations is a law not above, but between Sovereign States."[30] Subjects of international law—states—have sovereignty, defined by Oppenheim as "supreme authority, an authority which is independent of any other earthly authority" and "independence all round, within and without the borders of the country."[31] States are completely free; their only constraint is the rules to which they have freely consented. But this liberty must be checked by the liberty of the other members of the world community.[32] Legally, all states are equal: the great powers are recognized as de facto political leaders by the smaller states, but not as legally superior.[33] One result of all states' sovereignty and legal equality is the rule that no state, no matter how small, can be bound by a rule to which it has not consented: "the Law of Nations must be a weaker law than Municipal Law, as there is not and cannot be an international Government above the national ones which could enforce the rules of International Law in the same way as national Government enforces the rules of its Municipal Law."[34]

The second difference is that in a national parliament, elected representatives decide on laws by majority votes, and once a law is passed, the citizens must submit to it. But in the international sphere, because of the principles of sovereignty and equality, no state and no minority can be bound by international resolutions to which it has not agreed; and resolutions must be ratified by the states before they can enter into force.[35] Still, a majority of states in a legislative conference can adopt rules that are binding only for that majority. Several states together can act as legislators by laying down positive legal rules in the international sphere, just as each of them can legislate within its national law.[36] Oppenheim calls this "general" not "universal" law; he is optimistic that international rules can arise not only from explicit but also from tacit consent: "General International Law has a tendency to become universal because such States as hitherto do not consent to its will in future either expressly give their consent or recognise the respective rules tacitly through custom."[37] His optimism is founded on his belief that international rules, the true interests of all states, and the interests of the global community are all compatible:

> Though the individual States are sovereign and independent of each other, though there is no international Government above the national ones, though there is no central political authority to which the different States are subjected, yet there is something mightier than all the powerful separating factors: namely, the common interests. And these interests and the necessary intercourse which serves these interests, unite the separate States into an indivisible community.[38]

This community of interests gives treaties between sovereign states their binding force. Here Oppenheim's reasoning comes close to Wolff's about a fictional world state.

But third, for Oppenheim, unlike for Wolff, individuals cannot be subjects of international law. Only states can create rules of international law, and they alone have rights and duties arising from them.

Finally, Wolff had assumed a worldwide law of nations;[39] but for positivists like Oppenheim, the international legal community is a product of history and therefore not necessarily worldwide. When dealing with states outside the "circle of the Family of Nations," the law of nations "does not contain any rules. . . . It is discretion, and not International Law, according to which the members of the Family of Nations deal with such States."[40]

In sum, positive law theory shared a fundamental assumption with the natural law school: that there *could* be a law outside the state and that a legal order could be binding on states in their international relations.[41] It was this core assumption that made universal organizations like the League of Nations and the United Nations possible. Oppenheim himself proposed a world organization that would lack executive functions but would have two tasks: international legislation and international administration of justice. Yet he was absolutely opposed to a world state if it deprived individual states of their sovereignty and equality, and made them mere provinces of a supranational polity: "There can, therefore, be no talk of a political central authority standing above individual states; and so the organization in question must be *sui generis* and cannot frame itself on the model of state organization. . . . All proposals for an international executive authority run counter not only to the idea of sovereignty, but also to the ideal of international peace and of international law."[42] But in theory Oppenheim did not rule out a universal government. "Whatever else can be urged against a universal federal state and the like, it is at the present day no longer a physical impossibility." He realized, long before the advent of television, fax machines, and the Internet, that modern technology had made the world smaller and a world legislative body possible: "Distance has been so conquered by the

Case 2.3   The League of Nations

After World War I had scorched the earth of Europe and had claimed many millions of lives in a needlessly violent and seemingly endless conflict, it became unavoidable that a world organization was needed to help states conduct their affairs in a reasonable manner and for the common good of the global community. It seemed possible that war could have been avoided in 1914 had there been an international forum that could have prompted open discussion and expressed world public opinion on the conflict and its causes. After the war, US president Woodrow Wilson said to the US Senate: "A great war cannot begin with public deliberation. A great war can begin only by private plot."[a] Over and over, Wilson asserted that war could have been averted if the conflict had been brought to an international conference.[b] At the Versailles Peace Conference in February 1919, he expressed the highest confidence in the public: "We are depending primarily and chiefly upon one great force, and that is the moral force of the public opinion of the world, the cleansing and clarifying and compelling influences of publicity." In complete opposition to James Madison and Alexander Hamilton, who had warned against the fickleness of the public, the president who had waged war to make the world safe for democracy declared that "public opinion gives judgment in a manner that is broader and more equitable" than even the decision of a court of law.[c]

Already in 1899 and 1907, international peace conferences had been held at The Hague; at the 1907 conference, forty-four countries had been represented—virtually all sovereign states at the time. Oppenheim had proposed that such conferences become permanent institutions that all member states could join. Such an international legislature would go beyond customary law and create international law consciously by deliberation and decisions; it would have to be more than a mere forum for governments and their elite diplomacy; it would have to listen to the world's peoples.

If the watchword of the nineteenth century had been "colonialism," in the twentieth it was "self-determination"—the root from which the entitlement to democracy grew. The Versailles Peace Conference after World War I undid the work of the Congress of Vienna, which a century earlier had utterly disregarded ethnic sensibilities in redrawing the map of post-Napoleonic Europe. In redrawing Europe once again, Wilson made self-determination his lodestar.[d] The resulting League of Nations was a remarkable attempt at true representation of the peoples of the world—in many ways it was more democratic than its successor, the United Nations. The League Covenant's Article 3(4) provided that each representation of the peoples of the member state would have three dele-

(continues)

Case 2.3   continued

gates but only one vote at Assembly meetings. Each state was free to select its delegates, which of course opened opportunities for distorting true representation, as Wilson recognized at the Versailles Peace Conference: "It was impossible to conceive a method or an assembly so large and various as to be really representative of the great body of the peoples of the world, because, as I roughly reckon it, we represent as we sit around this table more than twelve hundred million people."[e] Although three delegates per member state taking their instructions from their government, much like diplomats do today, was hardly direct representation, it was a valiant attempt at building democracy into the first global organization in history.

With the League's creation, a long historical era finally seemed to come to a close. When Western Christendom had dissolved in the Middle Ages, international unity had become fragmented. Now it had been restored, and on a worldwide scale. At last, virtually all independent states had consented "to limit their complete freedom of action on certain points for the greater good of themselves and the world at large."[f]

There was of course a limit to the limiting of freedom of action. The League Covenant explicitly protected the autonomy of its member states: Article 15(8), inserted on US initiative, provided that if a dispute that would likely end in rupture was submitted to the League Council, the Council was not allowed to recommend a resolution if the dispute arose from a matter solely under the domestic jurisdiction of one of the parties. Under international law, the world community could not intervene—not even with a nonbinding recommendation.[g] The newly created Permanent Court of International Justice (PCIJ) followed suit in granting all states full sovereignty: in the *Lotus* case of 1927, the world court held that a state can extend its criminal jurisdiction to any case whatsoever, unless a rule or principle of international law forbids it.[h]

On the other hand, Article 11 of the League Covenant stated: "Any war or threat of war, whether immediately affecting any of the Members of the League or not, is hereby declared a matter of concern to the whole League." This proclamation meant that the League was a unit with concerns of its own.[i] In one early session, Italian delegate Tomasso Tittoni declared that "the Council was not a Conference of Governments, but that the Delegates, once appointed, were free to act as members of an international body as independent as the magistrates of a court."[j] Still, it would take the League's demise and another generation until the UN would be accorded the status of a legal person.

The League's founders were happy to leave state sovereignty untouched; they assumed that if they could just keep the peace, all other

(continues)

problems in the world community could be resolved.[k] In addition to raising hopes for peace, the League and its world court made it possible to envision a global organization through which international problems could be solved on their technical merits, not by raw power and politics. International entities like the Universal Postal Union had solved technical problems through organs guided by reasonable standards. It was a world in which progress seemed ensured if only the members of the global community could live by the universal standards of morality, expertise, and civilization.

But of course they would not. The failure of the League was programmed into its original premises. The optimistic assumption that reason and good faith would prevail conflicted with the pessimistic one that the world needed an institution to keep from going to war. Already Pufendorf had written that agreements between states were unnecessary when states behaved reasonably—but if they did not, agreements were useless. This was a contradiction in terms: where avoiding war was concerned, the League's success depended on the very conditions that, if they had existed, would have made the organization superfluous.[l]

A similar contradiction showed itself in the arena of democracy. Optimistic progressives believed that states had become more democratic, and that governments expressed the will of their respective peoples. But the problem of giving the peoples representation in the League Assembly had arisen precisely because it seemed that governments could not be trusted and that some authority was needed above them. This was another fundamental contradiction built into the League[m]—one that could be resolved only if and when every single country in the world was truly democratic. Only then would the community of states be one with the community of humankind. But almost a century after the League's founding, this still seems far off.

Notes: a. US Senate 1919: 141.

b. Schiffer 1954: 191.

c. Miller 1928, vol. 2: 562.

d. Franck 1992b.

e. Cited in Miller 1928, vol. 2: 561.

f. Great Britain 1919.

g. Schiffer 1954: 231–232.

h. Case of the S.S. Lotus (*France v. Turkey*), Permanent Court of International Justice (1927), P.C.I.J. Ser. A, no. 10. See Henkin et al. 1993: 63–72.

i. Schiffer 1954: 202.

j. League of Nations 1924: 320.

k. Schiffer 1954: 195.

l. Schiffer 1954: 199.

m. Schiffer 1954: 240.

telegraph, the railway, and the steamboat, that in fact the annual assembly of a world-parliament would be no impossibility, and in any case a world-government, wherever its seat might be, would be able to secure almost immediate obedience to its behests in the uttermost parts of the earth."[43]

To be sure, Oppenheim proposed a world organization without executive functions, but only legislation and administration of justice,[44] including the eventual codification of all international rules, until international law would become, at some point in the future, as positive and effective as national law. The League of Nations was to be the first laboratory for testing Oppenheim's theories.

Building on the principle of self-determination promoted by the League, a remarkable process started after World War II and the founding of the United Nations. Starting in the early 1960s, some 80 former colonies and protectorates became independent. Decolonization, which was to be virtually complete by the end of the twentieth century, fundamentally changed the international system and was one of the UN's indisputable successes. By 1991, 113 states had ratified or acceded to the International Covenant on Civil and Political Rights, which made the right of self-determination applicable to the citizens of all nations and binding on all states as customary law.[45]

Another key postwar process was the creation of a human rights regime. As recently as 1945, there was no word for the phenomenon now known as genocide. But before the war, a Jewish lawyer from Poland named Raphael Lemkin had begun a personal crusade to make international law against racial massacres. In a 1933 conference sponsored by the League, Lemkin proposed that an international treaty should be negotiated making "destruction of national, religious, and ethnic groups" an international crime. But his proposal met with howls of derision led by the delegates of Nazi Germany.[46] Lemkin came to the United States as a refugee in 1941, right after Franklin Roosevelt had incorporated human rights into the postwar order with his State of the Union speech on the "Four Freedoms"—freedom of speech and expression, freedom of worship, freedom from want, and freedom from fear. In 1944, Lemkin published a book in which he coined the word "genocide"; after the war, he served on the staff of the chief US prosecutor at the Nuremberg war crimes tribunal, where he introduced the term. Although it was not included in the court's judgment and sentence, a *New York Times* story carried the headline "Genocide Is the New Name for the Crime Fastened on the Nazi Leaders" and gave Lemkin full credit.[47]

Genocide was only the most prominent provision of the 1948 Universal Declaration of Human Rights; another was democracy. The declaration provided the first detailed democracy standards in an international instrument. Article 21(3) stated that "the will of the people shall be the basis of the authority of government"[48] (the article did not say whether this meant national government alone). While it does not have formal treaty status, the declaration has been enormously influential for international law and now, for some commentators, expresses legal rights and duties.[49]

It has not gone unchallenged, though. For Senegalese international jurist Babacar Ndiaye, the international community must accept the principle of noninterference if a country's citizens genuinely support a particular system of government for cultural or religious reasons—even if such a system goes against generally accepted principles of democracy or human rights. Ndiaye takes Islamic *sharia* law, the Islamic legal code derived from the Quran, as an example, in which a large Muslim majority wants to be governed by a religious system, not by secular law. In his view, the principle of "shared humanity" does not apply in such cases.[50]

But how can we know—if not through democratic processes—whether a people "genuinely supports" a nondemocratic government or *sharia* that grants criminals no due process and instead cuts their hands off? Cultures clashed in May 2002 when the UN Committee Against Torture urged Saudi Arabia to end corporal punishments like flogging (for certain sexual offenses and drinking alcohol) and amputation of limbs (for theft). The ten-member committee said that such punishments are prohibited under the 1987 Convention Against Torture, which Saudia Arabia had signed along with 128 other countries. This drew an outburst from the Saudi delegates, who said that the committee had no jurisdiction over *sharia* and that corporal punishment is not torture.[51]

The International Covenant on Civil and Political Rights walks the tightrope between global standards of democracy and human rights on the one hand, and the right to self-determination on the other. The covenant grants self-determination to the citizens of all nations and entitles them to determine their collective political status through democratic means. Ratified by 113 states in November 1991 but binding on other states as customary law, the treaty provides in Article 1: "All peoples have the right to self-determination. By virtue of that right they freely determine their political status and freely pursue their economic, social and cultural development."

Pooling State Sovereignty

As we will see in the next chapter, the UN Charter left the sovereignty of its member states intact. Despite the fact that it was written in the name of "We the People," the Charter was signed by representatives of governments; it contained no requirements about their legitimacy to speak on behalf of those peoples. Over and over, in Articles 2(3)(i), 2(4), 39–42, and

2(7), the Charter repeated that nothing shall infringe on the sovereignty of its member states.

On the other hand, whenever any country joins an international institution, its very accession shows its willingness to trade some sovereignty for other advantages. So even if the UN rarely if ever meddles in its member states' affairs, the relative gravity of competencies can be expected to shift gradually from the states to the UN.[52] A pathbreaking theory had anticipated this development already in 1943, at the height of World War II. David Mitrany found authority no longer in a territory or a state alone, but in activities and functions between states—hence the name of the theory, functionalism. He wrote:

> Sovereignty cannot in fact be transferred effectively through a formula, only through a function. . . . It would indeed be sounder and wiser to speak not of a surrender but of a sharing of sovereignty: when ten or twenty national authorities, each of whom had performed a certain task for itself, can be induced to perform the task jointly, they will to that end quite naturally pool their sovereign authority insofar as the good performance of the task demands it.[53]

Mitrany made clear that functionalism did not subordinate member states to the union itself—only to some of its services. In fact, just like in a national democracy, in the international sphere "the only possible principle of democratic confirmation is that public action should be undertaken only where and when and in so far as the need for common action becomes evident and is accepted, for the sake of the common good."[54] Still, as functions are pooled, this can lead to more or less autonomous bureaus, and the UN was no exception: it leapt quickly from a mere intergovernmental treaty to being an independent actor in its own right. Already in 1949, only four years after the UN's founding, its new judicial arm, the International Court of Justice (ICJ), had ruled that the world organization had the capacity to bring an international claim against a government, and obtain reparation for damage caused either to the UN or to the victim. This precedent-setting decision established the principle of international personality.[55]

Still, the ICJ did not touch the bedrock of state sovereignty either. Even today, the ICJ has no power to bring a lawsuit; only states may sue states. And Article 59 made it clear that ICJ decisions have no binding force other than for the parties bringing a case. Unlike the European Court of Justice (ECJ), which systematically grew its supranational powers over time, the ICJ has had relatively little opportunity to do so. While the ECJ created a caseload so vast that it was forced to create its Court of First Instance (CFI) to tackle the backlog, as we will see in Chapter 7, the ICJ has had few cases. Since its inception in 1946 to the turn of the century, the ICJ dealt with fewer than a hundred contentious suits,[56] of which twenty-seven were withdrawn; in another ten cases, the Court found itself without jurisdiction. The ICJ has tried fifty-four cases, and given only twenty-one advisory opinions.[57]

Today the ICJ is no longer the only international judicial actor on the international stage. The International Criminal Court (ICC) began operating in March 2003 (see Case 3.2 in the next chapter). Other avenues exist for parties seeking legal recourse in international affairs—for example, in commercial disputes. We have seen how arbitration through merchant guilds flourished in medieval Europe. After virtually disappearing in the era of nation-state ideology during the nineteenth century, international commercial arbitration made a formidable comeback in the last decades of the twentieth century. The number of arbitration forums grew from a dozen or so in the 1970s to more than a hundred in the 1990s.[58] In the domestic context, when parties seek binding dispute resolution by a third party, they can either go to a national public court or seek private arbitration. Since there are—at least so far—no international public courts (with the exception of the ECJ), parties can choose between a national court and international commercial arbitration, either by private courts like the International Court of Arbitration of the International Chamber of Commerce and the London Court of International Arbitration, or so-called alternative dispute resolution techniques like conciliation or mediation. Private mechanisms hold several advantages compared to public courts, including flexibility, technical expertise, privacy, and confidentiality.[59] But while privacy and confidentiality may be advantageous to the disputing parties, their secret dealings can be harmful to transparency and thus to democracy.

Even international commercial arbitration has so far left state sovereignty untouched, but it is no longer uncontested; there are trends toward supranational policymaking. In the final decades of the twentieth century, regional organizations, above all the EU, and multilateral institutions like the IMF, the World Bank, and most recently the WTO, began making supranational rules, dictating policies to member states. A few examples: In an environmental judgment in August 1999, the new Law of the Sea Tribunal ordered Japan to cease all fishing for southern bluefin tuna for the remainder of that year.[60] In 1999 a US district court upheld the constitutionality of the North American Free Trade Agreement (NAFTA) against claims that its dispute resolution provisions violated US sovereignty.[61] And the Montreal Protocol on Substances Depleting the Ozone Layer is now close to hard law: a legally binding and precise agreement with a system of compliance review by third parties.[62]

One key function of the state is national security—specifically its territorial monopoly on organized violence. But monopoly need not mean control by a single actor. We will see in Chapter 9 that NATO is a case in point: it is a collective security system, involving joint control of organized violence in a transnational space.[63] NATO's intervention in Kosovo was a potentially far-reaching precedent, and arguably the first direct challenge by an international organization to the internal sovereignty of a state. Legally, Kosovo was part of Serbia, whose president was Slobodan Milosevic, but the NATO member states decided to violate Serbia's sovereignty rather than letting Milosevic continue to violate the human rights of Kosovars. NATO's act was unprecedented: never had an international organization attacked a country unless that country had attacked another. It remains to be seen whether this action was exceptional, or whether it marked a precedent for the end of state sovereignty under international law. (That was not all: in 1999, during the NATO bombing campaign, the International Criminal Tribunal for the Former Yugoslavia indicted Yugoslav president Slobodan Milosevic, and Austrian police, bearing a secret indictment from the International Criminal Tribunal, arrested a Bosnian Serb general who was attending a conference in Vienna.[64])

Already in 1991, the leaders of the thirty-four states of the Conference on Security and Cooperation in Europe (CSCE) had reaffirmed in Moscow that "human rights, fundamental freedoms, democracy and the rule of law are of international concern, as respect for these rights and freedoms constitutes one of the foundations of the international order." The participating states "categorically and irrevocably declare that the commitments undertaken in the field of the human dimension of the CSCE are matters of direct and legitimate concern to all participating States and do not belong exclusively to the internal affairs of the State concerned."[65] While it is an exaggeration to speak of a withering away of the state, national sovereignty has become porous.

These trends away from absolute claims of state sovereignty are not new. Already from 1833 to 1865, the Anglo-American campaign to end slavery in the United States had joined forces across borders to change a nation's policy against the will of its government. Another was the international suffrage movement between 1888 and 1928 to secure the women's vote. In both cases, domestic actors allied with activists in other countries to compel a change in their government's policies or practices. Antislavery groups in Britain and the United States exchanged letters, publications, and speakers, and were honorary members of each other's activist groups. This prototype of today's transnational advocacy networks mobilized and succeeded in making abolition a pressing moral and political issue in the United States; and when the issue contributed to the US Civil War, the network became a crucial factor in preventing the British government's recognition of the slave-owning South.[66]

The women's suffrage movement was even more international: ideas and tactics migrated from place to place as individuals in different countries— often despite vastly different cultural, social, and political backgrounds—

"traveled, looked for helpful models, and set up networks of reform"[67] that ultimately changed state policies. The International Council of Women (ICW), founded in 1888, promoted links among women's organizations in many countries and worked actively with intergovernmental organizations. In 1907 the president of the Second Peace Conference at The Hague agreed to receive the ICW's delegation—perhaps the earliest example of granting NGOs a special role in international conferences.[68] The outcome: women's voting moved from impossible to possible, then to imperative, and finally to standard state policy.

To be sure, state sovereignty remains untouched in many other areas, and the legalization of world politics is hardly uniform. Military interventions, most recently the war of the United States and its allies in Iraq, continue to happen without clear international legal authority; neither exchange rates nor multilateral aid are subject to precise international legal rules; for decades, regimes like the one for international whaling have been locked in the same degree of legalization; and Asian and Latin American countries have been cautious about pooling their sovereignty in supranational institutions. More international legalization may or may not be the wave of the future and may or may not change world politics. But in the legal literature we see more and more about "constitutionalization" (above all in the EU, but also in an emerging "international economic constitution" for the world trading system) or at least a "judicialization" (of commercial arbitration agreements to facilitate foreign direct investment) that emphasizes the delegation of disputes to independent courts or arbiters.[69]

Individual Standing

In this age of national sovereignty under siege, where states may no longer serve as the sole guarantors of individual rights and welfare, a profoundly important question for transnational democracy arises: Can individuals have rights directly by international treaty—and independently of domestic law? For a long time, individuals did not have international standing; they were not subjects but objects of international law, did not enjoy procedural rights, and were never allowed to appear before the ICJ unless represented by their state, since only states can sue in the world court. This is likely to remain the case in the foreseeable future. As long as the global community is made up of states, it is only through the exercise of their will, by treaty or international authority granted by states, that a rule of law becomes binding on an individual. Only if and when some kind of international assembly or world parliament is formed, with a mandate to represent the will of the world's population and with the authority to legislate, will it be possible to assert that international law obtains authority from a source outside the states—even if states become the original creators of such a representative legislature.[70]

And yet the world community's interests are represented by human rights, which by definition lie above state interests and whose rise in international relations was prompted by several key events. We have seen that, already in the nineteenth century, movements had formed to protect victims of slavery and war; in the early twentieth, other movements took on laborers, refugees, and prisoners of war. We have also seen that the single most important event to catapult human rights onto the international agenda involved the atrocities by the Axis powers in World War II; at the Nuremberg trial, for the first time in history, individuals were punished under international law for war crimes, crimes against peace, and crimes against humanity. Before this precedent, human rights had been the exclusive competence of states; now individual responsibility had become a key concept in international law, and individuals had become carriers of inalienable human rights.

Today, under international human rights law, any state may bring a case against any other before a special human rights committee. But the European Community has gone further. Its 1950 Convention on Human Rights, ratified by twenty-seven European countries, established a commission with delegates of all its members, plus its European Court of Human Rights, in Strasbourg. The convention provided for universal jurisdiction: any state *or* individual can sue—although individuals require the consent of their respective government. This provision gave individuals legal standing while leaving the sovereignty of member states intact. Twenty years later an international jurist was to write: "The individual as the end of community is a member of the community, and a member has status: he is not an object. . . . For example, in the areas of black and white slavery, human rights and protection of minorities, international law has selected the individual as a member of the international community for rights and duties, even against a national State."[71]

In 1979 the Court followed suit and set a precedent for individual standing in regard to pregnant women who had taken the drug thalidomide and later given birth to deformed children. The parents of the deformed children negotiated with the manufacturers of the drug, but were unable to get effective redress, so the *Sunday Times* of London launched a series of articles to help the parents obtain more generous settlements. One proposed article was to deal with the history of the drug's testing, manufacturing, and marketing. But the British attorney general obtained an injunction against the article on the grounds that it constituted contempt of court. The injunction was granted in the High Court, rescinded by the Court of Appeal, but restored once again by the House of Lords.

In an unprecedented action, the publisher, editor, and a group of journalists at the *Times* decided to bypass the UK authorities and go directly to the European Community. They filed an application with the European Commission of Human Rights, claiming that the injunction infringed on their freedom of expression guaranteed by Article 10 of the European Convention on Human Rights. The commission, by a majority, found indeed a breach of Article 10 and referred the case to the European Court of Human Rights, which ruled for the *Times* and the individuals. This landmark decision confirmed the legal standing of individuals for the first time ever under European Community law.

In 1999 the Court followed the *Sunday Times* precedent and ruled that Britain's ban on homosexuals in its armed forces violated the right to privacy, secured in Article 8 of the European Convention on Human Rights.[72] These precedents have shown that individuals have rights and obligations regardless of their nationality, and have made possible a form of global citizenship transcending the state.[73] A threshold has been crossed: if an individual sues a state, that lawsuit is considered to lie within the scope of public international law governing relations between states, not just within private law governing relations between individuals.

International Law and the Global Commons

Another field where the human community has interests superior to those of states is the global commons: the oceans and the deep seabed, Antarctica, and outer space. The depletion of nonrenewable resources alone, from rain forests to oil, calls for intergenerational accountability—accountability to future generations.[74] This is also true for space exploration. In 1962 the UN created its Legal Principles Governing the Uses of Outer Space, stating that space is the "common legacy of mankind." In 1967 this was codified in the Treaty on Principles Governing the Activities of States in Exploration and Use of Outer Space, Including the Moon and Other Celestial Bodies, which ninety-eight states ratified; in 1972 the Convention on International Liability for Damage by Space Aviation followed. The deep seabed was addressed with similar rules in 1982, when the international community agreed on the Third Convention on the Law of the Sea, marking off the deep seabed from appropriation by any nation-state. The convention created the International Seabed Authority (ISA) and gave it the dual powers to regulate exploration by private and sovereign state actors, and to explore the seabed itself. (The United States signed the convention but has not ratified it.)

Perhaps the most prominent example of the evolution in managing the global commons is climate change. Scientists and environmental activists have warned that excessive carbon dioxide emissions lead to global warming and threaten to disrupt the environment, from air to water to earth. In 1987 the Montreal Protocol on Substances That Deplete the Ozone Layer was adopted as an international treaty to eliminate the production and consumption of ozone-depleting chemicals, with developing countries benefiting from a ten-year grace period. In 1992 more than 178 states met in Rio for the UN Conference on Environment and Development (UNCED). As its name implies, UNCED built on the premise that economics and ecology cannot be separated. Maurice Strong, secretary-general of the 1992 Rio Summit, put it simply: "Hungry people chop down trees."[75]

Five years later, in December 1997, more than 160 nations met in Kyoto, Japan, to check progress on the 1992 Framework Convention on Climate Change and negotiate binding limitations on greenhouse gases for the developed nations. The result was the Kyoto Protocol, in which industrialized countries agreed to curb their greenhouse gas emissions relative to the levels emitted in 1990. The United States, for example, agreed to reduce emissions by a relative 7 percent during the period 2008 to 2012. (The George W. Bush administration announced right after its election that the Kyoto Protocol was based on faulty science and that it did not intend to honor the treaty. It remains to be seen whether future US administrations will cooperate with or defect from the protocol.)

Conclusion

Several major developments in international law and organization have produced a unique situation. First, globalization has called into question the sovereignty of states, while nonstate actors—international, multinational, and nongovernmental organizations—have gained power. Global issues like AIDS, terrorism, the environment, trade, finance, poverty, and migration, to name but a few, have become relatively more important to states, and now matter at least as much as traditional domestic issues. This rise of global issues has caused a profound shift in international relations. The nineteenth- and twentieth-century balance of power was based on a constellation of states with conflicting interests; now common interests are becoming more and more important. Second, in the mid–twentieth century, institutions like the UN and the EU attained legal personhood; today many international organizations act as quasi-legislative bodies making international law. Third, in certain legal contexts, individuals now have legal standing under international law. And even where they do not, geoeconomics means less international (state-to-state) interaction and more transnational (state-to-firm or state-to-individual) dealings.

Together, these three factors mean a strengthening of international law and international organization. Early in the twentieth century Oppenheim had written that "much, if not all, depends on whether the *international* interests of individual states become stronger than their *national* interests, for no state puts its hand to the task of international organization except when, and so far as, its international interests urge it more or less irresistibly to do so."[76] Based on the tectonic shifts mentioned above, we can say that Oppenheim's threshold has been crossed: international law could be reconceived as public law, oriented to the principle that all social power—including international power—be accountable.[77]

In *Perpetual Peace* and *The Metaphysics of Morals,* eighteenth-century philosopher Immanuel Kant had rejected both world government and a world federation of states. But in both *The Idea for a Universal History* and *Theory and Practice,* he embraced a universal political system and a federation with the power to enforce the law.[78] Pufendorf and Grotius agreed that a world state would be too big for effective government; but Pufendorf also declared that "government, indeed, is a natural thing, and it was nature's intention that men should set up governments among themselves."[79] Even Hans Morgenthau, who had become an adamant realist while watching power-hungry Germany gobble up half of Europe before and during World War II, toward the end of his life refused power politics as being fatally defective in a nuclear age, and embraced the idea of world government. (After all, Albert Einstein had not been alone in his advocacy.)

To deserve the name and the attention of lawyers, "law" must have been set up by a sovereign—meaning a person or persons usually obeyed by the bulk of a territorial community, and not themselves obedient to any other authority; it must be a rule for the general conduct of its subjects; and it must be supported by a threat of punishment by the sovereign in case of disobedience.[80] To what extent, then, can international law be called "law"? Pufendorf's doctrine was that international law cannot be built on customary law, because that would lower the level of law to whatever was most expedient for states. But is it possible that over the centuries since Pufendorf presented his views, and given the rise of international organization in the second half of the twentieth century, international law has taken on a lawlike character comparable to that of municipal law?

Wolff granted that his world state, where all nations were free and equal, deliberated in a world parliament, and made decisions by majority voting, was a fiction. But he wrote at a time when most people rarely traveled beyond their town or village, and when a diplomatic pouch from one state to another took weeks or months to arrive at its destination by horse, coach, or boat. In such a world, it took a fertile imagination to envision a popular deliberative world body. Perhaps today, in a world of the Internet, instant communication, and video conferences, such a body has moved from fictitious to feasible. Certainly the United Nations is a precursor of such a world parliament. For years, one of its founders, US president Harry

Truman, had carried folded in his wallet several stanzas of his favorite poem, Tennyson's "Locksley Hall," which ended:

> For I dipt into the future,
> Far as human eye could see,
> Saw the Vision of the world, and all the wonders that would be . . .
> Till the war-drum throbbed no longer, and the battle flags were furl'd
> In the Parliament of Man, the Federation of the World.

Let us see whether the UN lives up to this lofty vision.

Notes

1. Boyle 1985: 6.
2. Jacobson 1979: 8.
3. Schiffer 1954: 16.
4. Krey 1923: 7.
5. Zimmermann 1933: 355.
6. Schiffer 1954: 29.
7. Schiffer 1954: 35.
8. Grotius 1913–1925 [1646]: 171.
9. Grotius 1913–1925 [1646]: 185.
10. Grotius 1913–1925 [1646]: 575.
11. Grotius 1913–1925 [1646]: 510.
12. Bederman 1992.
13. Schiffer 1954: 42–43.
14. Pufendorf 1931 [1660]: 165.
15. Pufendorf 1935 [1672]: 227.
16. Pufendorf 1935 [1672]: 983.
17. Hobbes 1651: chap. 12.
18. Schiffer 1954: 53.
19. *New York Times,* June 8, 2004: A19.
20. Wolff 1934 [1764]: 16.
21. Schiffer 1954: 319.
22. Nussbaum 1954: 156–158.
23. Stone 1954: 16.
24. Cited in Janis 1984: 408–409.
25. Bentham 1843: 535.
26. Oppenheim 1921: 4.
27. Oppenheim 1912, vol 1: 8.5.
28. Oppenheim 1912, vol. 1: 13.9.
29. Oppenheim 1912, vol. 1: 26.21.
30. Oppenheim 1912, vol. 1: 26.20.
31. Oppenheim 1912, vol. 1: 109.64.
32. Schiffer 1954: 89.
33. Oppenheim 1912, vol. 1: 171 n. 1.116.
34. Oppenheim 1912, vol. 1: 13.9.
35. Schiffer 1954: 170.

36. Schiffer 1954: 85.
37. Oppenheim 1912, vol. 1: 18, 23.
38. Oppenheim 1912, vol. 1: 11.7.
39. Schiffer 1954: 82.
40. Oppenheim 1912, vol. 1: 34.29.
41. Schiffer 1954: 95.
42. Oppenheim 1921: 16, 21.
43. Oppenheim 1921: 12.
44. Schiffer 1954: 169.
45. Franck 1992b.
46. Korey 1989: 46.
47. *New York Times,* October 20, 1946: sec. 4: 13.
48. UN General Assembly Resolution 217A (III), adopted December 10, 1948.
49. Crawford and Marks 1998: 74 n.; Reisman 1990: 867.
50. Ndiaye 1992: 25–29.
51. *New York Times,* May 19, 2002: A1.
52. James Hsiung, professor of international law, New York University, personal communication.
53. Mitrany 1946: 6–8. See also Haas 1958, 1964.
54. Mitrany 1946: 39–40.
55. Henkin et al. 1993: 348.
56. The exact number of cases is debated.
57. James Hsiung, professor of international law, New York University, personal communication. The ICJ's caseload has picked up since the end of the Cold War; as of 2004, there had been 131 cases.
58. Brown 1993.
59. Mattli 2001.
60. Southern Bluefin Tuna Cases (*New Zealand v. Japan; Australia v. Japan*) (order of August 27, 1999) (Int'l Trib. for the Law of the Sea), available at http://www.un.org/depts/los/itlos/orgs/tuna34.htm.
61. *Made in the USA Foundation v. United States,* 56 F. Supp. 2d 1226 (n.d. Ala. 1999).
62. Victor 1998.
63. Wendt 1994.
64. *New York Times,* August 26, 1999: A10.
65. Conference on Security and Cooperation in Europe, Document of the Moscow Meeting of the Conference on the Human Dimension of the CSCE, October 3, 1991 (unofficial text of the US delegation).
66. Keck and Sikkink 1998: 39–78.
67. Scott 1994: 234.
68. Keck and Sikkink 1998: 55.
69. Goldstein et al. 2000: 386–387.
70. Jessup 1948: 17–18.
71. O'Connell 1970: 108–109.
72. See *Lustig-Prien and Beckett v. The United Kingdom,* App.Nos. 31417/96 and 32377/96; and *Smith and Grady v. The United Kingdom,* App.Nos. 33985/96 and 33986/96 (Eur. Ct. H.R., September 1999), available at http://www.echr.coe.int/eng/judgments.htm.
73. Linklater 1998.
74. Some American Indians believed that we should consider all our decisions from the standpoint of how they will impact the next seven generations to come.

75. Strong 1989.
76. Oppenheim 1921: 17, emphasis in original.
77. Allott 1990.
78. Hurrell 1990.
79. Pufendorf 1935 [1672]: 164.
80. Stone 1954: 13.

3

The United Nations

After Iraqi dictator Saddam Hussein was ousted in 2003, the oil-for-food program—the largest in the UN's history—received more scrutiny than ever in its six years of operation. Created in 1996, the program had been an ambitious attempt to keep pressure on the Iraqi government to disarm, while at the same time helping the Iraqi people survive the international sanctions imposed on the rogue state after its 1990 invasion of Kuwait. The idea had been to enable Iraq to sell oil and have the money go to the purchase of food, medicine, and other goods; instead it ended up in payoffs and kickbacks. On a $500,000 contract for trucks, for example, Iraq would tell the supplier to prepare a contract for $550,000, with a side agreement to transfer the $50,000 add-on to an Iraqi-controlled bank account.

Such embezzlements happened with up to $33 billion worth of goods ordered by Iraq from mid-2000 until the US-led invasion in March 2003. All in all, a US Government Accountability Office report accused the Hussein government of having pocketed more than $10 billion of $64.2 billion in Iraqi oil sales. More important here are the questions that arose as to whether senior officials at the UN had taken advantage of the organization's being way over its head in Iraq. The UN's total annual budget for all its operations worldwide was $1.5 billion, but it found itself in charge of collecting and disbursing $10 billion a year in Iraqi oil revenues. Had UN bureaucrats aided Hussein's government in this corrupt scheme, profited illegally, and taken multimillion-dollar bribes? Even Secretary-General Kofi Annan's son Kojo was embroiled in the scandal, and it seemed like the entire UN Security Council knew what was going on, but that there had been a conspiracy of silence. While UN auditors over the years produced fifty-five reports, diplomats on the sanctions committee said they never even saw them.[1]

Is the oil-for-food scheme an exception, a bad apple in an otherwise healthy yield, or does the UN system itself makes this type of corruption possible? When Annan and the UN had won the Nobel Peace Prize in 2001, just after September 11, this had boosted the organization's legitimacy. On the other hand, even if the oil-for-food program was just a $10 billion exception, it is inexcusable for an organization that must instill trust in its good governance to carry out its mission. This brings us to question the UN as an international organization. How accountable and how independent is it? All in all, does it serve the world's peoples or the interests and agendas of a few?

A Brief History

Already in the midst of World War II, in January 1942, the twenty-six Allies, united against the Axis powers, had signed a "Declaration by the United Nations." A year later, two years before the inception of the UN itself, the first "United Nations" agency was founded: the Relief and Rehabilitation Administration (UNRRA) began work in 1943 to ensure postwar reconstruction. In 1944 the Allied powers held a conference at Dumbarton Oaks to negotiate the principles of a new postwar intergovernmental organization to replace the League of Nations, which was blamed for failing to prevent military aggression and war. In early 1945, Latin American states met in Mexico City to discuss proposals by the Great Powers for a "United Nations" body. And in April 1945, while the war was still raging, the UN founders met in San Francisco to produce the UN Charter, signed by fifty nations in June—six weeks before the United States dropped its atomic bombs on Hiroshima and Nagasaki and forced the unconditional surrender of Japan.

In February 1946 the UN General Assembly met for the first time in London and, still awed by the destructive power of the nuclear bombs the United States had just dropped, immediately established the Atomic Energy Commission (AEC). Rapidly a host of other UN institutions followed, among them the International Court of Justice and the UN International Children's Emergency Fund (now known as the UN Children's Fund, or UNICEF) before the end of the year. In 1948 the World Health Organization was brought into the UN system, and the General Assembly passed the Genocide Convention and the Universal Declaration of Human Rights. In 1949 the Assembly set up the Office of the High Commissioner for Refugees (UNHCR).

By the end of the century, the UN had become a multipurpose, universal IGO to which effectively any nation could belong (even Switzerland, the steadfast holdout, joined in 2002). The UN commits members to the nonuse of force and the peaceful settlement of disputes. Its central purpose is to maintain international peace and security, but also to develop friendly relations among states; to address economic, social, cultural, and humanitarian problems; and to promote respect for universal human rights. Its six principal organs are the General Assembly, the Security Council, the Economic and Social Council (ECOSOC), the Trusteeship Council, the International Court of Justice, and the Secretariat. These organs are an umbrella to dozens of other UN agencies and autonomous bodies (see Figure 3.1). The Security Council has launched over a dozen peacekeeping operations and special commissions over the years.[2] ECOSOC alone houses some forty agencies, functional and regional committees, and expert and ad hoc bodies. Some of these are hotly debated in the media, others are virtually unknown to the broader public: the World Bank (the focus of the next chapter) provides lending for developing countries; the Universal Postal Union ensures safe and cost-effective delivery of mail to and from Timbuktu or other remote areas that would be prohibitively expensive to reach if left to the free market; the World Food Programme (WFP) and the International Fund for Agricultural Development (IFAD) address the pressing needs of world hunger and food security; the International Atomic Energy Agency is designed to regulate nuclear energy and ensure its peaceful uses; and the UNHCR, the UN Development Programme (UNDP), the UN Development Fund for Women (UNIFEM), the UN Environment Programme (UNEP), the UN Population Fund (UNFPA), and UNICEF all address humanitarian issues.

The Trusteeship Council has virtually finished its task of decolonization and is one of the great success stories of the twentieth century; its phasing-out marks the end of an imperial age that for centuries dominated world history.[3] The Trusteeship Council is now a candidate for a new historic task: its mandate might become protecting the global commons and human rights.

Despite the wide-ranging language of its Charter ("We the Peoples . . ."), the UN was founded mainly to prevent the recurrence of large-scale war and to protect states against aggression. Representing the interests of the world's entire population was a welcome side effect, but democracy was not integral to the UN's purpose. The word "democracy" does not even appear in the Charter.

In his *Agenda for Development,* former UN Secretary-General Boutros Boutros-Ghali wrote in 1994 that "democracy is a fundamental human right."[4] In 1995 he stressed that "the United Nations must act to promote democracy not only within states and among states, but also within the global society in which we shall be living. These are three levels of the policy of democratization pursued by the UN."[5] In 1996, Annan published a long essay, *An Agenda for Democratization,* in which he referred to "a growing interest among the Member States themselves in the democratization of the United Nations itself."[6] But the vast heterogeneity of "We the

Figure 3.1 The United Nations System

PRINCIPAL ORGANS OF THE UNITED NATIONS

Security Council[a]	General Assembly[a]	Secretariat[a]
Subsidiary Bodies: Military Staff Committee Standing Committee and ad hoc bodies International Criminal Tribunal for the Former Yugoslavia International Criminal Tribunal for Rwanda UN Monitoring, Verification, and Inspection Commission (Iraq) UN Compensation Commission Peacekeeping Operations and Missions	Subsidiary Bodies: Main committees Other sessional committees Standing committees and ad hoc bodies Other subsidiary organs	Departments and Offices: OSG: Office of the Secretary- General OIOS: Office of Internal Oversight Services OLA: Office of Legal Affairs DPA: Department of Political Affairs DDA: Department for Disarmament Affairs DPKO: Department of Peacekeeping Operations OCHA: Office for the Coordination of Humanitarian Affairs
Programs and Funds: UNCTAD: UN Conference on Trade and Development ITC: International Trade Centre (UNCTAD/WTO) UNDCP: UN Drug Control Programme[b] UNEP: UN Environment Programme UNICEF: UN Children's Fund UNDP: UN Development Programme UNIFEM: UN Development Fund for Women UNV: UN Volunteers UNCDF: UN Capital Development Fund UNFPA: UN Population Fund UNHCR: Office of the UN High Commissioner for Refugees WFP: World Food Programme UNRWA[c]: UN Relief and Works Agency for Palestine Refugees in the Near East UN-HABITAT: UN Human Settlements Programme (UNHSP)	Research and Training Institutes: UNICRI: UN Interregional Crime and Justice Research Institute UNITAR: UN Institute for Training and Research UNRISD: UN Research Institute for Social Development UNIDIR[c]: UN Institute for Disarmament Research INSTRAW: International Research and Training Institute for the Advancement of Women Other UN Entities: OHCHR: Office of the UN High Commissioner for Human Rights UNOPS: UN Office for Project Services UNU: UN University UNSSC: UN System Staff College UNAIDS: Joint UN Programme on HIV/AIDS	DESA: Department of Economic and Social Affairs DGACM: Department for General Assembly and Conference Management DPI: Department of Public Information DM: Department of Management OHRLLS: Office of the High Representative for the Least Developed Countries, Landlocked Developing Countries, and Small Island Developing States UNSECOORD: Office of the UN Security Coordinator UNODC: UN Office on Drugs and Crime UNOG: UN Office at Geneva UNOV: UN Office at Vienna UNON: UN Office at Nairobi

Figure 3.1 continued

PRINCIPAL ORGANS OF THE UNITED NATIONS

Economic and Social Council[a]	Trusteeship Council	International Court of Justice

Functional Commissions:
Commission on Human Rights
Commission on Narcotic Drugs
Commission on Crime
  Prevention and Criminal
  Justice
Commission on Science and
  Technology for Development
Commission on Sustainable
  Development
Commission on the Status of
  Women
Commission on Population and
  Development
Commission for Social
  Development
Statistical Commission

Regional Commissions:
Economic Commission for
  Africa (ECA)
Economic Commission for
  Europe (ECE)
Economic Commission for
  Latin America and the
  Caribbean (ECLAC)
Economic and Social
  Commission for Asia and the
  Pacific (ESCAP)
Economic and Social
  Commission for Western
  Asia (ESCWA)

Other Bodies:
Permanent Forum on
  Indigenous Issues (PFII)
UN Forum on Forests
Sessional and standing
  committees
Expert, ad hoc, and related bodies

Specialized Agencies[g]:
ILO: International Labour Organization
FAO: Food and Agriculture Organization
UNESCO: UN Educational, Scientific, and Cultural Organization
WHO: World Health Organization
World Bank Group:
  IBRD: International Bank for Reconstruction and Development
  IDA: International Development Association
  IFC: International Finance Corporation
  MIGA: Multilateral Investment Guarantee Agency
  ICSID: International Centre for Settlement of Investment Disputes
IMF: International Monetary Fund
ICAO: International Civil Aviation Organization
IMO: International Maritime Organization
ITU: International Telecommunication Union
WMO: World Meteorological Organization
WIPO: World Intellectual Property Organization
IFAD: International Fund for Agricultural Development
UNIDO: UN Industrial Development Organization
WTO[d]: World Tourism Organization

Related Organizations:
WTO[a,d]: World Trade Organization
IAEA[a,e]: International Atomic Energy Agency
CTBTO Prep.Com[f]: PrepCom for the Nuclear-Test-Ban-Treaty
  Organization
OPCW[f]: Organization for the Prohibition of Chemical Weapons

Source: UN Department of Public Information, DPI/2342, March 2004, http://www.un.org/aboutun/chart.html.

Notes: a. Shaded areas indicate a direct reporting relationship, except in the case of the Secretariat, which lists the departments and offices of the Secretariat. Nonsubsidiary relationships include: Security Council—IAEA; General Assembly—IAEA, CTBTO Prep.Com, OPCW; Economic and Social Council—programs and funds, research and training institutes, other UN entities, specialized agencies; the WTO and IAEA—specialized agencies.

b. The UN Drug Control Programme is part of the UN Office on Drugs and Crime.

c. UNRWA and UNIDIR report only to the General Assembly.

d. The World Trade Organization and World Tourism Organization use the same acronym.

e. IAEA reports to the Security Council and the General Assembly.

f. The CTBTO Prep.Com and OPCW report to the General Assembly.

g. Specialized agencies are autonomous organizations working with the UN and each other through the coordinating machinery of ECOSOC at the intergovernmental level, and through the Chief Executives Board for Coordination (CEB) at the intersecretariat level.

Peoples" governed by the UN system and the vast distance between rulers and ruled stretch traditional concepts of democracy.[7] To what extent does the UN live up to its democratic aspirations?

And who is in charge? Is the organization accountable to the citizens of its nearly 200 member states; only to their governments; to the Group of 77 (which has grown to some 130 developing and emerging member states); to the five permanent members of the Security Council; to the sole remaining superpower, the United States; or not to states at all, but to powerful non-state actors—for example, large multinational corporations? To answer, this chapter matches the UN against the seven dimensions of transnational democracy from Chapter 1: appointment, participation, transparency, reason-giving, overrule, monitoring, and independence. It pays particular attention to the three most prominent actors at the heart of the UN: the Security Council, the General Assembly, and the Secretary-General. The chapter also reviews two cases: the International Labour Organization, the UN's oldest agency, which boasts a unique governance structure that might point to best practices in transnational democracy; and the UN's youngest institution, the International Criminal Court.

Appointment

We saw in Chapter 1 that appointment and removal power is a key feature of checking bureaucratic discretion. What are the rules for selecting key UN officials? Are they vetted? Is there a legislature that can throw them out if they fail to deliver their mandates? The most highly visible person in the UN system is the Secretary-General, "the chief administrative officer of the Organization" according to Article 97 of the UN Charter. Secretaries-General have been not only heads of the organization's Secretariat, but also de facto spokespersons for the world community. Trygve Lie, Dag Hammarskjöld, U Thant, Kurt Waldheim, Javier Perez de Cuellar, Boutros Boutros-Ghali, and Kofi Annan have all sought to rise above particular state interests and be quintessential global statesmen.

The Secretary-General is elected by the General Assembly upon the Security Council's recommendation. (Only once in the history of the UN has there been a proposal to have more than one person head the organization. In 1960, the Soviet Union, unhappy with Dag Hammarskjöld's handling of his role, formally proposed a "troika" arrangement of heading the UN with three leaders, but the member states rejected it.) The geographic regions (Africa, the Americas, Asia, Europe, and Oceania) may each nominate one candidate for the position. There is an unspoken rule that Secretaries-General should come from rotating regions, but there have been exceptions. Kofi Annan, a Ghanaian, succeeded Boutros Boutros-Ghali, an

Egyptian, resulting in the unusual outcome of two successive UN heads from Africa. Annan was chosen, nevertheless, because there had never been a Secretary-General from sub-Saharan Africa, and more important, because he had some thirty years of wide-ranging experience in key management positions across the Secretariat and was widely seen, not least by the United States, as being well equipped to tackle the UN's financial and organizational problems.

The Secretary-General is ultimately responsible for the recruitment of employees and other professionals at UN headquarters in New York and Geneva. This staff does all the substantive work of analyzing global, economic, social, human rights, and environmental concerns, as well as direct peacekeeping and other emergency operations. They prepare the Secretary-General's reports to the General Assembly, the Security Council, ECOSOC, and related organs and agencies. Article 101 of the UN Charter provides the two main principles for recruiting UN workers: the highest standard of efficiency, competence, and integrity; and the widest possible geographical spread. But in practice, the majority of workers hired by the Secretary-General have been from the United States and Western Europe. The basis for staff quotas was originally budgetary contributions; member states with higher contributions got more positions for their citizens. But in 1962 the General Assembly adopted a new formula, taking into account not only the monetary factor, but also membership and population size.[8] Another positive trend in appointment has been gender equity: by 2002, women accounted for 39.2 percent of the professional staff positions subject to geographical quotas and 36.5 percent of positions with appointments for one year or more.[9] While the UN's treatment of women is still far from equitable—appointments of women at higher levels had actually slowed during the preceding twelve months—it is more equal than in most national governments.

The UN Security Council, the organ charged above all with settling disputes peacefully and preventing war through collective action, is made up of five permanent members (China, France, Russia, the United Kingdom, and the United States) and ten nonpermanent members. The General Assembly chooses ten nonpermanent members for staggered two-year terms, five each year. On retirement from the Council, elected members cannot immediately run for reelection. (Enlarging the Council was one of the few changes made in the UN structure by formal amendment, from the original nine to the current fifteen members.)

The Council makes two types of decisions, procedural and substantive. Procedural decisions need a yes vote by any nine of the fifteen members; the permanent and the elected members have equal voice. Substantive decisions are a different story: according to the Charter they are made "by an affirmative vote of nine members including the concurring votes of the permanent members," and cannot be reached without yes votes by all of the Permanent Five. A permanent member's abstention does not count as a veto; it must vote no to block a decision. (One pitfall is the "double veto," in which a permanent member disputes the decision to declare an issue substantive and then vetoes the vote to declare that issue procedural. But since the end of the Cold War, this special [ab]use of veto power has not been a problem.)

Because the permanent members have more powers than other countries on the Security Council, it is often viewed as undemocratic,[10] and there have been many calls for its reform (especially by actors who have no seat on it). Annan himself has pushed for the Council's enlargement, with new members added both to the group of permanent members and to the elected nations that serve two-year terms. The argument usually goes like this: the Council reflects the balance of power at the end of World War II, but not today's world; the Permanent Five all owe their membership to winning the war; neither powerful losers (Germany or Japan) nor powerful and populous emerging nations (India or Brazil) are represented. If the UN were created from scratch today, the only claim the original five could make on dominating the Council would be that they are still the only five declared nuclear powers and the five leading arms exporters. A Security Council created anew could combine leading states (for example, the United States, China, Russia, India, and Brazil) with regional representation (for example, Europe, Africa, the Middle East, and South Asia) based on some system of rotation.[11] One proposal would add six permanent members; likely candidates would be Brazil, Egypt, Germany, India, Japan, and either Nigeria or South Africa.[12]

But not all commentators agree. There are those who say that any large-scale international action depends on the resources and goodwill of the permanent members, which still dominate international affairs; that increasing the size of the Security Council would reduce the UN's efficiency and make any meaningful decision more difficult;[13] or that reform proposals are thinly veiled attempts to reduce rightful US influence and would only reinforce Washington's penchant for dismissing the organization and looking elsewhere to pursue its interests.[14] "The worst fear of any of us," said Undersecretary-General Shashi Tharoor, who has spent his entire career at the UN, "is that we fail to navigate an effective way between the Scylla of being seen as a cat's paw of the sole superpower, and the Charybdis of being seen as so unhelpful to the sole superpower that they disregard the value of the United Nations."[15]

The General Assembly does not have the decisionmaking and executive powers of the Security Council, but it is crucially important for the UN's transnational democracy—it is the only organ in which there is an equal one-state, one-vote representation for the UN's nearly 200 member states, and has some agenda-setting power since it can put items on the Council's table. The Assembly president is elected by a two-thirds majority vote for a one-year term. As with all other Assembly votes, each member state casts one vote to elect the president.

The accession of member states to the UN is fairly democratic. The Council first makes a recommendation to the General Assembly that a vote be taken on admission. The Assembly then admits or refuses that country through a two-thirds majority vote. But the UN Charter contains no provisions on how member states are to elect or select their individual General Assembly representatives. Problems for democracy arise when a candidate country is not democratic, since the UN Charter fails to specify democracy as a precondition for UN membership or as a basis for suspension of rights or outright expulsion. Article 4 states merely that membership is open to "peaceloving states" that accept "the obligations contained in the present Charter and . . . are able and willing to carry out these obligations." And even these criteria are never rigorously applied in practice; so far no country has ever been expelled from the UN. Since Assembly delegates are not elected by their country's citizens but appointed by their government, the Assembly's appointment process does not guarantee that the respective UN delegate represents the people of his (or much more rarely, her) country. The democracy of the Assembly's appointment process stands and falls with the democracy of the member states.

Participation

Are nongovernmental actors entitled to become involved in UN decisions? Secretary-General Annan opened new doors for nonstate actors—above all, nongovernmental organizations and lobbyists from multinational corporations—to influence UN policymaking. Annan courted NGOs aggressively to make them "welcome partners" in UN efforts on human issues and to enlist their services. The UN partners with NGOs to help carry out programs in hard-to-reach regions of the world like North Korea and Iraq, and they can have some impact on UN resolutions by presenting high-quality research or proposals at the right time.[16] The Assembly has also come to rely on nonstate actors for information it would otherwise have to provide itself. UNICEF and ECOSOC both maintain strong working relationships with NGOs and multinationals, and often invite them to their sessions for input and feedback. ECOSOC has grouped over 1,500 NGOs into three categories according to the Assembly's areas of interest. Many NGOs and semigovernmental organizations, such as the Palestinian Authority (and before it the Palestinian Liberation Organization [PLO]), enjoy observer status.

The Assembly has also sought to strengthen the voice of regional organizations in the UN. It granted formal consultative status to the EU, the Arab League, the African Union (AU), the Organization of American States, and others working with ECOSOC and other organs. EU spokespersons often address UN forums. Just like with NGOs, giving a formal voice to regional organizations saves the Assembly a fair amount of fact- and opinion-gathering. Their access to the UN system legitimizes them in the international realm and strengthens their importance.[17]

The Security Council is organized to amplify signals from the member states through its rotating membership. Though representatives of countries not on the Security Council cannot vote there, they are invited to participate in any discussion where their interests may be affected. Similarly, even if a country is not a UN member state, it must still be invited to participate in discussions regarding any dispute to which it is a party. But the Assembly has no official voice or power in the Council and must rely for representation on the nonpermanent members, which not only have no veto power but also have generally less political muscle than any of the Permanent Five in shaping decisions.

Can private actors participate in UN decisionmaking? Not yet. But the upsurge of ethnic conflicts after the Cold War, from the Balkans to Rwanda to East Timor, has renewed the sense that the UN must protect not only its member states, but also minorities within them. In 1992 the Assembly adopted its Declaration on the Rights of Persons Belonging to National, Ethnic, Religious, and Linguistic Minorities, which includes the right "to participate effectively in cultural, religious, social and public life."[18] And under Secretary-General Annan, the UN launched the Millennium Assembly to bring the system closer to the world's peoples. When Annan was sworn in for his second term, he expressed the hope "that five years from now the peoples of the world—whom the organization was founded to serve—will feel that it is closer to them, working better to fulfill their needs and putting their welfare at the center of everything it does."[19] The initiative is likely to combine government bureaucracies with private organizations from the social and economic sectors, and lower the threshold for broader popular representation.[20] In that sense the UN is returning to the values of one of the oldest international organizations still in existence today: the International Labour Organization (see Case 3.1).

Transparency

Are the UN's deliberations and rules transparent and open to scrutiny by citizens and member states? Though debates do take place in the Assembly, the more significant work of the UN happens in quiet consultation and negotiation. What the public hears is not the deliberation but only the reso-

Case 3.1   The International Labour Organization

In 1919, when the ILO was founded during the Versailles peace negotiations at the close of World War I, it became part of the UN's predecessor, the League of Nations, along with the International Institute of Commerce. While the League eventually died, the ILO continued to function and found a new home in 1946 as the UN's first specialized agency.

The ILO is unique among international organizations. Not only is it the oldest international body still in existence, but it has also been associated with some of the most important and ambitious accomplishments of the twentieth century—universal worker rights, labor laws, and work standards, not least improving the lives of women and children. Immediately after its founding, the ILO took up the work and social status of women, who have been the subject of ILO agreements ever since. For example, soon after the UN's founding, in 1949, the ILO adopted the Convention Concerning Equal Remuneration for Men and Women Workers for Work of Equal Value.

Since children are the most vulnerable members of society, adults can easily engage them in hazardous and exploitative labor or sexual abuse, or traffic them across borders. According to the ILO, some 250 million children ages five to fourteen work in all regions of the world, 50–60 million of them in hazardous environments. Most of them live in Asia (61 percent) and Africa (32 percent). Over two-thirds of them work in agriculture.[a] Of course, children who work go to school less, if at all. Worse, working children of today are likely to become the parents of working children tomorrow, perpetuating a vicious cycle of ignorance and oppression. To break this cycle, 174 ILO member states in 1999 unanimously adopted a new convention (No. 182) to supplement the ILO's 1973 Minimum Age Convention (No. 138) on the Worst Forms of Child Labor. As of July 2005, 156 countries had ratified the updated convention, making it the fastest-ratified in the organization's history.[b] Recent ILO success stories include tougher child labor regulations in the Bangladeshi textile industry and in Pakistani soccer ball manufacturing.

Work lies at the heart of human activity, so the ILO is active in all parts of the globe and cooperates with many other UN bodies. It worked with the Food and Agriculture Organization (FAO) to regulate fishing in international waters. It has sought to protect workers from environmental hazards, prevent early disability, and promote vocational training or job placement. It contributed its Fundamental Principles on Rights at Work to the Global Compact, a pathbreaking initiative launched by Secretary-General Annan in 2000 to engage corporations in making globalization work for all. Already in 1969 the ILO had received the Nobel Peace Prize for its work.

(continues)

Case 3.1   continued

The ILO's rules and structure differ from those of other international bodies. As an agency under the ECOSOC umbrella, it is a functional organization much like the IMF and the World Bank; but while the IMF and the Bank create their own guidelines for how they will assist countries in need, the ILO enjoys advisory status and answers requests for technical assistance by member states. It resembles more the General Assembly or the Security Council than the Bank or the Fund: its conventions and resolutions build a body of universal labor laws and worker rights. In this way, it is a quasi-legislature.

There are clear rules for joining or leaving the ILO. The admission of a new member state needs a two-thirds majority to pass. (Both superpowers were in and out of the ILO in the twentieth century: The Soviet Union left in 1939, when it was expelled from the League of Nations after its attack on Finland, but rejoined in 1954. In 1970 the United States cut off its 21 percent payments of the organization's budget to push against the appointment of a Soviet delegate as assistant director-general and to express its anger at the ILO as a forum for ideological grandstanding; it rejoined in 1980 under President Jimmy Carter.) A unique appointment rule helps the ILO ensure transnational democracy: each member state sends to the three ILO organs (the International Labour Conference, the Governing Body, and the International Labour Office) one delegate from each of three groups—its government, employers, and labor unions. By bringing representatives from all three sectors to every level of decisionmaking, the ILO enhances participation by subnational actors. This triangular cooperation also makes the ILO transparent, because the negotiating opponents with a stake in labor issues face off on every issue under discussion. For example, member governments cannot push through a convention that would give too much to employers, because worker delegates are also there to safeguard their rights and act as check against excessive powers, and vice versa. The ILO's relative transparency and overrule procedures allow for monitoring by outside groups and parliaments.

The ILO's very mission makes it a guardian of democracy, since it looks out for worker rights everywhere. Despite its successes, much work remains to be done, especially in terms of the ILO's independence, given the lopsided funding by the United States of over one-fifth of its budget. But its tripartite decisionmaking, which puts contentious issues on the agenda and has helped parties resolve them, is worth emulating by other international organizations.

Notes: a. http://www.ilo.org/public/english/standards/ipec/simpoc/stats/child/stats.htm.

b. http://www.globalmarch.org/campaigns/conventioncampaign/index.php.

lutions. That most talks take place behind closed doors does not bode well for transparency. This is true most of all for the Council.[21] Key decisions are hammered out in informal gatherings among the representatives of the Permanent Five.[22] The Assembly also obscures its work, but not intentionally; its policymaking style is simply a bit meandering. One British observer described the General Assembly, with a healthy dose of Anglo sarcasm, as "a herd of grazing cattle, that moves as it chews, head down, gets through its day (or more often its morning) without any particular drive, yet not without a certain diffused sense of purpose."[23]

The Assembly has sought to strengthen its transparency by informing NGOs, media, policymakers, businesspeople, educators, and the general public on its activities. Its Department of Public Information (DPI) cultivates relationships between the UN and NGOs and spreads information on the UN and specifically on Assembly or Council votes and resolutions. Unofficial voting tallies first become available in press releases immediately after meetings; official information goes into the record of the meeting at which the vote was taken or into the Council's annual reports of its votes.[24] This public record enhances transparency, particularly in countries whose media are less free and/or less likely to cover international organizations.

Reason-Giving

Are UN organs required to give reasons for decisions? While the DPI is there to provide information, some of it tends to be biased. For example, the UN system's wide-ranging website often seeks to advocate or promote programs, causes, or points of view. The DPI tends to present the organization in its most favorable light.[25] This is of course its job; but a more independent information agency would make the UN more credible.

As long as a Security Council member is a democracy, it can be expected to explain Council decisions at least to its own electorate. If on the other hand its information policy is more closed (think of China or Russia among the Permanent Five, or Angola or Pakistan in the 2003–2004 slate of nonpermanent members or Tanzania in the 2005–2006 slate), this limits the reason-giving of the whole Council, which itself has no explicit reason-giving requirement; it relies on the Assembly to provide the reasoning behind its decisions, since the Assembly is the body recommending items for the Council's agenda.

As the UN's chief spokesperson, the Secretary-General has a unique role in explaining policy decisions of the Council or Assembly to the world public. Some, like Dag Hammarskjöld, Javier Perez de Cuellar, and Kofi Annan, have gone beyond the call of duty to give reasons and have in fact provided moral guidance to the world community. They have sought to bring a vision of human dignity and the peaceful resolution of disputes to a world of uncertainty, violence, and war. In that sense, they have embodied the very principles on which the UN was founded, and have attempted to make up for the organization's insufficient reason-giving procedures.

Overrule

At the 1945 San Francisco conference that launched the UN, the founders preferred to let each organ interpret its own competence.[26] Are there checks and balances—can some UN actors check others? Does the Assembly (as a quasi–world legislature) or the ICJ (the quasi–judicial branch) have the power to overturn decisions by the Council (the quasi–executive branch)? The Assembly cannot overrule the Council; dissenting member states have no recourse except Article 109, which allows them to convene a general conference to review the UN Charter as a whole—an arduous mechanism, to say the least: in the UN's first fifty years the Charter was amended only three times. And unlike in the League of Nations, dissenters cannot unilaterally withdraw from the organization.[27]

Ever since the powers of the League's Permanent Court of International Justice were transferred to the ICJ in 1946, all UN members have always automatically been ICJ parties according to its statute. Nonmembers of the UN may join the ICJ as well;[28] for example, Switzerland was an important member of the Court for decades before finally joining the UN itself in 2002. The ICJ consists of fifteen judges who each serve nine-year terms; elections for five of these seats are held once every three years and are voted on by both Assembly and Council. Judges are asked not to speak merely for their nation, but to be "independent magistrates" in performing their judicial duties. No two judges may be from the same country, and the UN attempts to select judges familiar with the full range of legal systems around the world.

As "the principal judicial organ" according to Article 92, the ICJ adjudicates disputes between member states, or between a member and a nonmember, under international law. Only states have access to its proceedings. (The new International Criminal Court, discussed in Case 3.2, opens the UN judicial process to individuals in a way that the ICJ was never designed or able to.) The ICJ gives advisory opinions to all six UN organs and sixteen specialized agencies. By employing an "expressive mode of review," the Court explains its position on Security Council actions in light of existing international law, and can lend legitimacy to—or withhold it from—the Council's actions.[29] But this check is highly indirect: at best, it affects future Council resolutions rather than existing ones. There is no institutionalized judicial review of the Council by the ICJ. The precedent for this lack of overrule powers was the case *Libya v. UK/USA*,[30] in which the ICJ decided implicitly that it is not entitled to supervise the Council acting under Chapter VII, and left it unclear whether the Council can be supervised if not acting under Chapter VII.[31] In sum, the UN system is lacking judicial review, legislative oversight, and other checks and balances that are essential for a democratic system.

Monitoring

Are legislative bodies or outside actors able to monitor UN organs, in particular the Security Council, the quasi-executive? As a quasi-legislature, the Assembly uses a system of annual reports on the work of each UN organ and agency to supervise the organization as a whole. Under Articles 60 and 85 of the Charter, the Trusteeship Council and ECOSOC operate "under the authority of the General Assembly." Major decisions on the Secretariat's personnel, funding, and policies are made by the Assembly.

Another monitoring tool is the budgetary process. Like many national legislatures, the Assembly uses its "power of the purse" to control programs and activities on which it does not have direct oversight—for example, those of the Security Council, to which the Assembly can make recommendations, but over which it has no formal power. According to Article 15(1), the Council must report to the Assembly on its activities. But in practice, reporting has been a mere routine: the Council presents an annual report that is not even discussed in the Assembly.

In turn, NGOs play an important role in monitoring not only the Assembly, but also the Secretariat, ECOSOC, various UN agencies, and member states' follow-up on their commitments—for example, the implementation of the 1990 World Summit for Children or the 1992 Rio Summit. Once the UN adopts a resolution or recommendation, NGOs can serve as watchdogs that publicize noncompliance by governments or lack of follow-up by Secretariat officials. This has happened in the human rights arena, where private humanitarian groups have been active in finding violations and making noise about them.[32]

Independence

Is the UN system immune or vulnerable to capture by powerful states, special interests, or even its own bureaucrats? The UN's priorities depend largely on who controls its agenda and on geopolitical power relationships at any given time.[33] The terrorist bombing of UN headquarters in Baghdad in August 2003 showed that, at least on the fringes of the Muslim world, the UN is not seen as neutral but as the stalking horse of US aspirations in the Middle East. The communications director of the UN's Baghdad mission, a survivor of the bombing, said: "It was clear to many of us in Baghdad that lots of ordinary Iraqis were unable to distinguish our U.N. operation from the overall U.S. presence in the country."[34] The corruption scandal discussed at the outset of this chapter, in which senior UN officials collaborated with Iraq's former government to embezzle billions of dollars meant for the UN's oil-for-food program, certainly calls into question the UN's impartiality. Reports of abuses—such as the 2005 accusations of UN peacekeeping soldiers raping women and girls in Congo and paying their victims $1 each, with similar abuses reported from Bosnia and Kosovo, Cambodia and East Timor, and West Africa—certainly do not help, especially since the UN has been reluctant to risk offending member states that contribute scarce peacekeeping troops.[35]

In the Security Council, the veto power of the Permanent Five threatens the UN's independence too. On several occasions, permanent members have used their veto to prevent the Council from stepping on their toes, effectively capturing its agenda. The UN's first decade, from 1946 to 1955, which was also the first decade of the Cold War, saw eighty-two vetoes, seventy-nine cast by the Soviet Union alone. The majority of the Soviet Union's vetoes in the UN's early years blocked admissions of new states to the UN, many of which ended up being admitted in 1955 anyway. By comparison, US vetoes reached that same number—seventy-nine—by 1997. Many other vetoes have been frivolous or inconsequential in their practical effects.[36]

The great powers have been much less able to dominate in the General Assembly, partly due to its one-country, one-vote rule. The subject of heated debate for decades, the rule has given all countries, regardless of their size, an equal voice. A population-weighted voting scale would change the power structure, but it would still be difficult for any one country to control Assembly decisions.

At times the Council or the Assembly has been dominated by opposing parties. Before the 1960s, Western powers controlled the Assembly. The United States, especially, used its credibility as a World War II victor, rebuilder of Europe through the Marshall Plan, and principal UN sponsor to lead the Assembly, while the USSR used its veto to hold the Council hostage. In more recent years, even before the end of the Cold War, the balance of power turned: third world nations gained leverage in the Assembly,[37] while the United States lost its monopoly of influence; it can no longer claim to be part of the majority within the Assembly, which some critics, particularly in the United States and Israel, sometimes deride as "Palestinian-occupied territory" for its frequent marginalizing of Israel, a key US ally and long the lone democracy in the Middle East. While many UN member states are ruled by dictators, we cannot expect the Assembly to

Case 3.2   The International Criminal Court

On July 17, 1998, at the UN Diplomatic Conference of Plenipotentiaries in Rome, 120 nations adopted the Rome Statute, creating the International Criminal Court. While ad hoc tribunals had been set up for specific cases ever since the 1946 Nuremberg trials, the ICC was to be broad in focus and permanent. It was to have jurisdiction over the most egregious crimes of concern to the international community: genocide, crimes against humanity, war crimes, and aggression. But the new Court would try individuals only when their respective national courts were either unable or unwilling to do so.

As of March 2005, ninety-eight states had ratified the ICC treaty and 139 had signed it. The Court's jurisdiction had begun in 2003, but it had yet to try a case. Three state parties—all in Africa—had brought cases to the ICC's prosecutor, who decided to open investigations into two of them (Congo and Uganda). There are no precedents for publication of Court rulings, the right of individuals to bring cases to the Court, or the Court's powers to indict, try, sentence, and enforce the sentencing of individuals. Other important issues remain unclear, such as how the Court will deal with citizens of countries that have not ratified the treaty, or how it will resolve conflicts between international and national law. Only by tackling cases will the ICC show whether it is effective, democratic, and independent. In the meantime, the best we can do is to inspect the treaty on which it is based. In this respect, the ICC is one of the most thoroughly designed international organizations ever; it stands on the shoulders of older international organizations in an attempt to learn from their best (and worst) practices.

Appointment

In February 2003 the member states began electing the ICC's eighteen judges, three of whom act as president and two vice presidents. The judges themselves select their president and vice presidents, and delegate their duties. The Court also includes a prosecutor and deputy prosecutors, plus a registrar and deputies. The ICC framers laid out meticulous procedures for appointment and removal through successive rounds of voting. The Assembly of States nominates candidates for the judicial positions and then votes in a one-country, one-vote secret ballot to elect the judges by absolute majority. The ICC

(continues)

Case 3.2   continued

treaty stipulates that judges represent the range of major judicial systems throughout the world, that they be ethnically diverse, and that both females and males be adequately represented. Member states can demand interviews with nominees, but there is no formal vetting process.

Participation

The ICC treaty provides for the Court's organs to communicate effectively with each other. Article 112, paragraph 5, states, "The President of the Court, the Prosecutor and the Registrar or their representatives may participate, as appropriate, in meetings of the Assembly [of States] and of the Bureau." In terms of public participation the Court is quite innovative too. It is the first permanent global tribunal in which individual citizens have standing (and can be sentenced). Citizens, no matter from what nation, can bring cases to the ICC. They can participate in Court proceedings and be compensated by Court order, though it is still unclear just how effective such compensation will be when a country is unwilling to cooperate with an order. (Reparations, according to the treaty, can include not only money, but also possessions, land, and other assets.) The ICC is designed not to preempt national judicial systems, but may aid individuals living under conditions that prevent them from bringing cases to the Court.

Transparency

The ICC provides for the greatest feasible transparency under existing political realities. Though its nomination process is public, as are its decisions, the votes by the eighteen judges are not—much like the procedure in the European Court of Justice, where there are no dissenting opinions, but unlike the procedure in the US Supreme Court, which publicizes dissenting opinions. However, unanimity makes sense for a criminal court: unanimous votes protect the accused—as well as the judges.

Reason-Giving

According to the Rome Statute, the ICC must fully explain its decisions to the international community and argue its cases to build a

(continues)

body of law based on precedents. The Rome Conference established a Preparatory Commission composed of state delegates[a] and charged with developing a clear definition of the crime of aggression, finalizing rules of procedure and evidence, and specifying the elements of crime that fall under ICC jurisdiction. Elements of a crime are the substantive parts that the prosecutor must prove in order for the accused to be convicted. The draft exhaustively catalogs the acts that constitute genocide, crimes against humanity, and war crimes. It forms a thorough and widely accepted definition of these heinous crimes that mirrors and adds to international law. In twelve chapters, the rules of procedure and evidence clarify issues like support for the defense (though they do not make clear which registry unit is responsible), the scope of protection for victims and witnesses (for example, when children testify on matters of sexual violence), the privilege against self-incrimination, and confidentiality. National delegations at the Rome Conference allowed the Preparatory Commission to delve into the progressive development of international law, but it was not to depart radically from existing customary law.[b]

Overrule

The Rome Statute did set up ICC appellate courts, but none of them are independent enough from the main judicial system for an appeal to be considered a check on an original ICC decision. The Court has the highest jurisdiction: no other body can check its powers—save the Security Council. According to Article 16, the Council may intervene if the ICC treats a case in which the Council itself is also involved. In such a case, a unique procedure proposed by Singapore comes into play: at least nine of the fifteen Council members must support a resolution to overrule the Court, and the Permanent Five all have to vote in favor of the resolution. In other words, no single permanent member has veto power in such a case, but by use of the Singapore procedure, the Council can overrule the ICC in matters of international security.

Monitoring

Article 112, paragraph 4, of the ICC treaty states: "The Assembly [of States] may establish such subsidiary bodies as may be necessary, including an independent oversight mechanism for inspection, evaluation and investigation of the Court, in order to enhance its efficiency

(continues)

Case 3.2   continued

and economy." Though this statement does not guarantee monitoring, it at least gives the Assembly of States the power to create monitoring bodies. Each ICC member state chooses and sends a delegation to the Assembly, a procedure that grants them some oversight. As long as most member states are democratic (for example, all EU and NATO states), this is not problematic: elected governments appoint delegates who presumably represent the wishes of their respective electorates. This is of course not true for dictatorships; but so far, many of them have been reluctant to join the ICC for fear of being sued.

Article 118 provides for audits: "The records, books and accounts of the Court, including its annual financial statements, shall be audited annually by an independent auditor." As long as it walks its talk, the ICC will have a system of monitoring that is more rigorous than that of any other existing international organization.

Independence

There is no easy way to determine whether or not the ICC will be independent. For example, it is unclear when it has jurisdiction to prosecute crimes of aggression and whether it can do so independently of approval by the Security Council, since crimes of aggression also fall under the purview of the Council's mandate to maintain security. Does the competence to determine an act of aggression lie exclusively with the Security Council, and does the UN Charter mandate this exclusive competence? Or is the Council only primarily competent for determining aggression, which would permit the ICC to play a role too, but might open the door for other actors such as the Assembly or the ICJ to step in?[c] These are still gray areas.

While the United States originally backed the idea for the ICC when it was first conceived, it backtracked as soon as the Pentagon expressed concern that a court outside the United States might try members of the US military. The "indispensable nation" voted against the Rome Statute in 1998 and insisted that the ICC would infringe on its national sovereignty by subjecting US citizens to politically motivated prosecution. Two years later, as one of his last actions while in office, US president Bill Clinton signed the statute on New Year's Eve 2000, the last day on which it was open for signa-

(continues)

ture. But his successor, George W. Bush, "unsigned" the treaty by doing nothing (signing the treaty by December 2001 would have indicated a country's intention to be involved in the framing process). Had Bush signed, the US Senate would still have declined to ratify the treaty anyway: Jesse Helms, the powerful chairman of the Senate Foreign Relations Committee, derided the ICC as a "kangaroo court." Resistance in Congress against joining the ICC was so strong that both chambers passed the 2000 American Service Members' Protection Act (H.R. 4654, S. 2726), which gives the US military the power to take back, if necessary by force, any American being held by the ICC. In an extreme case, this would mean a military invasion of the ICC's facilities, so some critics of the United States, with a bit of sarcasm, call the act a "law on the invasion of The Hague."[d]

Though it seems unlikely that US soldiers will be storming the UN prison anytime soon, even the possibility of such an action casts doubt on the ICC's ability to function effectively. Without the support of the world's only remaining superpower, how global can the Court be? Skeptics believe the ICC might turn into another League of Nations and be whittled away, but proponents respond that such fears are unfounded. They point to the fact that the Court has rules allowing national judicial systems to try cases first, and would step in only when a country's national system is not intact, or could not (or would not) deal with war crimes or crimes against humanity committed by its citizens. Proponents insist that because the Court will comprise judges from nations with well-developed judicial systems, trials will be fair.

Nonetheless, that the United States, a nonmember (though the most powerful by far), can threaten to hamper the entire enterprise shows a weakness in the Court's independence. US rejection of the ICC has meant that other nations, led by Germany, France, and Britain, will have to pick up a greater part of the Court's budget than would occur under normal UN formulas; this could further damage the Court's impartiality and credibility. Worse, the Court has no troops to enforce decisions—it depends on member states to implement its rulings.

Notes: a. Final Act, Annex I.F., s.1, A/CONF.183/10.

b. United Nations Association of the USA 2002: 276–277.

c. United Nations Association of the USA 2002: 277.

d. *Die Zeit,* June 27, 2002: 2.

represent world public opinion. For example, the 1975 "Zionism Is Racism" resolution against Israel, introduced by Somalia, could be carried only because of the votes of a consortium of dictatorships—fifteen Arab, twenty-seven African, and one socialist.[38] To its credit, the Assembly revoked the resolution in 1991—this was only the second revocation in its history—and Annan was to describe it later as "the low point" in UN action concerning Israel.[39]

Conclusion

Table 3.1 quantifies this chapter's findings about transnational democracy in the UN and the ICC. Admittedly, the ratings are rudimentary and crude, ranging from –1 (undemocratic) to +1 (democratic). But they do give a clear impression of transnational democracy in these two organizations, and show leverage points for possible improvements.

Does the UN represent the world's peoples? This simple question calls for a complex response. Almost from its inception, the organization has been criticized for its mandates, competencies, administration, and finances. But the UN is based on a treaty signed by member states; individuals have no formal representation in any UN decisionmaking body (with the possible exception of the ICC). UN reform is ultimately up to the member states overseeing the Secretariat.[40] As the plurality of its name implies, the United Nations can achieve only the level of competence that member states permit it to achieve, no more and no less. Take one UN agency, the WHO, for example: "The World Health Organization isn't the world health police," said one American observer. "It's a club, like a club in Boston where everyone's a member and they slap each other on the back. Every member's a sovereign country, and if they don't want to report something, they don't." (To its credit, despite China's initial lack of cooperation, the

Table 3.1   Transnational Democracy Ratings, UN and ICC

Dimension	UN	ICC
Appointment	–1	0
Participation	–1	+1
Transparency	0	0
Reason-giving	0	+1
Overrule	–1	0
Monitoring	–1	0
Independence	–1	+1
Total rating	–5	+3

Note: Ratings for the UN are based on the Security Council.

WHO still "did a fantastic job" and acted swiftly in 2003 to alert the world community to the SARS outbreak and to contain the disease.[41]) And the United States plays a gatekeeper role in reforms: in the UN's history, there have been just two major reform processes, both forced by the United States—one by President Ronald Reagan in the 1980s, the other by US-backed Secretary-General Kofi Annan starting in the late 1990s. No reform process has yet been undertaken without backing from the United States. This in itself raises questions about the UN's accountability and independence.

But there are hopeful signs for transnational democracy too. The Secretariat's internal accountability is improving; a joint inspection unit examines internal processes and seeks to give UN staffers recourse to a system of justice. The catalyst for many changes like these has been Secretary-General Annan, who has made use of the fact that not all UN reforms are subject to a formal amendment rule. Only a few months into his tenure, in July 1997, Annan proposed a host of innovations, several of which point in the direction of stronger transnational democracy, and most of which have since been implemented. First, the Secretary-General called for decentralizing decisionmaking to the country level; each in-country office would consolidate UN agencies on the ground under "one flag" instead of in separate silos. Not only is this more efficient, but it also brings the UN closer to the end-users it is sworn to serve, which is good for participation. Second, Annan urged greater transparency, less paranoia about maintaining confidentiality, and more openness in sharing information. Third, he proposed an ombudsman to monitor UN agencies for the public. Fourth, forced by arrears owed the UN by the United States, and by a reduced US pledge from 25 to 21 percent of the overall UN budget, Annan and his finance officials accomplished major reductions in the UN budget while attempting to maintain or even expand service quality. There are limits to this. The UN budget compared to the mandates and functions the UN has been asked to perform is really quite modest—little more than that of the New York City Fire Department. All the specialized agency budgets together do not amount to the allocations of a medium-size city.[42]

Though these reforms are needed, they are not enough. Commentators have proposed a flurry of other changes. A second chamber—"a forum in which people rather than governments are represented"—might sit alongside the UN General Assembly and enable fairer decisionmaking.[43] Building on the model of the European Parliament (see Chapter 7), such a UN parliamentary assembly would be consulted by the General Assembly and ECOSOC; major draft resolutions would be presented to it before being voted on by the Assembly; it would give opinions and have a procedure for questioning principal UN organs; and it could request amendments to policies adopted by the Assembly, or itself propose new policies.[44]

A conference on creating a more democratic United Nations has suggested that accountability of the Security Council to the General Assembly (or to a revitalized ECOSOC) needs to be strengthened—for example, by extending reporting mechanisms, or through "a standing committee of the General Assembly of 15 rotating, geographically representative members, [who are] not at the same time members of the Security Council, to report to the Assembly on the adequacy of efforts made by the Council."[45] Another proposal calls for the Security Council to appoint an independent and impartial commission that would evaluate preventive uses of force (like the 2003 Iraq War) after the event, and apply sanctions if the claims made before the event proved to be false.[46]

Another idea, giving the General Assembly the power to make international law, is controversial. If the Assembly were to become a full-fledged legislature, its current one-state, one-vote rule would hardly be democratic, given global demographics. When 0.5 percent of the world population carries more than 25 percent of Assembly votes,[47] this distorts the representation of large and small countries and violates the principle that individuals are the subjects of democracy. But proposals to change the voting weights of member states based on their populations (much like in the European Parliament) run into a dilemma: if voting weights were reapportioned according to populations, four states alone—China, India, the United States, and the former Soviet Union—would together carry an absolute majority.[48]

Currently each member state appoints five delegates to the General Assembly. Other proposals involve having country delegates to the Assembly represent both their government *and* the opposition, with one or two national delegates being directly elected; giving civil society representatives a consultative vote in the Security Council; and granting the ICJ compulsory jurisdiction over UN member states[49] or over all UN political agencies, even the Security Council.[50] One proposal even advocates a formal global citizenship under which individuals would have rights and representation bypassing the state.[51]

As long as the international state system and its underpinning, state sovereignty, remain in place, the UN is likely to remain as it is today: not a quasi-government, but a place where sovereign states can negotiate their interests. Of course, powerful states can bypass the UN altogether, as the United States and Britain did when they led a coalition in the 2003 Iraq War, prompting a visibly concerned Annan to ask, "Who decides? Under what circumstances? Did what happened in Iraq constitute an exception? A precedent others can exploit? What are the rules?"[52] And of course the veto power not only of Britain and the United States, but of all the Permanent Five, is likely to prevent any change in the Charter.[53]

Still, some agencies within the UN, especially the old ILO, one of the first modern international organizations, and the new ICC, the youngest, can serve as examples of transnational democracy. This brings us to the subject of Chapters 4–6: functional organizations. There are many of them, ranging from the International Air Traffic Association to the World Health Organization. I have chosen three prominent examples, each of which deserves a separate chapter, because these are the functional organizations that are most often and most publicly criticized for their lack of accountability and independence: the World Bank, the International Monetary Fund, and the World Trade Organization.

Notes

Yoram Wurmser, Elliott Bernstein, and Richard Radu assisted with research for this chapter.
1. *New York Times,* April 12, 2004: A9; August 10, 2004: A12; August 13, 2004: A1.
2. In the Middle East, the UN Truce Supervision Organization (UNTSO), established in 1948 and headquartered in Jerusalem; the UN Disengagement Observer Force (UNDOF), in the Golan Heights since 1974; the UN Interim Force in Lebanon (UNIFIL), since 1978; the UN Iraq-Kuwait Observation Mission (UNIKO), since 1991; and the UN Special Commission on Iraq (UNSCOM), to inspect Iraq for weapons of mass destruction. In Europe, the UN Peacekeeping Force in Cyprus (UNFICYP), since 1964; and missions in Georgia, Macedonia, Bosnia-Herzegovina, and Croatia. In Asia, the UN Military Observer Group in India and Pakistan (UNMOGIP), since 1949. In Africa, the UN Mission for the Referendum in Western Sahara (MINURSO), since 1991; the UN Observer Mission in Angola (MONUA), since 1997; and the UN Mission in the Central African Republic (MINURCA), since 1998. And in the Americas, the UN Civilian Police Mission in Haiti (MINPONUH), since 1997.
3. Ziring, Riggs, and Plano 1994: 476.
4. UN Doc. A/48/935 (1994): para. 120.
5. United Nations 1995.
6. Boutros-Ghali 1996: 3.
7. Bienen, Rittberger, and Wagner 1998: 292.
8. Ziring, Riggs, and Plano 1994: 115–117.
9. United Nations Association of the USA 2002: 319.
10. Archibugi 1993: 311.
11. Falk 1998: 310.
12. *New York Times,* March 21, 2005: A1.
13. Caron 1993: 563, 573.
14. Luck 2003: 51.
15. *New York Times,* September 19, 2003: A5.
16. Ziring, Riggs, and Plano 1994: 74.
17. Ziring, Riggs, and Plano 1994: 76–77.
18. UN General Assembly Resolution 47/135, adopted December 18, 1992, Art. 2: 2. Reprinted in *Human Rights Law Journal* 14 (1993): 54. See Crawford and Marks 1998: 77.
19. *New York Times,* June 30, 2001: A4.

20. Ziring, Riggs, and Plano 1994: 359.
21. Ziring, Riggs, and Plano 1994: 215; Carlsson 1995: 6.
22. Caron 1993: 564.
23. Nicholas 1975: 104.
24. http://www.un.org/depts/dhl/resguide/scvote.htm.
25. Ziring, Riggs, and Plano 1994: 326, 365.
26. Higgins 1963: 66.
27. Luck 2003: 3.
28. Ziring, Riggs, and Plano 1994: 56.
29. Alvarez 1996: 9, 34.
30. Aerial Incident at Lockerbie Case (Provisional Measures) *(Libya v. UK/USA),* International Court of Justice Reports (1992): 3.
31. Reisman 1993: 243; Franck 1995: 243.
32. Ziring, Riggs, and Plano 1994: 74.
33. Knight 2000: 63.
34. Salim Lone, interview in *New York Times,* September 19, 2003: A5.
35. *Seattle Post Intelligencer,* March 24, 2005.
36. Ziring, Riggs, and Plano 1994: 88.
37. Ziring, Riggs, and Plano 1994: 99.
38. Gorman 2001: 264.
39. United Nations Association of the USA 2002: 177.
40. Gorman 2001: 315.
41. Jack Woodall, moderator, ProMED, the Federation of American Scientists' Program for Monitoring Emerging Diseases. *New York Times,* May 4, 2003: A1.
42. Gorman 2001: 321.
43. Franck 1998: 483.
44. Childers with Urquhart 1994: 176–181. Erskine Childers and Brian Urquhart anticipate that endowing such an assembly with budgetary powers that most parliaments (even the European Parliament) enjoy will meet with too much opposition to succeed.
45. Second Conference on a More Democratic United Nations (CAMDUN 2): 19.
46. Buchanan and Keohane 2004: 15.
47. Ortega Carcelén 1991: 401.
48. Newcombe 1991: 227.
49. Archibugi, Held, and Köhler 1998: 221.
50. Crawford and Marks 1998: 84.
51. Archibugi 1993: 307.
52. *New York Times,* July 31, 2003: A16.
53. Bienen, Rittberger, and Wagner 1998: 295.

4

The World Bank*

I n recent years, the World Bank and its institutions have been under almost constant fire from transnational coalitions of civil society organizations—nongovernmental organizations, churches, indigenous peoples movements, and international networks—for inefficiency, nontransparency, and nondemocratic decisionmaking. The dissatisfaction has been most glaring during annual meetings of the Bank and its sister, the International Monetary Fund, when a heterogeneous network of antiglobalization protesters organize mass demonstrations against Bank and IMF policies and practices. And street protesters have not been alone; scholars and policymakers have joined the chorus. In 2001 the dean of Harvard's School of Government wrote that "these (international) institutions can look like closed and secretive clubs."[1] Former US treasury secretary Paul O'Neill, not exactly an antiglobalization activist, said in 2002 with characteristic bluntness that the Bank had driven poor countries "into a ditch" by lending instead of donating funds to fight poverty.[2]

Insiders attack the Bank too. Both economists in senior positions within the Bank's hierarchy and its shareholders have voiced dissent and demanded more accountability and more open decisionmaking.[3] An internal team reported in 2002 that the Bank did not undertake proper assessments of a $4 billion oil pipeline it backed in Chad and Cameroon, two of the world's poorest countries. The Bank's independent Inspection Panel praised the details of the Bank's environmental impact assessment, but warned that the ambitious project could damage the environment and rob the local population of a fair share of profits.[4]

On the whole, the protests have had a democratizing effect. They have

---

*This chapter was coauthored with Jillian C. Cohen, assistant professor in the Faculty of Pharmacy at the University of Toronto.

catalyzed public debate inside and outside the Bank—about the Bank's mandate, its functioning, and its impact on development. They have compelled the Bank to be more accountable to all its stakeholders, from governments to villagers.

There is little doubt that for hundreds of millions of people living far from the corridors of power in Washington, institutions like the World Bank matter a great deal. A Bank decision to make girls' education a priority can catalyze personal and community development.[5] At the same time, critics charge that the Bank has had little impact on the development process despite its vast lending. For example, sub-Saharan Africa as a region saw no increase in its per capita income between 1965 and 1999.[6] But it is too easy to blame this lack of results on the Bank alone. The regime type of a recipient country—whether that country is a dictatorship or a democracy—has a significant independent effect on that country's welfare. A study of 138 countries observed annually between 1990 and 1997 showed that if recipient countries were dictatorships, aid actually hurt the well-being of their populations as measured by their infant mortality rates: with increasing aid, *more* children died in dictatorships.[7] International aid can help bad as well as good governments survive.[8]

At any rate, this chapter does not evaluate the impact of the World Bank on the development process, a wholly different field of debate.[9] Rather, it attempts to understand the Bank's architecture and processes and to investigate the level of institutional democracy within the Bank. Put simply, this is *not* an output but an input analysis. The questions are: What inputs go into Bank decisions, and what is the process from which Bank policies are derived? If the Bank's internal decisionmaking procedures are democratic, then the policy outcomes—its output—will better reflect the views of its member countries and their citizens. Conversely, the Bank's outputs will fail to represent member countries' and citizens' interests if it suffers from weak internal democracy.

A Brief Background

In July 1944 the Bretton Woods agreement, signed at the UN Monetary and Financial Conference, established the International Bank for Reconstruction and Development (IBRD or World Bank). In 1945 the Bank moved into its headquarters in Washington, D.C., and began with an authorized capital of $10 billion, most of which was quickly lent to Western Europe for rebuilding its economic infrastructure, which had been ravaged by World War II. The original purpose of both Bank and IMF was to prevent the monetary insecurity that had arguably led to the Great Depression and trade-war policies in the interwar years, and had perhaps even contributed to the outbreak of the war itself.[10]

Both Fund and Bank were created at a time when it was widely recognized that governments and international regimes should correct for market failures in the economy. John Maynard Keynes, the economist whose ideas inspired the creation of both institutions, envisioned the Bank as a sort of global credit and development arm of the international community whenever the free market would not ensure adequate lending to a country to aid its development. In its initial decades, the Bank focused on "brick and mortar" projects that included building countries' basic infrastructures, initially in Europe but soon in developing countries. By the 1980s, when a global debt crisis swept the world, the World Bank started to change its lending focus. Slow global economic growth led to overcapacity in many economies while the number of viable new projects the Bank could finance went down. And since poor debtor countries needed substantial funds that could be disbursed quickly, it provided more adjustment loans to streamline economic sectors such as agriculture and telecommunication. At the same time, the United States, the Bank's main "shareholder," sought to involve it in solving the debt problem. At the 1985 annual meeting of the World Bank and IMF in Seoul, then secretary of state James A. Baker III proposed to solve third world debt by boosting economic growth instead of imposing domestic austerity. The intention was for debtor countries to pursue market-oriented growth, for commercial banks to provide more money, and for the World Bank to disburse loans more quickly.[11]

Today the World Bank counts 184 member states and offers cumulative lending of $371 billion—in 2004 it loaned $20.1 billion for 245 projects in developing countries.[12] It now includes a number of institutions (see Figure 4.1): the IBRD, the International Development Association (IDA), the International Finance Corporation (IFC), and the Multilateral Investment Guarantee Agency (MIGA). The focus here is primarily on the IBRD, the institution that provides loans to governments of low- and middle-income countries.

The Bank classifies countries according to their gross national income per capita, which can be low, middle, or high. The low-income economies in 2000 were defined as having $755 or less per capita, lower-middle income $756–$2,995, upper-middle $2,996–$9,265, and high $9,266 or more. Less than 5 percent of IBRD financing comes from member countries. The other type of loan is through the IDA, which uses interest-free loans or long-term credits for which borrowers pay less than 1 percent interest. IDA loans must be paid back in thirty-five to forty years and have a ten-year grace period on the repayment of principal.[13] Some forty countries contribute to IDA funding.

The Bank has broadened its mandate to "fight poverty and improve living standards for people living in the developing world."[14] It now includes providing loans to governments for health, education, governance, and social protection programs. But this makes the results of its projects much

Figure 4.1 World Bank Organization Chart

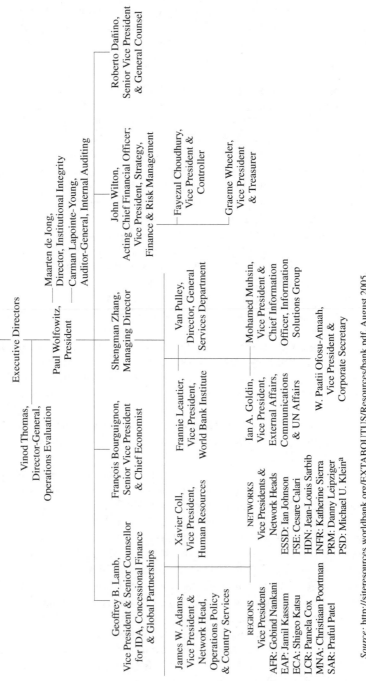

Board of Governors

Executive Directors

Paul Wolfowitz, President

Maarten de Jong, Director, Institutional Integrity
Carman Lapointe-Young, Auditor-General, Internal Auditing

Roberto Dañino, Senior Vice President & General Counsel

Vinod Thomas, Director-General, Operations Evaluation

Shengman Zhang, Managing Director

John Wilton, Acting Chief Financial Officer; Vice President, Strategy, Finance & Risk Management

Fayezul Choudhury, Vice President & Controller

Graeme Wheeler, Vice President & Treasurer

François Bourguignon, Senior Vice President & Chief Economist

Van Pulley, Director, General Services Department

Mohamed Muhsin, Vice President & Chief Information Officer, Information Solutions Group

W. Paatii Ofosu-Amaah, Vice President & Corporate Secretary

Geoffrey B. Lamb, Vice President & Senior Counsellor for IDA, Concessional Finance & Global Partnerships

Frannie Leautier, Vice President, World Bank Institute

Ian A. Goldin, Vice President, External Affairs, Communications & UN Affairs

Xavier Coll, Vice President, Human Resources

NETWORKS
Vice Presidents & Network Heads
ESSD: Ian Johnson
FSE: Cesare Calari
HDN: Jean-Louis Sarbib
INFR: Katherine Sierra
PRM: Danny Leipziger
PSD: Michael U. Klein[a]

James W. Adams, Vice President & Network Head, Operations Policy & Country Services

REGIONS
Vice Presidents
AFR: Gobind Nankani
EAP: Jamil Kassum
ECA: Shigeo Katsu
LCR: Pamela Cox
MNA: Christiaan Poortman
SAR: Praful Patel

Source: http://siteresources.worldbank.org/EXTABOUTUS/Resources/bank.pdf, August 2005.
Note: a. Reports to IFC Executive Vice President on IFC Business.

harder to determine compared with a traditional loan for building, say, a bridge. An internal Bank analysis of health, nutrition, and population (HNP) projects admitted difficulties in finding a clear impact.[15]

The literature on the Bank tends to be split between studies of internal organizational or policy shifts, and studies of the Bank's external output. Both are necessary to understand transnational democracy, and neither is complete without the other. The first approach focuses on policies but not performance, the second on practices and impacts, often without explaining the institutional dynamics that led to them.[16] But output accountability is linked to the seven input indicators of transnational democracy. Bank officials have become sensitized to public embarrassment if they fail to comply with their own policies. Compliance improved dramatically, for example with the Bank's resettlement policy, when it became clear that the Bank's Inspection Panel would publicize lack of compliance. Greater accountability and independence at the input stage enhance greater output accountability, and it is easier—and cheaper—to reshape projects in the design stage than later, when a variety of national and transnational interests are vested in project completion at all costs.[17] Because inputs and outputs are connected, a separate output accountability indicator is unnecessary.

Appointment

A selection committee recruits and hires professional and technical Bank staff. These appointments are usually transparent: open positions are advertised, for example in *The Economist,* and posted on the Bank's intranet and public website. Most positions are filled based on merit and not on logrolling by member states, but there are weaknesses. Sometimes job descriptions are designed to shoe in internal candidates; internal announcements say only that "a suitable candidate has been identified"; the reasons for hiring one person over another are not always publicly stated; and often governments provide funds designated only for their own nationals. This effectively bars full competition from the hiring process. The firing process is problematic too: generally, it takes egregious acts to compel the Bank to terminate staff, particularly those who are on open-ended contracts.

Appointments of upper-level managers are different: they are political positions filled not internally but by member countries through the Bank's Board of Directors. There is no formal rule governing the appointment of the World Bank president, and candidates have come from countries other than the United States; but ever since the Bank's inception, the men who have landed the top job have always been Americans.

The president is assisted by a team of managing directors who oversee the Bank's regional and sectoral networks, such as the HNP Network and the Public Research and Economic Management Network, which are organized regionally (such as for Latin America and the Caribbean). The president is appointed by the Executive Board, comprising twenty-four country representatives, but with direction from the United States. The US executive director nominates the candidate; the executive directors then appoint the president, usually by resolution.[18] (The US government established a search committee that reviewed recommendations from member countries before recruiting former president James Wolfensohn. In March 2005, the George W. Bush administration nominated its deputy defense secretary, Paul Wolfowitz, a known hawk, democracy advocate, and architect of the war on Iraq, to succeed Wolfensohn, prompting Bank staff to joke that the Bank's conditionality guidelines would be streamlined to one article: "You do what we tell you, or we invade you." But after quizzing Wolfowitz in Brussels, European development ministers unanimously endorsed him, based on his commitment to development and democracy, and the Bank's executive directors unanimously approved his presidency.[19])

The Board of Governors is made up of finance ministers from member governments, who meet at least annually. It is charged with general oversight and sets the Bank's de facto policy direction. But the board is heterogeneous and subject to catering to the political will of those member countries with the largest share of voting rights, above all the United States and Japan. It tends to delegate much of its authority to the Executive Board, which is involved with the Bank's internal operations. There are questions about how representative of the member countries the executive directors are. The Executive Board supposedly represents all of the Bank's 184 member states, but in practice representation is imperfect because country interests are clustered. The Canadian executive director is responsible for representing the interests and policy directions not only of Canada, but also of a cluster of other countries with varied interests and policy directions that are grouped under Canada: Antigua and Barbuda, the Bahamas, Barbados, Belize, Dominica, Grenada, Guyana, Jamaica, St. Kitts and Nevis, St. Lucia, and St. Vincent and Grenadines. Executive director positions are typically controlled by member states' finance ministries, which are often highly insulated and able to resist dissent—for example, from their peers in environmental protection agencies. (Adding to the complexity of this structure, the Bank's Development Committee, comprising yet another twenty-four members, also makes policy decisions. Appointed by the Board of Directors, the committee meets twice a year to set broad Bank policy and advise the Board of Governors on development issues.[20])

The Bretton Woods system gives each state a base of 250 votes, but votes are weighted by financial contribution, which is in turn based on the size of a country's economy. For example, the United States contributes some 22 percent of the Bank's capital and holds 20.6 percent of the total vote, while the Maldives have 0.3 percent.

What makes the Bank's activities contentious is that the great majority of voting rights belong to a small number of industrialized countries—the principal shareholders in terms of paid-up capital. For example, the seven wealthiest national economies (Canada, France, Germany, Italy, Japan, the United Kingdom, and the United States) together command 45 percent of voting shares. The voting weight of the United States gives it the power to veto any changes in the Bank's capital base and Articles of Agreement, since 85 percent of shares are needed to effect such changes.[21] In contrast, the much greater number of developing and emerging economies enjoy a small proportion of the voting rights, although they are the principal stakeholders and pay interest to the Bank.[22] This arrangement has led critics to charge that the Bank is not accountable to developing countries, but to the United States and other creditor nations.[23]

Participation

"When we talk about good governance, we don't mean Japan gets a few percentage points more in voting rights, we mean that the meetings are open to the public and the media," said Njoki Njoroge Njehu, director of 50 Years Is Enough!, a network of over 200 US grassroots and policy organizations dedicated to the transformation of the Bretton Woods system. "We mean that when civil society participates in PRSP [Poverty Reduction Strategy Paper] process, as in the case of Tanzania, people there are able to get the draft document outlining national economic plans, without needing to rely on allies in Washington to obtain the documents somehow and send them to Tanzania—documents that were drafted in Tanzania in the first place."[24]

In theory, interested parties on the ground have ways to participate in the Bank's decisionmaking—they can go to their elected representatives and make their views known—but local representatives and their country representatives at the Bank rarely communicate directly. Still, the Institute for Development Research reported just before the turn of the century that transnational coalitions of NGOs, international issues networks, and internal reform alliances can have an impact on World Bank policies, and sought to establish guidelines for such lobbyists.[25] Globalization and environmental activists have indeed produced some change—for example, the Bank now needs to complete environmental and social assessments for all projects, at the identification stage. The Bank itself has undertaken studies that suggest the value of public participation in client countries (in 1999 it published a manual on public participation in environmental decisionmaking and created an internal Participation and Civic Engagement Group). But critics have charged that this is lip service. Perhaps the most telling sign of the Bank's efforts to improve participation is the large-scale presence of external parties from NGOs, business, and the media in its annual meetings.

A major improvement the Bank has made with public participation is the creation of its Inspection Panel, launched in 1993. The panel consists of three members who are non-Bank experts and who are barred from seeking future employment with the Bank. It is an independent forum for private citizens of borrowing countries to voice their concerns about Bank policies or their impact—directly, without having to go through their national government. The panel has a website with detailed instructions about who can participate and how. For example, persons must

- live in the project area (or represent people who do) and be likely to be affected adversely by project activities,
- believe that actual or likely harm results from failure by the Bank to follow its policies and procedures, and
- have discussed their concerns with Bank management without satisfactory outcome.[26]

The Bank's executive directors even felt obliged to grant panel claimants a direct hearing as a group before making their 1999 decision to change the panel's mandate.[27] But the costs and risks of a claim can be substantial, since the preparation, filing, and lobbying for it are highly technical and require specialized policy language that few if any claimants master.[28]

Transparency

In the twentieth century, international organizations worked mostly in club-like fashion. Cabinet ministers—trade ministers in the GATT, finance ministers in the IMF, defense and foreign ministers in NATO, or central bankers in the Bank for International Settlements (BIS)—met and made rules in secret. They used to run international institutions largely unchallenged, but that has changed. Since 1994, responding to demands from its member countries, the Bank has promoted greater transparency, largely through spreading the knowledge it produces and influences. Its website is a comprehensive storage of information, including annual reports, project reports, research, and presentations prepared by its staff. Its annual meetings with the IMF are visible forums to give information about itself directly to the public and the media.

Can private citizens get access to the minutes of the Executive Board?

Minutes are not posted; interested parties have to get them informally. The decisionmaking processes are described and outsiders can find out how they work, but cannot get information on specific decisions. Reports by the independent Inspection Panel are confidential too. This secrecy has prompted activists to demand that the Bank open all its meetings to the public and media, and that it make all its lending documents public.[29] Even senior Bank officials themselves concede that transparency is woefully lacking. Edward Jaycox, the Bank's former vice president for Africa and a senior adviser to former president Wolfensohn, said in an interview: "I don't think we can make these deals in the old way, in the back room, with a series of agreements that don't get published. I think it would be prudent, in the circumstances, to insist on public education as part of the lead-up to a major reform effort."[30]

The Inspection Panel is a key guardian against such opacity. When the panel receives a claim, it sends a copy to Bank management, asks it to respond within twenty-one days, and notifies the Executive Board. Once management responds, the panel weighs the evidence from both sides and determines whether to recommend an investigation into the alleged policy violation. During this preliminary review, the panel may visit the site of the project under scrutiny. It then makes another recommendation to the board, which decides whether to permit the investigation. After the board's decision, management's response and the panel's recommendations are both made public. If the investigation proceeds, the panel sends its final report and findings to the board and management, which has six weeks to prepare recommendations. The Executive Board makes a final decision on whether to take action, and both the panel report and management's recommendations are again made public.

These procedures would go a long way toward ensuring transparency; the only problem is that panel votes themselves are confidential. Worse, most civil society actors are still unaware of the panel and its potential for bureaucratic democracy, and Bank-funded projects appear to people in client countries as projects sponsored by their respective national government, not as Bank projects. The result: many affected people never even think of holding the Bank accountable.[31]

Reason-Giving

Not least in response to widespread anti-Bank protests, former president Wolfensohn was very public and argued his case in the media and on the Internet, for example by highlighting the conflict between the pressure to lend and the need for quality results. Also, the Bank's Operational Evaluation Department (reviewed in detail below) forces the Bank to explain its decisions. Most recently, under increasing pressure to improve its accountability, the Bank agreed to disseminate drafts of its Poverty Reduction Strategy Papers prior to Executive Board approval. These papers are comprehensive plans for economic growth and the alleviation of poverty, prepared by member countries, Bank staff, and consultants.[32]

Over the years, the Bank's reason-giving rhetoric has undergone significant change, often as a result of intense internal debates over whether to comply with policy reforms. While in the 1980s its language emphasized structural readjustment, the Bank now describes virtually all its activities in terms of poverty alleviation. But activists charge that these rhetorical changes are mostly window-dressing—that they have yet to be matched by substantive policy changes.[33] A leaked internal memo gives the impression that high-level Bank environmental officials see project safeguards merely as public relations exercises to "buy time from our critics."[34]

Overrule

The Bank's Inspection Panel has been called a de facto "court of last resort"[35] that might induce Bank managers to improve policy compliance in projects far beyond the few actually under inspection. But "court of last resort" is too optimistic: the panel can make only recommendations and no binding rulings. Worse, the Bank's Executive Board has the power to overrule these recommendations and even to prevent the inspection of projects. It has often rejected panel recommendations.

There is no comprehensive judicial review of World Bank decisions, and there are no adequate internal checks and balances.[36] The only actors with the power to overrule the Bank are its principals, the member states. A famous example was the Three Gorges Dam in China: the Chinese government, prodded by widespread domestic resistance against the giant project, pushed through a change in World Bank policy. The problem is that the Board of Governors, the body wherein the member states can overrule Bank policies, meets only once a year—an insufficient cycle for assessing a myriad of policy decisions.

Monitoring

Monitoring occurs in the Bank's operating divisions, rather than in its central research and policy units.[37] Some critics stress the lack of individual (as opposed to organizational) accountability at the Bank: virtually all Bank bureaucrats, except for the president, operate in anonymity and away from the public eye. The Committee on Development Effectiveness (CODE) was set up in 1994 in response to demands from member countries and external parties that the Bank needed to be more accountable for its operations and project financing.[38] CODE oversees evaluation of the Bank's and the International Finance Corporation's operations. It is a standing eight-member committee staffed by members of the Bank's Executive Board and having a triple mandate: to review the work and reports by the Operations Evaluation Department and Operations Evaluation Group—and management's responses to them—and identify policy issues for the board's consideration; to verify that the Bank's evaluations and self-evaluations are adequate and efficient; and to bring up issues in operations evaluation and development effectiveness for the board's review and decision.[39]

In short, CODE is a self-evaluation tool. But self-evaluation is always susceptible to distortion; the more independent monitor is the Operations Evaluation Department, which continuously audits both IBRD and IDA. It does three different kinds of audits: project reviews, country assistance evaluations, and process reviews. Here is how the process works. The Bank funds projects in member countries that typically last five to eight years. Projects may be related to sectors (such as agriculture or health), thematic areas (such as poverty or gender), or countries. The Operations Evaluation Department does not evaluate all projects; for example, it might audit Bank performance only in the health or energy sector. Whenever a Bank project is completed, Bank staff must prepare a self-evaluation—an Implementation Completion Report (ICR)—for that project and rate its performance. Department staff then review every report, confirm or reject the rating by Bank staff, and choose projects with good potential for Project Performance Assessments (PPAs) to check on results, sustainability, and institutional development. To reduce assessment costs, they cluster projects for PPAs. The Bank says that one in four completed projects are evaluated by the department.

The Operations Evaluation Department also does Country Assistance Evaluations to check the Bank's performance in a particular country. These evaluations focus on whether performance matches the Bank's Country Assistance Strategy (CAS) and whether that strategy is productive. There are two kinds of evaluation: Sector and Thematic Reviews audit performance and experience in a sector or thematic area; Process Reviews examine ongoing activities such as grants or coordination between donors. The latter are done in response to an Executive Board request or to other demands. Finally, the department also prepares the Annual Review of Operations Evaluation (AROE) of the Bank's evaluation processes themselves; and the Annual Review of Development Effectiveness (ARDE), an analysis of the Bank's overall performance.

One weakness of the Operations Evaluation Department is that its audits are still internal: none of them guarantees objective analysis by an independent body. That is why the Inspection Panel is an important monitoring tool. In the case of Planafloro, a natural resource project in Brazil from 1989 to 1995, international NGOs such as the Environmental Defense Fund protested the lack of local participation in the project design. An NGO forum asked the Inspection Panel to review the project in 1995, which it did.[40] In another case, the Bank's resettlement policy (1986–1994) came under review as a result of revelations by the Morse Commission on the controversial Narmada Dam project. An internal team was authorized to assess the Bank's resettlement policy; it found that the Bank's 1986 policy had shown only about 30 percent compliance in its first five years. Compliance improved rapidly under external and internal scrutiny, though the review team had to use outright guerrilla tactics to get good information from reluctant task managers. Only intense negotiation and threats of leaks to the press by external advocates forced the Bank to publish its final report in 1994.

Member countries—the Bank's principals—can monitor the organization too. If a member state is unhappy with Bank policies, it can threaten to cut off its funding. Member states—above all the United States, the largest Bank donor—can wield this "club behind the door" as a last resort. The US Congress in particular has budget power. Threats by a congressional committee to cut off future funding spurred the Bank to make more project information available earlier and compelled the Inspection Panel to investigate project abuses. Right after its inception, the new panel was asked to investigate the proposed Arun III Dam in Nepal; it raised serious questions about the dam, and the new president canceled the project.[41] But Arun turned out to be the exception to the rule: normally the executive directors overturn panel recommendations.[42]

Last but not least, can private citizens or nongovernmental actors monitor decisionmaking at the Bank on their own? Compared to other multilateral agencies, the Bank permits citizens relatively good access to activities. NGOs like Environmental Media Services have websites with sections devoted to monitoring Bank decisions. One NGO official reported that she was able to monitor the Bank through "participant observation."[43]

Independence

We have seen that the Operations Evaluation Department is quite autonomous within the Bank. Still, most of its evaluations are not based on independent field studies, but "desk reviews" based on official project files created, by definition, by interested parties.[44] So the independence of its evaluations is not beyond doubt. And the Operations Evaluation Department is not alone: the Bank's Executive Board has yet to reject a single Bank loan proposed by management—not a good sign of independence.

The Bank is arguably beholden to the United States, its largest sponsor. As mentioned above, the Bank president has always been an American, at least by informal convention if not by formal rule. Other nation-states usually retain powerful levers to block enlightened World Bank policies, especially at the final implementation stage. Their delegates sit on the Bank's Executive Board, which decides whether the Inspection Panel can even investigate a case. Of fourteen panel claims from 1993 to 2000, the board approved three.

Conventional wisdom says that the Inspection Panel is beholden to the donor governments. But this widely believed story is far from true in practice. Ironically, not donor but *borrowing* states have led a backlash to weaken the powers of the panel and block transnational accountability reforms. For example, in the Itaparica case, all borrowing-country blocs voted against an inspection by the panel, while all the Northern-only votes (except France) supported the panel's recommendation. The final vote was 47.1 percent in favor of inspection and 52.9 percent against—so a coalition of Bank members from the South, the East, and a divided North successfully resisted independent inspection. At least in this case Bank critics have clearly exaggerated US hegemony,[45] and two Bank critiques got mixed up: the legitimacy critique by human rights activists and end-users, and the use of that critique by nation-states (not least third world countries, many of which are still ruled by dictators) to block transnational democracy in order to preserve their sovereignty for their own ends.

In sum, the Inspection Panel's scope is limited, and it works at the Executive Board's discretion. Many problems with Bank projects are not even subject to the panel's mandate. And the International Finance Corporation, the Bank's private sector branch, is officially exempt from panel scrutiny. But on balance the panel has been a remarkably autonomous body. As we saw above, its three non-Bank development experts must reject any possible future Bank employment. It is the biggest hope for the Bank's independence.

Conclusion

Bank policies and procedures allow some transparency, participation, public dialogue, and dissent. But they fall short in most transnational democracy indicators. It is not surprising that the Bank gets a rating of +1 (strong democracy) in only one indicator (reason-giving), a rating of 0 (medium democracy) in four other indicators (appointment, participation, transparency, and monitoring), and a rating of –1 (weak democracy) in the last two (overrule and independence) (see Table 4.1). In sum, the Bank has yet to improve its transnational democracy in six of the seven indicators.

There are many ways in which the Bank can, and must, do so. First, it

Table 4.1   Transnational Democracy Ratings, World Bank

Dimension	World Bank
Appointment	0
Participation	0
Transparency	0
Reason-giving	+1
Overrule	−1
Monitoring	0
Independence	−1
Total rating	−1

should strengthen the individual accountability of officials. One Bank social policy analyst said that there has been "too much focus on structures rather than incentives and individuals. I would find three or four terrible cases and fire them, plus recruit those who believe in the policies." Robert Picciotto, director of the Operations Evaluation Department, said: "Jim Wolfensohn would like to connect staff incentives with development results. The question is how to do it without unintended consequences. . . . Incentives and penalties should start with the managers. This is where the buck stops."[46]

Second, the Bank should create additional channels for public inputs into the policy processes. Bank managers can make greater efforts at engaging grassroots participation. For example, the Bank could hold public hearings in selected member countries on projects prior to approval. While such a procedure would be time-consuming and costly, it would maximize ownership by affected stakeholders, be a good investment in democracy, and yield better outputs.

The Bank is not without a track record in this area. One example is its Development Marketplace,[47] a biannual event held since 1998 to capture novel ideas for alleviating poverty. The forum, held in the atrium at the Bank's Washington, D.C., headquarters, is designed to connect providers of new antipoverty ideas—not only Bank staff, but anyone, anywhere—with potential funding sources. Starting in 2000, since many applicants had impressive ideas but no funds to travel to Washington, the event team held teleconferences with fifty-two proposal teams from countries such as Egypt, Uganda, and the Philippines (often at 11:30 P.M. or 4:30 A.M. to accommodate groups in other time zones, and videotaped for all judges to see) so they could still present their ideas to the jury. The panel of judges deciding on the grants included respected leaders of NGOs like Oxfam International and World Vision; executives of private sector companies such as Asea Brown Boveri and Battelle; and senior World Bank executives. At another forum in February 2002, the judges distributed a pool of $5 million among forty-three competitors for microfunding; grants ranged from $29,000 to $380,000. Since 2001, the process has decentralized: Country Innovation Days have been held in Thailand, Peru, Ukraine, Brazil, and Guatemala.[48] But a few million dollars in grant money is minuscule compared to the Bank's annual lending of over $20 billion. The Bank must find ways to move processes like the Development Marketplace from the periphery to the center of its work, and break the hold of tradition-bound managers and processes.

Third, the Bank should allow more discussion with dissenters. To that end, it could invite critics to a public debate with Bank staff so that a "marketplace of ideas" is promoted. Another possibility would be to set up and empower a World Bank ombudsman.[49] Even better, the Bank could invite dissenters to participate in projects with Bank staff. Their views could be documented throughout the life-cycle of a project (typically five years), giving Bank staff and outside parties opportunities for substantive discussions at the project's conclusion and opportunities for distilling best practices and recommendations based on reality and not just hearsay or ideology.

Fourth, the Bank should shorten the lead-time between top-level decisionmaking and outcomes on the ground. Long lead-times may well create a disconnect in perceptions: policymakers at the top insist that newly designed projects have improved—for example, potential disasters like the Narmada Dam or the Three Gorges Dam tend to be much more scrutinized and dropped early in the project cycle—while affected groups on the ground still smart from the results of past decisions.[50]

Finally, the Bank should strengthen the authority and autonomy of the Inspection Panel and expand its powers to all projects and processes. Perhaps the panel's mandate should go beyond merely inspecting the status quo, and include finding solutions.

Is the World Bank capable of renewing and democratizing itself? Although Ernst Haas has asserted that the Bank's shift toward poverty alleviation in the 1970s was an example of institutional learning,[51] the evidence so far suggests that such moves are driven more by institutional adaptation to political threats than by true learning.[52] But there are encouraging signs. If it builds its transnational democracy, the World Bank could become a truly global institution that better reflects the interests of all its member states, and ultimately of all people whose lives it affects.

Notes

1. Nye 2001: 3.
2. "Treasury Chief Accuses World Bank of Harming Poor Countries," *New York Times,* February 21, 2002.
3. Woods 2003.
4. "Bank Team Attacks Own Oil Project," *Financial Times,* August 19, 2002.
5. O'Brien et al. 2000: 1.

6. World Bank 2002: xi.
7. Navia and Zweifel 2002.
8. Rodrik 1997.
9. See, for example, World Bank 2002.
10. Krugman and Obstfeld 1994: 523–557.
11. Hormats 1987: 48–50.
12. http://web.worldbank.org/wbsite/external/extaboutus.
13. http://web.worldbank.org/wbsite/external.
14. "What Is the World Bank Group," http://webworldbank.org.
15. World Bank 1997: 15.
16. Fox 2000.
17. Brown and Fox 1998.
18. http://web.worldbank.org/wbsite/external.
19. *New York Times,* March 30, 2005: A1; April 1, 2005: A1.
20. http://www.bicusa.org/ptoc/htm/saul_infodisc.htm.
21. http://www.ems.org/banks/wb_basics.html.
22. "New Roles and Functions for the U.N. and the Bretton Woods Institutions," http://www.wider.unu.edu/research/1998-1999-5.1.publications.htm.
23. "Toward a New Washington Consensus," *Multinational Monitor,* September 2001.
24. Interview, *Multinational Monitor,* September 2001: 28.
25. Brown and Fox 1998.
26. http://www.worldbank.org.ipn.
27. World Bank 1999.
28. http://worldbank.org/ipn.
29. "Toward a New Washington Consensus," *Multinational Monitor,* September 2001.
30. "Are World Bank's Africa Policies Working?" *African Farmer,* July 1994.
31. Fox 2000.
32. Blustein 2001: A2.
33. "Toward a New Washington Consensus," *Multinational Monitor,* September 2001.
34. Cited in Brown 1999.
35. Fox 2000: 297.
36. Rich 1994.
37. Brown and Fox 1998.
38. http://www.worldbank.org.
39. http://www.worldbank.org.
40. Brown and Fox 1998.
41. Brown and Fox 1998.
42. Fox 2000.
43. Covey 1998: 115.
44. Fox 2000.
45. Fox 2000.
46. Confidential interview and interview with Picciotto cited in Fox 2000: 300.
47. http://www.developmentmarketplace.org.
48. Wood and Hamel 2002.
49. Bradlow 1993.
50. Fox 2000.
51. Haas 1990: 142–145.
52. Fox 2000.

5

The International
Monetary Fund*

Since its inception after World War II, the International Monetary Fund has become far more powerful than its modest staff and budget would suggest. Reaching beyond strictly monetary matters, it now manages the economies of more than eighty developing countries, pushes for their fiscal austerity, affects their money supply, and ultimately shapes the financial lives of their citizens. From taking the dollar off the gold standard in the early 1970s to Argentina's financial meltdown in the late 1990s, from the second oil crisis in the late 1970s to the sovereign bankruptcy debate in the early 2000s, the IMF's influence has always been visible.

But not always welcome. Opponents in social and environmental movements as well as in conservative think tanks have raised fundamental questions about the organization's premises and policies. This chapter analyzes the IMF's rules and processes, and reviews criticisms from the socialist left and the libertarian right of its power structure. By assessing its transnational democracy systematically, the chapter aims to help shape a reform agenda for a new, democratic IMF.

A Brief History:
From Monetary Police to Lender of Last Resort

The IMF, like the World Bank, emerged from the UN Monetary and Financial Conference at Bretton Woods in July 1944. With the disastrous interwar period—massive unemployment, hyperinflation, trade wars, and economic disintegration—still burned into their minds, representatives of

---

*This chapter was coauthored with Johannes van de Ven, senior consultant at Swiss Consulting Group and research associate at the Center for Economics and Ethics, University of Louvain, Belgium.

forty-four countries sought to design a stable monetary framework that would foster price stability without dampening international trade.

According to its Articles of Agreement, the IMF exists to promote international monetary cooperation; facilitate the expansion and balanced growth of international trade; promote foreign exchange stability; create a multilateral system of payments between members; assist in the correction of maladjustments in members' balance of payments; and reduce the duration and severity of disequilibria in members' balance of payments (see Figure 5.1). Bretton Woods set up fixed exchange rates against the US dollar and an unchanging price of gold at $35 an ounce. This gold standard, with the dollar as its principal reserve currency, played a key role in the monetary stability the world saw after 1945. Member governments committed themselves to the rules of the monetary regime as long as other countries in their region did so too, and tended to keep their commitments if their region valued the rule of law domestically.[1]

But this regime did not last. Stability received a serious blow when the United States unilaterally decoupled the dollar from the gold standard. In August 1971, to rein in excessive spending on the Vietnam War, US president Richard Nixon announced that the US Federal Reserve would no longer automatically sell gold to foreign central banks for dollars. This surprise led to the end of the stable dollar-centered fixed-rate regime. A new agreement was reached in December that year at the Smithsonian Institution in Washington: on average, the dollar was devalued by 8 percent, and the United States imposed a 10 percent import surcharge to force the realignment, which eventually led to the floating of all major currencies, financial deregulation, and an explosion of cross-border short-term capital flows. Although a temporary measure to correct for speculative capital movements, free floating has survived until today.

In 1978, an amendment in its Articles of Agreement led to the Fund's growing role in policing the world economy in general and the economic performance of individual member states in particular. So-called Article IV consultations are currently completed with almost all member states. In 1987 the IMF launched the Structural Adjustment Facility (SAF) and Extended Structural Adjustment Facility (ESAF). All these packages imposed conditionality: the Fund expects members to implement certain structural policies to qualify for funds. So-called high-conditionality requirements include further trade liberalization, deregulation of capital markets, across-the-board privatization of publicly owned industries, a shift of social security from the state to the market, fiscal reform, and slashed government budgets.

IMF membership rose sharply from 62 nations in 1960 to 184 by 2004. Staff numbers quadrupled from 750 in 1966 to almost 3,000 in the late 1990s. Like the UN, the IMF posts so-called resident representatives to

Figure 5.1 IMF Organization Chart

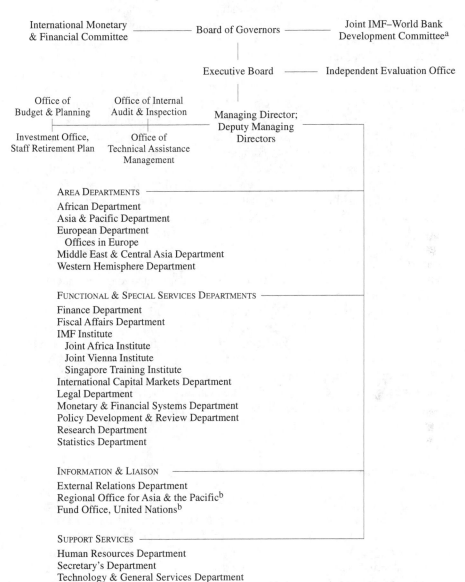

Source: http://www.imf.org/external/np/obp/orgcht.htm, November 2003.
 Notes: a. Known formally as the Joint Ministerial Committee of the Boards of Governors of the Bank and the Fund on the Transfer of Real Resources to Developing Countries.
 b. Attached to the Office of Managing Director.

over sixty countries. Besides its head office in Washington, D.C., it has opened offices in New York, Tokyo, Paris, Geneva, Vienna, and Singapore. In addition to granting loans, it has increasingly been involved in training and technical assistance activities. Starting in 1964 these trainings were organized out of Washington, after 1992 out of Vienna, and since 1998 they have been offered out of Singapore. Now Fund staff carry out over 600 technical assistance operations each year.

After the fall of the Berlin Wall, the IMF found itself at the front lines of the effort to rebuild Eastern Europe and the former Soviet Union; in the second half of the 1990s, massive bailout packages for Asian, Eastern European, and Latin American countries followed. It became a so-called lender of last resort; by 2000 it was extending some sixty loans annually, each running into the billions of dollars and lasting up to fifteen years. More than half its member states have borrowed money from the Fund. In 1999 the IMF broadened its scope once again: conditional lending now included an explicit focus on poverty reduction—but still in the context of growth-oriented strategies. Based on its Poverty Reduction Strategy Papers, the IMF set up the Poverty Reduction and Growth Facility (PRGF), with an emphasis on good governance; as of March 2005, eighty-four low-income member countries were eligible.

Most mainstream political parties in the United States and Europe, from Social Democrats on the left to Christian Democrats on the right, support the Fund's neoliberal approach: they see the global free market as the best framework for liberty, democracy, and prosperity. Significant support comes from investment banks, chambers of commerce, business schools, mainstream mass media, and policy think tanks. Pitted against them are groups like 50 Years Is Enough!, which have called for the abolition of the IMF. Who is right?

Appointment

The IMF's internal power structure was laid bare in November 1999, when its then-chairman, Michel Camdessus, resigned after twelve years at the Fund's helm. His surprise announcement prompted a prolonged and messy power struggle over his succession. Under an informal rule, a European is the Fund's managing director while its acting director is an American. (As discussed in Chapter 4, a symmetrical gentlemen's agreement dictates that an American gets the World Bank presidency.) France found itself on the sidelines when its obvious candidate, Bank of France governor Jean-Claude Trichet, preferred to take over from Wim Duisenberg as head of the European Central Bank. Before long, German chancellor Gerhard Schröder nominated a German: Caio Koch-Weser, a twenty-five-year World Bank veteran and for a few months German finance minister. To plead Koch-Weser's case, the German government took the unusual step to summon ambassadors from forty IMF member countries to its chancellery, but the candidate didn't fly for two reasons: his relative inexperience at diplomacy, and more important, US reluctance toward another European "socialist." US officials also questioned whether Koch-Weser would be able to stand up to his former boss, then–World Bank president James Wolfensohn.

Since the Europeans failed to rally around one candidate, then–US treasury secretary Lawrence Summers seized the opportunity to break the informal rule and nominated the IMF's number two man, Stanley Fischer. But despite being widely respected for his track record, policy acumen, and commitment, and immediately backed by several African and Arab nations, Fischer's US citizenship became a hurdle he could not jump.

Japan proposed a way out of the "Eurocentric gentlemen's agreement" by nominating its former vice minister of finance, the skilled economist and politician Eisuke Sakakibara, better known as Mr. Yen. But that did not work either, and by March 2000 negotiations were still deadlocked. Prospects looked so bleak that the IMF Executive Board organized a crisis meeting to break the impasse amid fears that the escalating US-EU row could unsettle financial markets. Newspaper headlines drew parallels between the appointment dispute and the transatlantic battle over interest rates that had triggered the 1987 stock market crash. The impasse was resolved only when all parties agreed to back yet another German, Horst Köhler, who until then had been running the European Bank for Reconstruction and Development. The agreement disguised the fact that the IMF suffers from an anachronistic appointment procedure—a highly informal and undemocratic process that pulls for power plays among the highly industrialized Group of Eight nations.

Yet there might be light at the end of the tunnel. After Köhler's surprise resignation (just like his predecessor's) in March 2004, a group of IMF executive directors, representing over 100 of the 184 IMF member states (mostly developing and emerging economies, but also Australia and Switzerland), demanded an open and transparent process to fill the post. Where a candidate was from was no longer to be the deciding criterion for appointment. (Nevertheless, as always, a European became IMF president in May 2004: Rodrigo Rato, former economy minister in Spain's conservative Aznar administration.)

The IMF describes itself as a cooperative providing global public goods like capital mobility, free trade, and financial stability, but such rhetoric is not credible without equitable voting shares. Much like the Bank's, the Fund's vote distribution has been a contentious issue. Representation is through quotas determined by a country's economic power. The United States alone holds 17.3 percent of the votes, substantially more than all of Latin America, South Asia, and sub-Saharan Africa combined. The Group of Seven and EU combined represent 14 percent of the world population but hold 56 percent of the voting shares. Africa, a continent heavily affected by IMF policies, accounts for only 2 percent of IMF votes. Under the current rules, the United States alone can block any motion to change the Articles of Agreement. A majority of 85 percent is needed, which means that the 17.3 percent voting weight of the United States is tantamount to de facto veto power. But according to one observer "it's inconceivable that those paying the IMF's bills would relinquish control over its leadership."[2]

Participation

What about IMF participation by nonstate actors and private citizens? Since the late 1980s, NGOs have pushed for greater involvement of poor and marginalized communities and directly affected groups. NGOs such as Bread for the World and Oxfam began writing environmental and social assessments and impact studies in the hopes that such analytic documents would reform Fund activity or halt it altogether, and with some success. In 1991, "stakeholder participation" focusing on consultation and information disclosure was included in the IMF's environmental assessment policy. This procedure was the first major victory for NGOs. Reform-oriented movements are now invited to the Fund's annual meetings and engage in more direct talks with IMF staff, along with corporate managers, investment bankers, and academics.

A breakthrough in the dialogue with nongovernmental organizations came in 1998 when the Executive Board reviewed the Fund's evaluation process. For the first time NGOs such as Rethinking Bretton Woods Project and Friends of the Earth participated in the review, and even published a joint paper with the Fund, recommending more independent evaluations and learning from previous ones.[3]

One key area for concerted activism has been debt relief; ever since the 1982 Mexican debt moratorium, NGOs have campaigned for debt forgiveness. Although the IMF is not the biggest lender by far, it has been the focus of attention, since it acts as a coordinator for rescheduling commercial, bilateral, and multilateral loans. The early 1990s saw the first globally coordinated effort to reduce the debt burden of emerging economies; even the rock star Bono raised his voice for the cause. In 1993 the European Network on Debt and Development (Eurodad) and religious groups like the US-based Maryknoll launched a global campaign with short films on the need for debt forgiveness. In 1995 the late Pope John Paul II entered the debate, and soon the Pontifical Council for Justice and Peace organized a Vatican conference with the major Washington-based multilateral institutions to highlight the socioeconomic impact of debt payments on developing countries.

The Catholic Church launched the Jubilee 2000 campaign, an appeal to world leaders for debt forgiveness, demanding a "fair and transparent process" of writing off debts in a global petition signed by 24 million people in more than sixty countries. The principles of Jubilee included a "survival in dignity" clause and a reasonable "burden sharing between debtor and creditor."[4] Persistent pressure for debt relief has been partially successful. At the Fund's 1996 annual meetings, the Interim and Development Committee endorsed exceptional debt relief for six countries; Uganda was the first to take advantage of the so-called Highly Indebted Poor Countries (HIPC) initiative. But by January 2002, less than $36 billion of the $100 billion pledged by donor nations for debt reduction had been scheduled. Nevertheless, the Jubilee movement was to obtain debt relief for more than twenty of the world's poorest countries.

Street protests are still the most visible expression of grassroots activism. In 1989, during the most violent "IMF Riots" in Venezuela, over 300 antiausterity protesters died. More recently, at the IMF and World Bank meeting in April 2001, over 20,000 people gathered in Washington, D.C., to demand more democratic decisionmaking—or the abolition of the Fund. Similar protests erupted later in Prague and Genoa.

Challengers from the left are not alone in believing that IMF intervention is counterproductive. The most vocal critic on the right is the Washington-based Cato Institute, which lobbies the US Congress against more IMF funding and tries to delegitimize the Fund's very existence. One of its adjunct scholars wrote that "the only cure for the IMF's ills is to pull the plug on that international bureaucracy."[5] Another critic from the right is the Heritage Foundation, also in Washington. Both think tanks assert that IMF assistance compounds "welfare dependency" and robs developing economies of incentives to take off.

Greater public participation in the IMF can be credited to activists' skillful use of electronic mail, the World Wide Web, and less expensive telephone usage to join forces and mount sophisticated campaigns on a global scale. On the other hand, radical efforts to delegitimize or abolish the IMF have had less impact. Remarks like "I always compare the IMF to the Communist Party: a vanguard, very ideological, very top-down"[6] have allowed the Fund to discredit or marginalize radical NGOs.

Transparency

To attack their credibility, the IMF has exploited democratic deficits in some NGOs themselves; several NGOs have failed to disclose their hidden political agendas, show their funding sources, or publish annual reports.[7]

Simultaneously, the IMF's External Relations Department has sought to disarm the opposition of trade unions, dissident NGOs, radical church movements, and environmentalists with information; but the highly technical language of IMF documents requires sophisticated knowledge of finance, which many nonstate actors lack.

The Fund's proceedings are virtually secret. Despite good intentions, most letters of intent, policy framework papers, and Article IV documents are not published. Minutes of Executive Board meetings are made available only after thirty years—although these meetings happen three times a week! True, there have also been glimpses of transparency. Three examples: In 1980 the IMF started to publish its influential biannual *World Economic Outlook*. In the early 1990s, under new internal compliance guidelines, IMF employees started to build an enormous paper trail (but have shelved most assessments and not incorporated them in future policy designs). And since 1998 the Interim Committee has encouraged member governments to implement the IMF's Code of Good Practices on Fiscal Transparency. In September 2001 the IMF cut Zimbabwe off from IMF loans on charges of massive fraud and macroeconomic mismanagement by Robert Mugabe's government. The IMF has been better at pushing for transparency in member states than in its own backyard.

Reason-Giving

In recent years, the IMF has massively increased its public information, and its public relations department has given much visibility to its activities. Since 1994 the Fund has published all its so-called Article IV consultations on its website, as long as affected member governments have not objected. In 1996 it established a special data dissemination standard and began publishing the statistics behind its policy proposals. And since the mid-1990s it has urged member states to publish their letters of intent or policy framework papers that contain the details behind stand-by agreements and short-term loans.

But IMF missions to member nations are very technical. Dehumanizing economic benchmarks has led to misguided policies with disastrous results. According to former World Bank chief economist and Nobel laureate Joseph Stiglitz, IMF staff often have alarmingly little experience with the affected country. They can present econometric models, but their analyses can be flawed or outdated and not geared toward the target country's needs.[8] Of course there are linkages between sound balance sheets and soaring social indicators, but IMF staff recruitment focuses too narrowly on economics PhDs who lack a full commitment to sustainable development. IMF staff turnover is even lower than at the World Bank, managers rarely get fired for nonperformance, and labor mobility between the IMF and other multilateral or nongovernmental organizations is rare. This leads to overly economic reason-giving.

Overrule

The checks and balances at the Fund are weak: no independent body is empowered to overrule decisions of the IMF's managing director, Executive Board, or Governing Board, and there is no judicial review. But this does not mean a total lack of checks and balances. The crisis unleashed by the devaluation of the Mexican peso in 1995 led to serious soul-searching within the Fund, especially in the area of evaluation, and led to a decision by the Governing Board to start evaluation missions through internal audits and inspection. In mid-2002 the IMF added in-house evaluations of technical assistance programs and resident representative offices. But the findings of these evaluations have yet to be published, and internal evaluations all too often merely justify policies already in place. IMF managers are still reluctant to submit the Fund's activities to systematic scrutiny, which happens too late in a project cycle to reshape project designs anyway.

But the board has also allowed two or three independent evaluations per year by outside experts. And during its 2000 spring meetings the IMF established its Evaluation Office (EVO) to "systematically conduct objective and independent evaluations on issues, and on the basis of criteria, of relevance to the mandate of the Fund."[9] The EVO is independent of IMF management and staff and operates at arm's length from the Executive Board. Its director is appointed for four years, renewable for a second term of up to three years, and may be fired at any time with approval of the Executive Board. Moreover, the EVO is free to consult with whomever and whichever groups it deems necessary, both within and outside the IMF.

Still, the IMF often wears too many hats at once, which goes against the principle of checks and balances. For example, sovereign bankruptcy procedures can create a conflict of interest within the IMF: they make the Fund simultaneously a major creditor and a judicial authority ruling on a country's bankruptcy.

Monitoring

We have seen that internal evaluations have little concrete impact on IMF policy. External monitoring, both by NGOs in the development or environment fields, and by think tanks in policy analysis, has been more effective.

The first signs of public scrutiny came in the late 1980s when several NGOs identified adverse social and environmental effects of the Washington-based multilateral development agencies and organized a highly visible campaign against the World Bank–sponsored Narmada Dam in India. Although the campaign focused on the dam, it indirectly targeted the IMF-led structural adjustment programs. An ever-growing chorus of criticism led to more and more impact studies until the Fund finally gave an institutional response: in 1999 it expanded the environmental assessment policy unit to include the so-called sectoral adjustment operations in areas like healthcare, education, and energy.

But in March 2000 a US congressional commission headed by economist Allan Meltzer launched another report sharply critical of the IMF. The bipartisan Meltzer Commission had been set up by Congress as a precondition for approving a further $18 billion IMF package in 1998. It charged that the IMF suffered from a chronic lack of transparency and accountability, and called for an independent evaluation unit and an ombudsperson.[10]

Independence

Although it comprises only 5 percent of the world population, the United States generates 30 percent of the world's gross product. The sole remaining superpower's global strategies seem to influence IMF lending policies. In 1998 the Clinton administration arranged a massive bailout package for Russia in return for its support in the Balkan War—while turning a blind eye to the country's endemic and large-scale corruption. US geopolitics was again the motive for bailout packages for Turkey and Pakistan; the administration reportedly told Pakistan that access to IMF-subsidized lending would depend on Islamabad's willingness to sign a nuclear nonproliferation treaty.[11] Another example of US influence is offshore banking. Before September 11, 2001, the United States repeatedly vetoed efforts to limit offshore bank accounts that can be used for sinister purposes: to avoid taxation, launder money, speculate with hot-money flows, conduct illegitimate money-wires, or fund the drug trade. After the terrorist attacks, the George W. Bush administration quickly made a U-turn when it became clear that offshore banking can also finance terrorism.

According to Stiglitz, US involvement in the IMF is often tainted by double standards—for example, free trade rhetoric combined with higher trade barriers to protect US steel or cotton industries—that breed resentment at what others see as US hypocrisy: "It is difficult to deal with a great power that is both schoolmaster and truant," the Nobel laureate wrote. "At the very least, it encourages cynicism."[12] This perceived discrepancy between word and deed has a history. When US secretary of state George

Marshall launched his major reconstruction plan for Europe in 1947, he said: "Our policy is directed not against any country or doctrine but against hunger, poverty, desperation and chaos."[13] But even the Marshall Plan was a Cold War initiative designed to prevent the rise of communism in Europe.

To be sure, the United States is an ideal candidate for enlightened global leadership by virtue of its drive for innovation, the openness of its society, and its capacity to reinvent itself. But as long as the United States holds the IMF's purse strings, controls Fund policies with its effective veto, pushes for Fund leaders whose ideology conforms with a neoliberal free market and antigovernment bias, and uses IMF lending as a carrot or stick for its own narrow interests, we cannot speak of true IMF independence.

Conclusion

To its credit, the Fund has substantially reformulated its conditional lending policy[14] and has encouraged "social safety nets" to lessen the harmful effects of structural adjustment in developing nations. It has paid attention to children and the elderly in education and healthcare programs. In a shift from the past, it has committed itself to targeting more spending on poverty reduction. And thanks to NGOs like Transparency International, it has also paid more attention to sound governance. For example, it halted credit disbursements to Kenya and Colombia in 1996 due to corruption charges, has urged both India and Pakistan to curb military expenditures over the years, and in September 2005 threatened to expel Zimbabwe unless it paid interest on its loans.

An increasingly accountable IMF would have to legitimize its actions, which would in turn improve them. As we have seen, constructive dialogue with outsiders has enhanced the accountability and effectiveness of IMF policies. But much remains to be done. Here is how the Fund performs in the seven dimensions of transnational democracy (see Table 5.1), and how it might speed up the reform process: In appointment it receives a rating of −1 (weak democracy). The highly informal appointment process for top IMF leaders pulls for manipulation by the great powers. An open selection process in which candidates present their intentions and proposed policies is a sine qua non for democratic accountability. The unequal voting weights of the member states may have worked in the past but no longer reflect global realities. A greater voice for developing and debtor nations is not needed just for democracy; it also means adapting the IMF to the realities of interdependence and interconnectedness under globalization. Large emerging economies like China, India, and Brazil deserve a bigger voice in debates. The current voting structure, which gives China about as many votes as the Netherlands, makes no sense. Some developing nations have campaigned for a one-country, one-vote rule like in the UN General

Table 5.1   Transnational Democracy Ratings, IMF

Dimension	IMF
Appointment	−1
Participation	0
Transparency	0
Reason-giving	−1
Overrule	−1
Monitoring	0
Independence	0
Total rating	−3

Assembly, but such a rule would make the IMF ineffective. To mitigate the democratic deficit at the heart of the IMF, a dramatic reform of the voting formula and rules is needed. In one proposed revision, a member country's voting weight would be based on three variables: its population, its economic potential, and its Human Development Index. Under such a rule, no country alone could exercise an effective veto, and the standing of developing nations would be greatly improved. Brazil's voting weight would rise from 1.5 to 2.2 percent; China's would almost quadruple from 2.3 to 8.7 percent, and India's would more than triple from 2.1 to 6.4 percent,[15] while that of the United States would sink from 17.3 to 11.2 percent.

In recent years the IMF has opened itself up, if reluctantly, to greater participation by nonstate actors, and so receives a rating of 0 (medium democracy) in participation. Although the Fund's transparency is on the rise, access to key information remains a tricky issue; its transparency rating is 0 (medium democracy). Just like the minutes of the US Federal Reserve, IMF minutes should be made available instantaneously to the public, and the transparency of the Fund's Executive Board and upper-level management can be ensured by full disclosure of all discussions after a short period of time, as central banks like the US Federal Reserve do. The board should make decisions based on consensus or majority vote. Only such public proceedings can make the IMF credible again. If it preaches transparency to developing nations as a precondition for loans, it should itself lead by example.

Reason-giving receives a rating of −1 (weak democracy). According to Stiglitz, "IMF policies stem not from economic analysis and observation but from ideology—specifically, an ideological commitment to free markets and a concomitant antipathy to government."[16] Reasons for Fund policies must be based on clear criteria and be free of biased agendas: "If there's one thing I've learned in government, it's that openness is most essential in those realms where expertise seems to matter most."[17]

In overrule, the Fund also receives a rating of −1 (weak democracy), since there are virtually no checks and balances. To prevent conflicts of interest, unambiguous legal procedures must be in force; statutory revisions of the IMF, for example to establish an international bankruptcy court, are a sine qua non for monetary stability in emerging markets. Judicial review of IMF decisions and policies would be crucial for the organization's credibility. Similarly, the IMF receives a rating of 0 (medium democracy) in monitoring, since it still gives outside groups little opportunity for scrutiny.

In independence, the IMF is relatively insulated against pressure, but prone to capture by corporate as well as US interests, and gets a rating of 0 (medium democracy). One proposal by British finance minister Gordon Brown is to divorce the IMF's evaluation department from its lending side; this would allow IMF staff much more freedom to speak out on emerging problems.[18]

Strengthening the Fund's accountability and independence is a major challenge. The solution is not to abolish the IMF but to reform it. Reform is all the more warranted because IMF policy failings are not just random blunders; bad outputs are directly correlated to undemocratic inputs. These changes are crucial if the IMF is to deserve the vast influence it wields over the global economy.

Notes

1. Simmons 2000.
2. Calomiris 2000a: A26.
3. Pollack 1997.
4. Pettifor 2002. In 2001, Jubilee 2000 was renamed Drop the Debt.
5. Hanke 2000.
6. Justin Forsyth, Oxfam policy director, cited in Crooks 2002: 11.
7. O'Brien et al. 2000: 159–205.
8. Stiglitz 2002a.
9. International Monetary Fund 2000a.
10. The Meltzer Report, Commission hearings, and background papers are available at http://phantom-x.gsia.cmu.edu/ifiac.
11. Calomiris 2000b.
12. Stiglitz 2002b.
13. George Marshall, speech delivered at Harvard University, 1947.
14. International Monetary Fund 2002.
15. Huffschmid 2000.
16. Friedman 2002.
17. Stiglitz 2000.
18. Beattie 2002.

6

The World Trade Organization*

The inhabitants of the small city Aurangabad, 150 miles northeast of Bombay, find themselves at a strange and unsettling juncture. In the early 1990s India began liberalizing its economy; a decade later, the weekly *India Today* celebrated the rise of India's new middle class. A poll conducted for the magazine found that 86 percent of respondents in five major cities now owned a color television, 72 percent a refrigerator, and 44 percent a washing machine. Another 32.5 million households, some 15 percent of the population, now belonged to a more modest "consuming class." The typical member of that larger group owned a television, a bicycle, and a wristwatch. After declining for almost four centuries, Aurangabad has seen new life in the past twenty-five years, but now it feels threatened by the powerful and inexorable forces of global capitalism. India dismantled myriad trade barriers (in March 2005 it tightened its 1970 patent law on everything from software to electronics to generic drugs, potentially choking off the supply of affordable drugs for half the world's AIDS patients, for example) as a condition for joining the World Trade Organization. Inhabitants fear that the WTO is a tsunami that will blow Aurangabad's economy to pieces. "The milkman is going to die," said one. "The grocer is going to die," said another. The most frightening word in the city's industrial zones has become "WTO."[1]

Why does the WTO instill such fears? Doesn't everybody want more trade? Since its very inception in 1995, the WTO has been the focus of global media attention and harsh criticism from left and right, from developing and industrialized nations alike. Despite these controversies, it is gaining momentum as the main global umpire reaching far beyond trade

---

*This chapter was coauthored with Johannes van de Ven, senior consultant at Swiss Consulting Group and research associate at the Center for Economics and Ethics, University of Louvain, Belgium.

disputes: investment strategies, people's production and consumption patterns everywhere, and even national sovereignty have come under its purview.

This chapter briefly reviews the WTO's roots and examines its rules for loopholes and pitfalls by matching them with the seven indicators of transnational democracy. It weaves in two hotly debated cases: the Multilateral Investment Agreement (MIA), adopted to pry open developing markets for multinationals; and the so-called trade-related intellectual property rights (TRIPs), the WTO's increased jurisdiction over which has come under fire in North and South.

From the GATT to the WTO

In the famous phrase of Charles Kindleberger, "For the world economy to be stabilized, there has to be a stabilizer, one stabilizer."[2] But in 1926, Britain suffered from imperial overstretch and could no longer act as a hegemonic power to sponsor the relatively free trade regime of the nineteenth century. And the other Great Powers that could have provided leadership had also been greatly weakened by World War I: Germany and Austria had lost the war, and France had won but lost some 6 million soldiers—much of its productive work force. The only exception was the United States: it had entered the Great War late, sustained relatively minor losses, and emerged from the war as the strongest power with the capability to sponsor freer trade. But Britain could not, and the United States would not, play the leadership role needed for international stability.[3] Since there was no one else to fill the vacuum, the result was catastrophe: tariff hikes by all great trading partners to protect their domestic industries, including the Smoot-Hawley tariff in the United States, bilateral trade agreements by Nazi Germany, trade wars, and finally World War II.

When the Allies met at Bretton Woods to build an institutional framework that would prevent similar disastrous policies in the future, one result was the WTO's predecessor: the General Agreement on Tariffs and Trade came into effect in January 1948. Originally, the Bretton Woods framers had planned an International Trade Organization (ITO) alongside the IMF and World Bank. The GATT was meant only as a provisional short-term agreement until the ITO could be launched at a 1947 conference in Havana. But the ITO never came into force for several reasons: though the Soviet Union had attended Bretton Woods, it stayed away from Havana, probably to protest the incipient Cold War and the Truman Doctrine, which called for containing communism anywhere in the world; thirty developing countries protested that the ITO draft treaty was solely in the interest of the Great Powers; and US president Harry Truman never submitted the treaty to the

US Senate. (Congress never voted on the GATT either, and when it did so later, only on tariffs *within* the GATT, since it saw the GATT as an executive agreement, a treaty not an organization; and treaties were none of its business but rather the job of the executive.)

The GATT was not a rulemaker. It operated under general principles: nondiscrimination (members agreed to treat other members equally), reciprocity (concessions made to one member were automatically available to all others), and trade expansion.[4] Decisions were usually reached by consensus, not through voting. From its inception, member states worked in eight rounds of multilateral trade negotiations (see Table 6.1) that substantially opened industrial markets (except in agriculture, where high trade barriers remained). The last was the longest: the so-called Uruguay Round, 1986 to 1994. Three major trading blocs, the United States, the EU, and Japan, dominated the talks. An agreement was finally reached in 1993, but the markets of these three economic powerhouses remained effectively closed to agriculture and textile imports from the South. Meanwhile, developing nations updated their laws on competition, intellectual property rights, customs systems, and foreign investment; and liberalized their capital accounts, industrial tariffs, and service sectors to give Northern multinationals access to their markets. The GATT is generally recognized as having contributed to economic growth in developing countries, especially those that qualified for most-favored-nation (MFN) status with each other.

Table 6.1   From the GATT to the WTO

October 30, 1947	In Geneva, 23 countries sign the General Agreement on Tariffs and Trade.
January 1, 1948	The GATT enters into force. China is a founding member, but will soon exit.
1949	Second GATT round: 5,000 tariffs are lowered or eliminated.
1950–1951	Third GATT round: 8,700 more tariffs are lowered, 38 countries participate.
1955–1956	Fourth GATT round (in Geneva): tariffs lowered by $2.5 billion.
1960–1965	Dillon Round: tariffs lowered by $4.9 billion.
1964–1967	Kennedy Round: tariffs lowered by $40 billion, 62 countries participate.
1965	The GATT adopts special rules for developing countries.
1973–1979	Tokyo Round: 102 countries discuss, for the first time, rules on lowering subsidies and dumping; tariffs lowered by $300 billion.
1986–1994	Uruguay Round: 128 countries participate, ending with the biggest steps toward trade liberalization so far.
1994	The World Trade Organization is founded, headquartered in Geneva. The GATT obligations are incorporated in the WTO (Charter Annex IA).
1999	The WTO meeting in Seattle fails to start a new negotiating round. Globalization opponents disrupt the proceedings.
2001	China becomes the WTO's 143rd member.
2004	Cambodia joins, raising WTO membership to 148, with 27 applications pending, including Algeria, Libya, Russia, Serbia, Saudi Arabia, Vietnam, and Yemen.

But the GATT's very success led to its downfall. As it grew beyond narrow trade issues, it became insufficient for resolving disputes. Often derided as the "Gentlemen's Agreement to Talk and Talk," it lacked the teeth—the institutional credibility and authority—needed for effective arbitration and rulemaking. A new institution was warranted to address the complexities of global trade. At the end of 1994, the GATT was history.

In its place, the WTO came into being in January 1995, with headquarters in Geneva, and within a few months its secretariat employed 630 people (see Figure 6.1). Its main functions are administering WTO trade agreements, providing a forum for trade negotiations, handling trade disputes, monitoring national trade policies, providing technical assistance and training for developing countries, and cooperating with other international organizations.

The WTO has enlarged its scope from mere trade liberalization based on tariff concessions (shallow, or "negative," integration) to a wider range of more intrusive regulations (deep, or "positive." integration).[5] It now includes services, trade-related intellectual property rights, foreign investment, competition policy, and a quest for harmonization of national rules in trade-related investment services.[6] This broader agenda lowers the risk of cross-border transactions for millions of entrepreneurs.[7] But the WTO's competencies differ sharply from those of the GATT. Member nations that signed the GATT agreements were called "contracting parties," for which GATT rules were legally binding only insofar as they agreed to each rule individually. The WTO, by contrast, is a stand-alone institution and a legal person with self-executing rules and procedures. With its vastly expanded jurisdiction, the WTO is more than a trade organization. Its rules have far-reaching effects on the socioeconomic environments of countries—even nonmembers—around the globe. The WTO's unprecedented powers have alarmed not only nongovernmental groups but also governments, which fear that their control of vital national decisions is being overtaken by supranational rules. They and other critics have raised questions about the organization's democracy and legitimacy. We look at their claims systematically.

Appointment

Unlike the IMF and the World Bank, which are dominated by their wealthiest member states through voting quotas, the WTO operates by consensus. (Already the GATT had this safeguard for national sovereignty. Binding any country to a rule required consensus, not majority votes on senseless resolutions—except if a decision could not be reached by consensus, but that occurred rarely if at all,[8] as member nations rarely objected to rulings

Figure 6.1 WTO Organization Chart

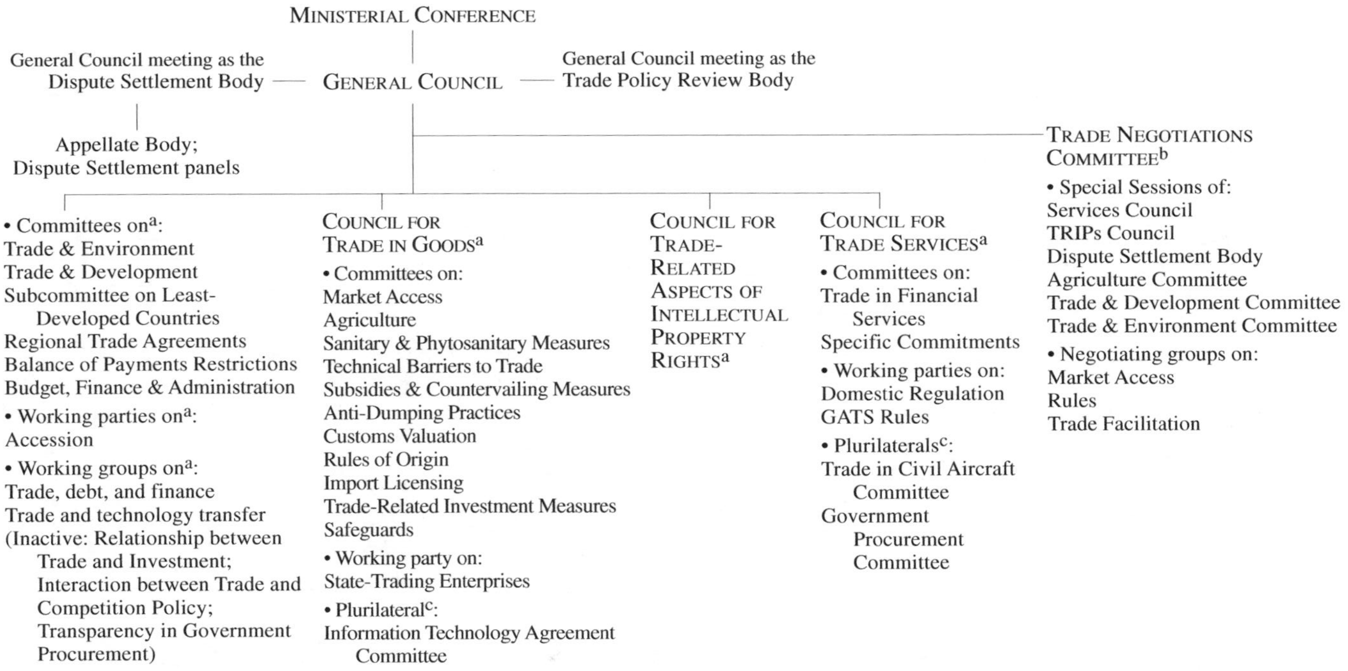

MINISTERIAL CONFERENCE

General Council meeting as the Dispute Settlement Body — GENERAL COUNCIL — General Council meeting as the Trade Policy Review Body

Dispute Settlement Body
Appellate Body;
Dispute Settlement panels

COUNCIL FOR TRADE IN GOODS[a]
• Committees on:
Market Access
Agriculture
Sanitary & Phytosanitary Measures
Technical Barriers to Trade
Subsidies & Countervailing Measures
Anti-Dumping Practices
Customs Valuation
Rules of Origin
Import Licensing
Trade-Related Investment Measures
Safeguards
• Working party on:
State-Trading Enterprises
• Plurilateral[c]:
Information Technology Agreement Committee

COUNCIL FOR TRADE-RELATED ASPECTS OF INTELLECTUAL PROPERTY RIGHTS[a]

COUNCIL FOR TRADE SERVICES[a]
• Committees on:
Trade in Financial Services
Specific Commitments
• Working parties on:
Domestic Regulation
GATS Rules
• Plurilaterals[c]:
Trade in Civil Aircraft Committee
Government Procurement Committee

TRADE NEGOTIATIONS COMMITTEE[b]
• Special Sessions of:
Services Council
TRIPs Council
Dispute Settlement Body
Agriculture Committee
Trade & Development Committee
Trade & Environment Committee
• Negotiating groups on:
Market Access
Rules
Trade Facilitation

• Committees on[a]:
Trade & Environment
Trade & Development
Subcommittee on Least-Developed Countries
Regional Trade Agreements
Balance of Payments Restrictions
Budget, Finance & Administration
• Working parties on[a]:
Accession

• Working groups on[a]:
Trade, debt, and finance
Trade and technology transfer
(Inactive: Relationship between Trade and Investment;
Interaction between Trade and Competition Policy;
Transparency in Government Procurement)

Source: http://www.wto.org/english/thewto_e/whatis_e/tif_e/org2_e.htm, February 2005.

Notes: Each year, new chairpersons for the major WTO bodies are approved by the General Council. All WTO members may participate in all councils, committees, etc., except the Appellate Body, Dispute Settlement panels, and plurilateral committees.

a. Reporting to the General Council or a subsidiary.

b. The negotiations mandated by the Doha Declaration take place in the Trade Negotiations Committee and its subsidiaries. This now includes the negotiations on agriculture and services begun in early 2000. The TNC reports to the General Council.

c. Plurilateral committees inform the General Council or Goods Council of their activities, although these agreements are not signed by all WTO members.

against them.) The problem is that WTO membership has greatly expanded: the GATT had 23 signatories at its 1948 inception and 84 by the end of the Tokyo Round in 1979. More than 110 countries signed the Uruguay Round accords in 1994; by the 2003 Cancun talks, there were 146 member states; and by March 2005 there were more than 20 candidates, including Russia and Saudi Arabia, with Iraq and Afghanistan (but not Iran, because of opposition by the United States) entering membership talks. The WTO's vast membership strains the consensus rule, especially when the number of states affected by a particular issue grows with global interdependence.

Two new WTO competencies are its strengthened dispute settlement system and its biannual ministerial meetings, neither of which was present in the GATT. Dispute settlement works as follows: (1) Parties are obliged to consult one another. (2) If parties cannot settle a dispute among themselves, they present it to the Dispute Settlement Board and request an ad hoc panel. (So far this is like the process under the GATT, but the WTO gives deadlines for dispute resolution.) (3) A panel has sixty days to write a report. (4) Disputants comply. (5) When disputants cannot accept a decision, they appeal. (6) The seven-member Appellate Body cannot "remand" a case back to the first-level panel.

Dispute panelists are appointed by the secretariat, but the parties in a dispute may veto their appointment. If a panelist is unacceptable, the chair of the Dispute Settlement Board and the director-general appoint alternates. Panelists are trade experts who have served in trade ministries or in GATT-like settings or have otherwise demonstrated their competence.[9] Their qualifications are laid out in WTO Article 8(1) and include past service on GATT panels, past representation of a country before a trade institution or tribunal, past service as a senior trade policy official of a WTO member country, and teaching or publishing on international trade law or policy. Only candidates who abide by the WTO philosophy qualify for appointment.

These criteria ensure the selection of panelists with track records, but also with a bias toward the status quo. No other requirements, like impartiality, judicial independence, or integrity, are selection criteria. Conflicts of interest are not explicitly ruled out.

Panel rulings are automatically binding and do not require unanimous consent to be adopted, which prompts fears by states wary of losing sovereignty. But the system has been productive: in the WTO's first three years alone, panels dealt with more complaints than the GATT had in all of its forty-seven years before. In its first five years, the Dispute Settlement Board took up 185 consultation requests, 144 distinct matters in which a single panel reviewed multiple claims, 32 active cases, 26 completed cases, and 39 settled or inactive cases. By March 2005, 329 cases had been brought to the WTO.

The WTO's top body, the Ministerial Conference, meets only every other year to set policy; daily operations are managed by the General Council, which also functions as Trade Policy Review Body and Dispute Settlement Body. It holds twelve official meetings a year and gives equal representation to all member states. Under its tight supervision, staff and management enjoy less discretion than their counterparts at the IMF or World Bank.[10]

In July 1999, member governments agreed to the appointment of Mike Moore of New Zealand as director-general for a three-year term. The General Council had determined already that Moore's successor would be Supachai Panitchpakdi of Thailand. These decisions were made by 134 member governments and took over a year to finalize. Members stressed that this unprecedented term-sharing arrangement did not constitute a precedent for future appointments. There are no comprehensive rules for appointing directors-general.

Participation

The long-standing "green-room" procedure is another area where reform is warranted. In the informal ritual a relatively small number of developed and developing nations meet on crucial issues. This old-boys network has pushed through decisions that might be impossible by consensus building. During the Tokyo Round of the GATT, back-room negotiations involved eight or fewer delegations; in WTO negotiations, more than twenty-five members participate. Industrialized members are usually represented by the United States, the EU, Canada, Japan, Australia, New Zealand, Switzerland, and Norway; developing nations include Brazil, Argentina, Mexico, Chile, Colombia, China, India, Korea, Pakistan, South Africa, Egypt, and at least one Association of Southeast Asian Nations (ASEAN) country. The problem with the green-room procedure is that most other developing countries stay outside the decisionmaking process for lack of resources or capabilities. (Eighteen WTO members have no representation in Geneva whatsoever.) Many developing countries were angered at being excluded from the decisionmaking in Seattle in 1999.[11]

Transparency

WTO dispute panels operate behind closed doors; documents of proceedings are confidential, and only the parties in the dispute can see them. Worse, the opinions of individual panelists remain anonymous. Disputes like the US-EU *Beef Hormone* case and the US Cuban Liberty and

Case 6.1   Multilateral Investment Agreement

Member state sovereignty came under attack in 1995, when industrialized nations—above all the United States, the EU, and Japan—pushed for a comprehensive Multilateral Investment Agreement that would essentially give multinationals free access to developing markets. Foreign firms would have the right to enter and set up shop with 100 percent equity in any sector of any national economy except national security. Legal scholars warned that such an MIA would go far beyond WTO rules, which were at the time limited to trade-related investment measures, and extend WTO scope and authority to domestic policies in developing nations. Developing nations added that an MIA would contradict the UN Charter and the UN declarations that guarantee member states sovereignty over their own national resources and activities. A worldwide network of Northern and Southern NGOs joined the chorus and sharply attacked the proposal; their statement, signed by over 200 development and environmental groups, stressed that "such a proposal would abolish the power and legitimate right of states and people to regulate the entry, conditions, behavior and operations of foreign companies and foreigners in their country. This is a prime and fundamental sovereign right which is essential for any country to determine its own economic and social policies."[a]

With an MIA in place, the WTO would become a securities and investment regulator, much like a global Securities and Exchange Commission, the agency that regulates firms in the United States. This would not necessarily be a bad thing, but developing nations would need the chance to accept foreign direct investment on their own terms, not only on those imposed by international capital markets or multilateral institutions. In the words of political economist Dani Rodrik, "The lesson of history is that ultimately all successful countries develop their own brands of national capitalism. The states that have done best in the post-war period devised domestic investment plans to kick-start growth and established institutions of conflict management."[b]

Notes: a. Cited in Khor 1999: 11.
    b. Rodrik 1999: 89–90.

Democratic Solidarity Act (also knows as Helms-Burton Act) are only two of many examples of opaque WTO procedures.

In July 1996 the WTO opened access to certain documents; later it began publishing material on the Internet. But such concessions are hardly more than cosmetic, and have done little to soothe the protesters around WTO ministerial meetings, from Seattle in 1999 to Cancun in 2003–2004. Full transparency—a prerequisite for meaningful participation in the WTO's decisionmaking process—would require more rigorous policies on disclosure of information.[12]

Reason-Giving

The WTO's dispute resolution system has been an effective tool in resolving trade rows, but there has been concern about how panels, especially first-level panels, evaluate the at-times-difficult scientific evidence in a case, for example in the *Beef Hormone* or the *Shrimp Turtle* cases. Here the WTO suffers from limited resources, and its rules give little guidance. The "dispute settlement understanding" text in Articles 21 and 22 is ambiguous, inconsistent, full of gaps, and in need of clarification.[13] And why is it that in certain cases panels promote a philosophy of deregulation and in others protectionism?

In theory it would not be inconsistent to push for deregulation in industrialized countries while at the same time demanding a stronger social safety net in developing countries.[14] But WTO officials seem to have a clear bias toward a one-size-fits-all approach of unfettered markets and dismantled governments. This so-called Washington Consensus seems to assume that the US market is the ideal governance model and that it should be adopted worldwide. It tends to confuse the size and makeup of the public sector in the United States with that of a typical developing nation. Most third world countries lack a social safety net; Western-style welfare states are so rare that there is little left to deregulate, if anything. By pushing for deregulation and prying all markets open for their multinationals, industrialized nations increase the burden for developing nations.

Overrule

A UN declaration has little or no rulemaking power, and signing it means mostly a moral (not a legal) commitment. Noncompliance does not have consequences (other than perhaps reputation costs). WTO rules are another story: they have real teeth. The WTO is both a rulemaking and a rule-supervisory body that implements agreements, resolves disputes, amends rules,

Case 6.2   TRIPs and AIDS

One of the Uruguay Round's hottest debates was on so-called trade-related intellectual property rights. In effect, the TRIPs agreement, signed by 142 countries in 1994, provided a minimum twenty-year period of patent protection for pharmaceutical products. Brazil, for example, claimed that the United States and EU, backed by their pharmaceutical lobbies, were putting profits above people's lives, but the concern failed to make it into the final agreement.

South Africa wanted to import generic antiretroviral agents that suppress HIV in the fight against AIDS and come at a small fraction of the cost of the original patented medicine. Thirty-nine pharmaceutical firms took legal action to prevent South Africa from importing the generics, but the lawsuit backfired: after a huge public outcry, the industry dropped the case in April 2001.

That same month, Brazil presented a motion to the UN Human Rights Commission concerning the right to affordable medicines. The resolution was meant to generate international support for Brazil's policy of freely distributing its generic AIDS drugs. All members of the commission, except the United States, voted for the motion. (Weeks later the commission voted the United States off the island. It was the first time it had thrown out a commission member since its 1947 inception.) When the George W. Bush administration realized it was not going to win at the UN, it took the Brazilian case before a WTO dispute panel. Backed by a pharmaceutical industry with a yearly turnover of $300 billion, the Bush administration argued that without patents protecting their brand-name products from generic competition, pharmaceutical companies would never have invested tens of millions of dollars in the research and development needed to make medical breakthroughs. But another public outcry forced the United States in June 2001 to drop the threat of trade retaliations. In Brazil, two multinational pharmaceuticals, the US firm Merck and the Swiss firm Roche, slashed their prices on antiretrovirals by 65 and 40 percent respectively after Brazil threatened to violate their patents and produce generics itself at a state-owned laboratory. Brazil now manufactures eight of the twelve drugs in the anti-AIDS cocktail locally, and distributes them for free as part of its widely hailed AIDS program. The country is seen as a role model in the war against AIDS because it has reduced HIV transmission rates

(continues)

dramatically—to below 1 percent of the population. AIDS-related deaths have fallen by about 50 percent; hospitalizations are down an impressive 75 percent.

Ironically, the anthrax scare in the United States after the September 11, 2001, terrorist attacks turned out to be a defining moment for amending the TRIPs rules. The US campaign against terrorism led to sweeping new legislation to override drug patents in the name of national security: in a desperate attempt to negotiate low-cost Cipro, the United States threatened to override Bayer's patent. Developing nations, equally vulnerable to their own pressing health concerns, immediately made the US action their showcase for generics. They argued that it smacked of hypocrisy to apply one rule for North American or European public health issues (such as the Anthrax scare) and another for pandemics in the developing world (such as AIDS). Brazil and India used this argument decisively in their fight to change the rules; in November 2001, developing nations won a fifteen-year grace period for implementing TRIPs. Immediately following this breakthrough, Médecins sans Frontières announced that it would work with Brazil to export the country's generic AIDS drugs and its anti-AIDS program to other affected countries worldwide.

and grants waivers. When a country signs on to a WTO regulation, it has to alter its national laws and policies to bring them in line with the new rules. Noncompliance can result in retaliations—trade sanctions by affected states. Unlike under the GATT, a WTO dispute settlement can allow cross-sectoral retaliation, meaning that a member nation may retaliate against the noncompliant party's key exports, not just against related products in the same sector. Noncompliance can even lead to expulsion from the WTO or loss of the coveted most-favored-nation status.

Given these vast powers, can the WTO be overruled? The Dispute Settlement Body decides by consensus,[15] which allows an objecting member to veto decisions, much like in the EU's informal Luxembourg Compromise. But dispute panels have the power to override national governments, and no outside appeal of panel rulings is available.[16] There is an internal appeal procedure: claimants who are unhappy with a ruling can appeal to the Appellate Body, as happened in late 2002 when a dispute panel had ruled in favor of seventeen countries as plaintiffs against the US Congress's Byrd Amendment. The panel had found that the amendment violated WTO rules on antidumping and subsidies, and had called for its repeal. The United States appealed that ruling.[17] But in January 2003 the Appellate Body upheld the panel's ruling that the Byrd Amendment indeed violated international trade law.

Monitoring

As a young and relatively untested institution, the WTO is rarely scrutinized from the outside, let alone by an elected body. By default, nonstate actors such as NGOs, the international media, and antiglobalization protesters have been the only ones to monitor it. The WTO in its early years failed to set up formal linkages with NGOs or civil society movements. But in 1996 the WTO secretariat began informal dialogues with NGOs. Article V(2) provides for such consultation: "The General Council may make appropriate arrangements for consultation and cooperation with NGOs concerned with matters related to those of the WTO." Article 13(2) of the Understanding on Rules and Procedures Governing the Settlement of Disputes adds: "Panels may seek information from any relevant source and may consult experts to obtain their opinion on certain aspects of the matter." Neither article is binding on the organization; NGOs have little voice except for occasional consultations on dispute settlement. But in the 1998 *Shrimp Turtle* case, the Appellate Body insisted on accepting amicus curiae (friend of the court) briefs from non-WTO members like NGOs and experts, and has since repeatedly asserted this procedural right—often over vehement objections of member states.[18]

Independence

The WTO, like the GATT before it, has no independent enforcement powers. If a country violates WTO rules or refuses to comply with a dispute panel ruling, the suffering country can demand compensation, or retaliate. In both cases the remedy is authorized by the WTO, but carried out bilaterally; the WTO cannot act independently. This rule gives some member states much more power than others: a big-market state can do significant damage to a smaller country by retaliating, while small states find themselves at the receiving end of terms of trade.[19] When the WTO gave Ecuador the right to impose sanctions of over $200 million a year on the EU in a banana dispute, Ecuador refrained because it did not want to jeopardize its other commercial interests.

How immune against capture by great powers or special interests is the WTO? Before its inception, domestic policies on healthcare, investment, and culture came under national jurisdiction; now countries have come increasingly under the thumb of dispute panels that are sometimes dominated in turn by powerful industry lobbies. This has narrowed the ability of national governments to determine their own socioeconomic destiny.[20] It comes as no surprise that the United States and the EU have used the dispute system the most, sixty-nine and fifty-four times respectively by early 2001. In the same period, developing countries together initiated sixty-six disputes (India, Brazil, Mexico, and Thailand have been the most outspoken).[21] Though the United States has brought more complaints than any other country, this has not automatically led to victory: it has lost cases involving sea turtle protection, Kodak, EU computers, clean-air regulations, and antidumping duties.[22] Nevertheless, already in the first years of dispute panels a clear pattern had emerged: the countries that could afford to lodge complaints generally won cases.

This is important because developing nations often lack the resources to take advantage of the WTO. Taking a case to a dispute panel requires the services of highly specialized and sophisticated trade lawyers. Using a private law firm can cost more than $300,000, far beyond the reach of many WTO members. All too often, a third world member like Bangladesh can barely afford one overworked and sleep-deprived attorney, who must face off in Geneva against dozens of well-rested and well-prepared lawyers from an industrialized member like the United States or the EU. Well-funded lobbies of multinational firms dominate much of the WTO agenda. To level the playing field, nine developing countries, including India, Pakistan, Cuba, and Malaysia, launched a proposal that would force industrialized members to pay part of a poor complainant's costs whenever they lose a WTO case.

Conclusion

Table 6.2 summarizes the transnational democracy ratings for the World Bank, IMF, and WTO. Overall, the World Bank is the most democratic of the three institutions, the WTO comes in second, and the IMF is the most undemocratic, but all three organizations have an overall negative rating.

The WTO has improved its transnational democracy in recent years. And it has done so with a relatively small annual budget of $91 million—roughly equivalent to the annual travel budget of IMF officials. Its appointment procedure has existed only since 1995; it is not an old-boys network like that of the IMF. Developing nations have more sway, as the appointment of Thai chairman Supachai in 2002 demonstrated. But appointment is opaque and informal, and so the WTO gets a rating of 0 (medium democracy).

Table 6.2   Transnational Democracy Ratings, World Bank, IMF, and WTO

Dimension	World Bank	IMF	WTO
Appointment	0	−1	0
Participation	0	0	−1
Transparency	0	0	−1
Reason-giving	+1	−1	0
Overrule	−1	−1	+1
Monitoring	0	0	−1
Independence	−1	0	0
Total rating	−1	−3	−2

NGOs, private practitioners who represent disputants, and others have suggested reforms of the dispute settlement system.[23] A steering committee of member states (twenty or so in number) would be charged with building consensus on trade issues. Much like at the World Bank and the IMF, membership in such a steering committee would be representative of the broader membership and be based on clear, simple, and objective criteria—for example, by absolute value of foreign trade, ranked by country or common customs region—and global geographic representation, with at least two participants from each major region. Such a reform would not undercut decisionmaking by consensus and would cause the least disruption to the existing green-room players, but bring on board previously excluded nations. Ironically, many small and least-developed nations have blocked these developments, claiming that they would have no substantial input.[24]

In participation, the WTO receives a rating of −1 (weak democracy). The WTO should find ways to reduce the cost burden of participation in dispute settlement for developing countries.[25] Above all, these nations should have a better chance to be represented; quite a few members do not even have a physical presence in Geneva.

In transparency, the WTO has realized that the less hidden its deliberations, the stronger its credibility. But panel hearings are still confidential, and the WTO gets a rating of −1 (weak democracy). Secrecy leads only to more mistrust of the institution and raises concerns about conflicts of interest. Panel meetings should be open not only to member governments, but also to NGO observers and perhaps even the media. NGOs should have the right to send memos to and receive information from panel proceedings. All documents in dispute resolution—expert memos, briefings, and rulings—should be accessible to the public. Publishing the minutes on the Web would be a cost-effective way to achieve transparency. This is so in other organizations; there is no reason why the WTO should be an exception.[26]

In reason-giving, the WTO gets a rating of 0 (medium democracy). It is not based on clear, objective criteria and seems biased toward the Washington Consensus. Its evaluation mechanism, especially, needs more scrutiny; it should overcome its inconsistent enforcement of rules. Instead, the WTO should establish a binding code of conduct for multinationals. And dispute panelists should be selected based on broader know-how. The WTO exists not merely for pressing member nations to abandon quotas and tariffs; trade is not an end it itself, but only a means to serve the fundamental goal of improving the quality of life for everyone.

In overrule, the WTO is the last resort in trade disputes; it cannot be overruled. But since the organization is largely a dispute resolution mechanism, the absence of a check on the WTO is not necessarily a problem; given this, and given the WTO's strong Appellate Body, it gets a rating of +1 (strong democracy). Still, not all is well in terms of checks and balances. Already in the final Uruguay negotiations, some delegates had expressed the need to curtail WTO decisionmaking that might be too "intrusive on sovereignty." This concern is reflected in Article IX and amendments to Article X. For example, Article IX(3) suggests that decisions cannot impose new obligations on members.[27]

In monitoring, the WTO is a young and hardly tested institution, and outside scrutiny is not institutionalized. It gets a rating of −1 (weak democracy). Like the IMF and the World Bank, the WTO should start granting consultative status to NGOs. Such a move would build trust with civil society and make WTO policies more accountable and legitimate.

Finally, in independence, the WTO gets a rating of 0 (medium democracy). It depends too much on government funding and is not impartial. Jagdish Bhagwati asserts that "poor countries see the WTO increasingly as the target of western lobby groups determined to exploit the WTO to their own advantage, using the specious argument that their causes have to do with trade in some intrinsic way."[28] Instead the WTO should, in partnership with developing nations, come up with hard-nosed proposals to remedy their problems. It should seize opportunities for reform, especially of trade-distorting agricultural policies in the EU and the United States.

While the WTO's dispute resolution system so far has been effective in resolving trade rows, sometimes developing countries are at a disadvantage even if they win. Retaliation is of little use to them and can even have disastrous unintended consequences when initiated by a much more powerful industrialized state or customs union. Developing countries should have the right to seek financial compensation in addition to the right to impose sanctions.

But developing countries need not be the victims of industrialized countries in the WTO. Brazil managed to use WTO rules of engagement to break a monopoly that keeps medicines excessively expensive for the people who need them the most. In the hands of a skillful developing country, the WTO treaty can be a powerful diplomatic and legal tool.

Notes

1. *New York Times Magazine,* April 15, 2001: 32.
2. Kindleberger 1973: 305.
3. Kindleberger 1973: 297–298.
4. Gilpin 1987: 74.
5. See Tinbergen 1965.
6. O'Brien et al. 2000.
7. Jackson 2000: 271–272.
8. Schott and Watal 2000: 284.
9. Dispute Settlement Understanding (DSU), WTO Charter, annex 2. See also Khor 2000: 40.
10. Woods and Narlikar 2001.
11. Schott and Watal 2000: 285–286.
12. Roberts 2004.
13. Jackson 2000: 275–276.
14. See Williamson 1990.
15. Jackson 2000: 279. WTO Agreement Article IX, footnote 1, defines consensus: "The body concerned shall be deemed to have decided by consensus on a matter submitted for consideration, if no member, present at the meeting when the decision is taken, formally objects to the proposed decision."
16. Palmeter and Mavroidis 1998.
17. Bhagwati and Mavroidis 2002.
18. The cause of the uproar by member states was the Appellate Body's publication on November 8, 2000, of procedures for nonparty submissions to the dispute between France and Canada over imports of chrysotile asbestos. The Appellate Body had published the procedures (http://www.wto.org/english/news_e/news00_e/ds135_9.doc) to provide an orderly process for the submission of amicus briefs, of which it had already received (though not accepted) five, and emphasized that it had adopted the procedures "for purposes of this appeal only." It refused to elaborate. See http://www.ictsd.org/html/weekly/story1.28-11-00.htm.
19. I owe this insight to an anonymous reviewer.
20. Khor 2000.
21. See World Trade Organization 2001: 10.
22. Wallach and Sforza 1999: 195–212.
23. See *Journal of International Economic Law* 1(2) (1998) and 2(2) (1999).
24. Schott and Watal 2000: 286.
25. Jackson 2000: 274.
26. Jackson 2000: 276–277.
27. Jackson 2000: 278.
28. Bhagwati 2002: 15.

7

The European Union

The previous three chapters focused on functional organizations—the World Bank, the IMF, and the WTO. We now take up regional organizations, most of which consist of mere treaties to foster collaboration in the economic or, less often, political sphere. The great exception is of course the unprecedented experiment of the European Union. In less than fifty years, the EU has evolved from being an intergovernmental club to a supranational body. Now it is a system of pooled sovereignty with many features of a federal state: its own territory and flag, its own currency and central bank, its own executive, legislature, and court, and now its own army (in June 2004 Europe agreed to take over peacekeeping duties from NATO in Bosnia).[1] Much like the United States, the EU is a "regulatory state"[2] in which a limited budget forces the government to rule by regulation rather than by taxation and spending, and in which extensive policymaking powers are delegated to nonelected government agencies not directly accountable to voters or to their elected representatives. EU institutions like the European Commission, the European Central Bank, and the European Court of Justice have established their authority over national courts and executives. The EU greatly influences how people live, work, and spend money, from Sicily to Scotland.

This unprecedented delegation of powers to the EU has spurred widespread concerns among policymakers and scholars—and a vast literature—on a democratic deficit of its institutions and decisionmaking. Critics argue that we must match the EU even more than other regional organizations against standards of democracy, because the EU—by making and imposing law—executes immediate sovereign might.[3] But the label "democratic deficit" includes so many claims that at first glance it is little more than a justification for all kinds of grievances and dissatisfactions with the European project.[4] Partly because the EU is a moving target that has evolved over the years, we meet a bewildering jungle of arguments and opinions with hidden assumptions. Charges of a democratic deficit can be bundled into five rough sets. Space does not permit a full analysis of these arguments; I refer the reader to a systematic evaluation elsewhere.[5] I present here just the bottom lines.

Lack of Transparency

EU institutions, especially the Council of Ministers (comprising member state ministers who serve as delegates to the EU, much like in the US Senate or the German Bundesrat, whose members represent the states), suffer from too much secrecy.[6] The Council hides proceedings from scrutiny, which raises problems of trust and allows for collusion by special interests.[7] More than the national state has already, the EU piles on layers of government and removes decisionmaking even further from concerned citizens.[8] A long chain of delegation reaches from voters in member states to their national governments, then to those governments' delegates in EU governing bodies, and finally to EU nonelected officials—and makes the EU opaque.

Lack of Consensus

EU enlargement—ten new countries joined in the spring of 2004—creates fears that new member states will reduce the voting weight of existing ones, like when a company issues new voting shares and the value of each share shrinks.[9] The decline of the unanimity principle fuels these fears only more: the 1966 Luxembourg Compromise used to give any member state— even tiny Luxembourg—the power to veto unwanted policies by invoking its vital national interest. This informal practice was "the single most legitimating element" of the European Community's constitution.[10] The rise of qualified majority voting (QMV) means that large member states can now outvote smaller ones in the Council of Ministers, which creates compliance problems when smaller states feel bulldozed.[11] The 2000 Nice Treaty reinforced the trend toward majoritarian QMV by changing voting weights in the Council. Now countries that together have a mere 38 percent of the EU's total population (for example, Germany and two other large member states, say France and Poland or Spain and the United Kingdom) have the power to block a policy.[12]

Lack of Social Justice

Some claim that both globalization and the EU structure favor negative integration—that taking down national barriers may lead to a "race to the

bottom," whereby the most competitive member states are the ones offering corporations the biggest tax breaks and the lowest labor or environmental standards, and hence minimal social policy, to lure highly mobile
companies and capital. This "regime erosion" in countries with high standards, unless kept in check there, might lead to further regime erosion in
countries with lower standards and exacerbate the rich/poor gap in the
Union.[13] So governments reduce their social spending—but EU social
policy is far from ready to protect citizens from this threat to their welfare.[14] (A "race to the bottom" is an unproven myth.[15] Dani Rodrik's
analysis of over a hundred countries has shown that the more open
economies are to global or regional integration, the *bigger,* not smaller,
are their governments, and hence their government services like schools
and healthcare.[16])

Lack of Legitimacy

Eurobarometer polls (opinion surveys gauging the attitudes of member
state citizens toward the EU) and low voting turnouts show mistrust in EU
institutions. Yet even if European institutions were democratized, the pre-
conditions for authentic democracy would still be lacking: there are no
European parties or political leaders, no European media for debates on
policy issues and choices, and no Europe-wide competition for government
offices.[17] The EU is far from a unified society, but a multitude of societies
and cultures. In addition to the now twenty official EU languages, significant minorities speak dozens of "lesser used" languages: Mirandese in
Portugal, Gaelic and Welsh in Britain, Occitan and Basque in France and
Spain, and Francoprovençal and Friulian in Italy. Europe is not one but
many national cultures and peoples; it is made of many "demoi, then, rather
than demos"[18]; and without one demos there can be no democracy. In this
view, European citizenship is a phony concept, an empty package, a brand
developed by EU "managers" to placate dissatisfied shareholders—
"Saatchi and Saatchi European citizenship."[19]

To make EU citizenship real, the EU would need a constitution. In an
intergovernmental conference in June 2004, EU member states agreed on a
new constitutional treaty that would confirm the European Commission's
legislative initiative but grant the European Parliament codecision powers
in virtually all policy areas. The constitution would extend QMV in the
Council, but taxation, social policy, and common foreign and security policy stay under unanimity, and would create a EU minister of foreign
affairs. It would give European citizens the right to ask the Commission
for a policy proposal to the Parliament if they "collect one million signa-
tures in a significant number of Member States."[20] Such a constitution

would be great for transnational democracy, but again, it is unclear whether it will ever become a reality or die a slow death in one of the national referenda.[21]

Lack of Accountability

The European Commission, the European Central Bank, agencies, and the European Court of Justice are agents unaccountable to their principal, the European electorate. The Commission, the EU executive, has successfully exploited the 1960 Rome Treaty's Article 155, which authorizes it to launch initiatives and debates, shape the agenda, garner support for its proposals, and shepherd policies through the maze of EU rules from draft to decision.[22] As a result, its powers have grown, and it now "combines the role of prosecutor and judge [which] has left the Commission the master of its own procedural destiny."[23] The European Central Bank makes rules that become law in European and member states without involving national parliaments, the European Parliament, or other elected institutions. For the most part, only treaty amendments can change the Central Bank's statutes and need the unanimous consent of all member states; national elected officials can override Central Bank decisions only through a very arduous procedure.[24] And the Court transformed the Rome Treaty into supranational law with direct effect on member states.[25] Commission and Court both have lawmaking powers in politically contested areas.[26] Despite its growing importance, the Parliament, the only supranational institution directly elected by EU voters, is still too weak to compensate for this democratic deficit of the other supranational institutions, whose unelected officials expand their powers away from the public eye.[27] "That this nonelective bureaucracy executes, legislates, and adjudicates raises questions of excessive power and accountability."[28]

*   *   *

With this debate in mind, we can now see how the EU functions in action. The heated debate around biotechnology—specifically, whether and how producers should label products that contain genetically modified organisms—lends itself as a fascinating case that we can match against our seven transnational democracy indicators.

Case 7.1   Regulating Biotech

Genetically modified organisms (GMOs) are life forms whose genetic material (DNA) has been altered in a way that does not occur naturally by mating or natural recombination, but through a technology used to isolate genes from one organism, manipulate them in the laboratory, and inject them into another. Supporters argue that genetic engineering offers significant benefits to producers and consumers, from cost savings for farmers passed on to consumers, to increased yields benefiting poor nations, to environmental protection through reduced use of pesticides, herbicides, and other chemical sprays, to improved human health through new vitamins, nutrients, and pharmaceuticals.[a]

There is so far no conclusive scientific evidence that the use of GMOs is inherently unsafe, but skeptics point to possible dangers. One former biotech engineer who became a vocal GMO critic asserted that they pose several health risks. Gene mutations can damage genes naturally present in an organism's DNA, alter the metabolism, produce toxins, and reduce the nutritional value of a food. They can alter normal genes, and lead to the production of allergens. Or they can interfere with other essential, but yet unknown, functions of an organism's DNA.[b]

Whatever the scientific merits of these claims, the evidence is growing that biotech foods and crops require stringent regulatory oversight. In 1999 the British Medical Association called for an immediate moratorium on GMO foods because of potential human health risks, including possible allergenic reactions and increased exposure to antibiotic resistance of genes that are spliced into every genetically engineered food.[c] A 1999 study reported in the medical journal *Lancet* that a specific genetically engineered potato was causing rats to suffer substantial health effects, including weakened immune systems and changes in the development of their hearts, livers, kidneys, and brains.[d]

The European public seems to share this skepticism. In 1999 the British survey institute Healey-Baker asked 6,700 Europeans in eight EU member states (plus in then–three candidates Czech Republic, Hungary, and Poland) whether they would eat GMO foods; 61 percent responded that they would prefer not to. Resistance was highest in Italy (79 percent) and lowest in the Netherlands (47 percent). More than 57 percent of respondents said they would like to see more organic foods on shop shelves.[e] Anti-GMO activists assert that the public is even more averse to GMOs than these numbers show.

(continues)

Case 7.1   continued

The Campaign to Ban Genetically Engineered Foods, for example, cites surveys according to which 97 percent of European consumers want clear labeling of all genetically engineered foods, and 80 percent do not want GMO foods at all. How responsive have EU institutions been to these consumer preferences?

The European application procedure for GMOs works roughly in nine steps: (1) The manufacturer or importer must submit a notification of a GMO product, with full risk assessment, to the member state competent authority (MSCA) where the product is first to be placed on the market. (2) The MSCA accepts or rejects the application. (3) If the MSCA accepts, the application goes to the European Commission and all other competent MSCAs, which have the right to object. (4) Unless other MSCAs object, the original MSCA grants consent to place the product on the entire EU market. (5) If other MSCAs object, the Commission seeks the opinion of the Scientific Committee. (6) The Commission submits a draft decision to the Regulatory Committee (comprising member state representatives) if the case is highly technical, or to the Council of Ministers if it is not, which votes under QMV. (7) Blocking an application in the Council requires unanimity. (8) If the Council does not decide within three months, the Commission decides. (9) Unless the Council rejects the GMO application unanimously, the Commission must authorize the GMO as long as it fulfills current EU legislation, and member states must comply. How democratic is this procedure?

Appointment

The key actors in the European GMO procedure are the member state competent authorities, the Commission, and the Council of Ministers or Regulatory Committee. The Commission has a near-monopoly on initiating proposals for rules or laws, but much of the authorization procedure itself is in the hands of ministers of member state governments on the Council. Democratically elected governments appoint the MSCAs, Council, and Regulatory Committee. By contrast, the Commission is vetted by the Parliament and approved wholesale (once its president is approved individually). Ideally the Parliament would vet the health or environment commissioners and have the power to dismiss each individually. But it does have the power to fire the whole Commission (which it did only once, in March 1999, when it pressured the Santer Commission to resign because of a corruption scandal).

(continues)

In 1985 the Commission launched its "New Approach" to technical harmonization among member states. Now the regulator could lay down only essential safety requirements, while standards were delegated to standardization bodies. Over the years, the scope of these standard-setting bodies has gone beyond purely technical standards and has come to include environmental and health objectives relevant to consumers. In 1990 the Commission charged the Comité Européen de Normalisation (CEN; European Standardization Committee) with the mandate to implement Directive 90/219/EEC, which covers contained use of GMOs. But CEN is only marginally charged with the issue of labeling GMOs.

One candidate for checking the Commission is the Council of Ministers, made up of delegates of the member states whose governments are all elected; it has not only control over GMO authorization, but also the last word on much European legislation. In 1990, Article 14 of Council Directive 90/220/EEC covered the deliberate release of GMOs into the environment, but left implementation to the member states, which were to "take all necessary measures to ensure that products containing, or consisting of, GMOs will be placed on the market only if their labeling and packaging is that specified" between member state and producer. Article 9 of the directive left it to member states—rather than requiring them—to work with diffuse interests: "Where a Member State considers it appropriate, it may provide that groups or the public shall be consulted on any aspect of the proposed deliberate release." Environmental and consumer organizations promptly criticized the directive for inadequate labeling rules, arguing that it neither protected the environment nor gave consumers a real choice.

In May 1998 the Council issued a regulation on GMO food compulsory labeling. It applied its earlier rule to biotechnology: "It is now urgent to lay down detailed uniform Community rules for the labelling" of foods. Article 2(3) says in great detail, down to the size and placement of lettering, that when the food consists of more than one ingredient, the words "produced from genetically modified soya" or "produced from genetically modified maize," for example, must appear in parentheses immediately after each ingredient.[f]

In October 1998, member states launched a de facto moratorium on GMO products. In June 1999, EU environmental ministers in the Council made it official: they moved to a three-year moratorium on any new approvals of GMO foods or crops. (In March 2000 the Parliament endorsed the moratorium in a nonbinding resolution.) Five member states then banned previously approved products under

(continues)

Article 16 of Directive 90/220/EEC, which permits member states on certain conditions to temporarily restrict the use or sale of specific GMO products.[g] The Council based its decision on its own regulation, for the approximation of member states' laws on labeling and presentation of foods, of a generation earlier. Article 5(3) of 1978 Council Regulation 79/112/EEC had stated: "The name under which the product is sold shall include or be accompanied by particulars as to the physical condition of the foodstuff or the specific treatment which it has undergone (e.g. powdered, freeze-dried, deep-frozen, concentrated, smoked) in all cases where omission of such information could create confusion in the mind of the purchaser." The Council held that the 1978 article was applicable to GMO labeling.

Participation

The protection of diffuse interests—environmentalists, consumers, women—from special, highly organized interests is a challenge in any system of governance; the EU is no exception. Still, the EU is not simply a "businessman's Europe" privileging concentrated and mobile capital over other interests. Rather, European institutions present opportunities as well as risks by offering multiple access points that diffuse interests can, and do, use effectively to get their preferred policies adopted and implemented. First, they can take the "national route" and lobby their member state governments for regulations and for representing these in the Council of Ministers. Second, they can take the "Brussels route" by lobbying the Commission to initiate a policy. The Commission and to some extent the Parliament strategically support the evolution of European interest groups, including consumer, environmental, and worker interests. The Commission's Environment Directorate has close ties to environmental activists such as Friends of the Earth Europe and Greenpeace,[h] and consumer groups have created a strong presence with the Directorate of Health and Consumer Protection.[i]

The Commission has a long-standing history of protecting consumer interests. Already in the early 1970s, it had established and funded its Consumers' Consultative Council, composed of both national and European consumer organizations and to be consulted on draft policies relevant to consumer concerns.[j] Today it includes these nongovernmental groups in advisory committees, grants them privileged access, and gives them considerable financial support—for example, to the European Bureau of Consumers' Unions (BEUC). The Commission's motives for doing so are not only altruistic: it gets

(continues)

expertise, legitimacy for its proposals, and partnership from interest groups in promoting its preferred policies in member states.[k]

Third, diffuse interests can go to the Parliament, which has often empathized with their demands, especially in its Committee on the Environment, Consumer Protection, and Public Health. The Parliament regularly restores crucial funds for consumer groups that the Council has cut out of the EU budget. Finally, interests can appeal to the national courts and to the European Court of Justice.[l] Together, these four access points constitute an "opportunity structure"[m] that allows advocates to place issues on the Community agenda, have them adopted by Council and Parliament, and backed by the Court.

Transparency

But the EU food safety system has so far been a relatively decentralized and incomplete regulatory patchwork,[n] which means high information costs for consumers and Parliament members alike. Worse, the Council does not even publish its proceedings. In May 1998 the European Commission's green paper "Efficiency and Accountability in European Standardization Under the New Approach" concluded tersely: "The management of the standardisation process and transparency can be improved." To compensate for the EU's lack of transparency, the Commission takes pains to publish comprehensive explanations of its decisions, both in print and on the Internet.

Reason-Giving

In April 1996 the Commission formally approved the import, storage, and processing of Monsanto's GMO soybeans, Roundup Ready, in the EU. Soybeans are used in 60 percent of all processed foods, such as bread, pasta, candies, ice cream, pies, biscuits, margarine, meat products, and vegetarian meat substitutes. GMO importers were not required to label their products as they entered Europe. The Commission also approved the sale in the EU of a gene-altered maize strain developed by the Swiss pharmaceutical Ciba-Geigy (now Novartis) without requiring specific labeling; as of fall 1996, those products were on shop shelves across Europe, unlabeled. The Campaign to Ban Genetically Engineered Foods asserted that the Commission took these actions without properly informing the public or listening to its wishes.

The Commission realized that it had gone too far. In 2000 it established a 1 percent threshold value above which operators must report GMOs on product labels.[o] On the same day, it reinforced the Council's regulation on labeling foodstuffs and food ingredients that contain additives and flavorings genetically modified or produced from GMOs.[p] Facing mounting resistance to GMOs in member

(continues)

states, it proposed to them "a strategy to regain public trust in the approval procedure for Genetically Modified Organisms" while improving the transparency of decisionmaking, addressing public concerns, and involving the public in GMO authorization. "The EU needs to re-establish public confidence in our approval systems," EU environment commissioner Margot Wallström admitted. "Citizens must be allowed to choose for themselves whether they want products containing GMOs or not."q Meanwhile, the EU had approved eighteen GMO products, and fourteen other approvals were pending.

Overrule

Where does the European Court of Justice stand with GMO regulation? Judicial review so far is rare: in March 2000 the Court ruled that France had no right to block the sale of three GMO crop strains after the Commission had already approved them.r The case dates back to 1998. The French government, faced with mounting public opposition to new GMO crops, had declined to ratify an EU decision clearing new types of maize developed by the Swiss manufacturer Novartis to resist corn borers. The Court ruled that France could not unilaterally withdraw its own earlier approval.

The ruling confirmed that once a member state approves a GMO, the EU institutions, not that member state, have the authority to approve that GMO for sale. But the Court also said that even if EU countries and the Commission have already approved GMO foods, the Commission can later remove them from the market: "New information indicating that a GMO constitutes a risk for human health and the environment allows the procedure for placing a GMO on the market to be stopped pending a fresh Commission decision." This left the door open for France to ask the Commission to retake its decision based on new information. The Court even permitted member states to restrict or prohibit use of a product on their territory, as long as they told the Commission, if they had good reasons to deem GMOs risky.

Monitoring

The Parliament, the only EU supranational actor directly elected by voters, does not have approval power in each individual GMO case, but shares with the Council the power to make laws that affect the GMO approval process. Under a new Article 129A, the 1992 Maastricht Treaty enabled consumer protection by introducing QMV and a codecision procedure of Parliament and Council for consumer protection directives.s Over the years, the Parliament has used its

(continues)

newfound power to issue a plethora of nonbinding resolutions, especially in response to public pressure to rein in GMOs. For example, in March 1996 it criticized the Commission for "glossing over" important elements, and asked it to urgently ensure the comprehensive labeling of GMO products, collect further information, launch a proper public debate, enforce existing GMO legislation, and create a stable legal climate on GMOs. But it also voted against full and complete labeling of GMO foods, and supported the Commission and Council's view that food labels should display only major changes in a product caused by GMOs. In April 1997 the Parliament voted with near unanimity (407 to 2, with 19 abstentions) to suspend the admission of the GMO variety Bt-maize.

Three months later the Parliament again called on the Commission to come up with clear labeling rules. Parliament members criticized the Commission's new rules on gene-altered maize for leaving member states too much wiggling room. In its Resolution 6/97 the Parliament complained that "the current rules of the WTO oblige importing countries to prove that a product is harmful, rather than requiring the exporter to demonstrate that it is safe, thereby emphasising that commercial considerations take presidence [sic] in decision making." It accused the Commission of "lack of responsibility" for deciding unilaterally "to authorise the marketing of GMO maize in spite of all the negative positions of most Member States and the European Parliament" and for acting prematurely "before the coming into effect of the European Parliament and Council Regulation on novel foods and novel food ingredients."

In March 1998 the Parliament's Committee on the Environment, Public Health, and Consumer Protection held a public hearing on GMOs. A year later, in February 1999, the Parliament demanded some 100 amendments to a Commission proposal and charged that producers were liable for human or environmental damage caused by GMOs.[t] In December that year, it called on the Commission again to come up with new proposals for coherent labeling to give consumers a clear choice and the option to buy GMO-free food. It asked the Commission to review its 1 percent threshold for GMO content within twelve months in light of new scientific evidence, and to add to any new legislation a list of GMO-free products.

That same month, the Parliament banned GMO foods from all its restaurants. Though largely symbolic, this new policy sent a clear message: the Commission was guilty of catering to the interests of the biotech industry—at the expense of European consumers.[u]

To be sure, the Parliament has not been consistently anti-industry. Though it revised its earlier labeling directive in April 2000 to make

(continues)

Case 7.1   continued

releasing GMOs into the environment harder, it could not agree on liability rules. Greenpeace responded immediately in a press release: "It is a scandal that the parliament failed to put the financial responsibility where it belongs, to the biotech industry. If these crops were as safe as companies claim them to be, they should have no problems in accepting full liability for them."[v]

Greenpeace might have barked up the wrong tree. Despite all the noise the Parliament makes, the body that has the last word on biotech regulation is the Council. Still, Council and Commission are subjected to much public scrutiny from watchdog groups and the media. Watchdogs, especially, have mobilized public skepticism toward GMOs. And the two supranational EU bodies, the Commission and to some extent the Parliament, strategically support the evolution of European interest groups, especially consumers, environmentalists, and workers. But they have not always been successful: there are many examples of interest group mobilization failing.[w]

Independence

The Commission has not delegated the GMO approval process to another agency; it suffers from a conflation of executive and bureaucratic functions. The Commission and the regulating agency are one and the same. This fundamental conflict of interest is bad for independence.

Notes: a. Pollack and Shaffer 2001: 162.
    b. Fagan 2000.
    c. British Medical Association 1999.
    d. Ewen and Puztai 1999.
    e. Ammann 1999: 18.
    f. Council Regulation 1139/98, May 26, 1998.
    g. Commission press release, July 13, 2000.
    h. Mazey and Richardson 1993.
    i. Maier 1993; Young 1995.
    j. Pollack 1997: 580.
    k. Eichener 1997: 605.
    l. Pollack 1997.
    m. Mazey and Richardson 1993.
    n. Pollack and Shaffer 2001: 158.
    o. Commission Regulation 49/2000, January 10, 2000.
    p. Commission Regulation 50/2000, January 10, 2000.
    q. Commission press release, July 13, 2000.
    r. Case C-6/99.
    s. Pollack 1997: 579.
    t. Friends of the Earth press release, February 11, 1999.
    u. Friends of the Earth press release, December 17, 1999.
    v. Greenpeace press release, April 12, 2000.
    w. Streeck and Schmitter 1991; Streeck 1996.

Conclusion

Now that we have reviewed its biotech regulation, we can analyze the EU's transnational democracy along each of the seven dimensions. While there is room for improvement and further democratization, EU institutions appear to be relatively well equipped to represent and protect diffuse interests (see Table 7.1).

The EU's appointment, participation, reason-giving, overrule, and monitoring all get a rating of +1 (strong democracy). In appointment, the EU is the only transnational organization with a directly elected and increasingly powerful parliament that vets the Commission—and can remove it if necessary. Democratically elected governments appoint the decisionmakers in the Council. In participation, the EU encourages and even funds consumer involvement, and the Council of Ministers—representing the member states—is strongly involved in GMO legislation and decisions. In reason-giving, the Commission publishes its reasoning both on paper and on the Internet. In overrule, the Council (and more and more the Parliament) checks the Commission's power as the EU executive; it can only propose, not ratify, legislation, and compared to executives in other systems, its agenda-setting process is quite open.[29] Also in overrule, judicial review of the EU's GMO decisions, though a bit spotty, has been effective when it happened. And because European decisionmaking needs a consensus among different actors that keep a suspicious eye on each other, every policy development involves "horizontal control"[30] among knowledgeable actors. Such checks and balances are often more effective than vertical control by citizens and their elected representatives.[31] Finally, in monitoring, member states, the Parliament, and watchdog groups all scrutinize both Council and Commission.

Other dimensions are less democratic. The EU's transparency dimension gets a rating of 0 (medium democracy), since policymakers are far removed from the electorate, and the Council's deliberations happen in secret. The Council should be more transparent and publish a record of its

Table 7.1 Transnational Democracy Ratings, EU

Dimension	EU
Appointment	+1
Participation	+1
Transparency	0
Reason-giving	+1
Overrule	+1
Monitoring	+1
Independence	−1
Total rating	+4

Note: Ratings for the EU are based on its biotechnology regulation.

proceedings. The only undemocratic aspect of the EU is independence, for which it gets a rating of –1 (weak democracy), for several reasons: The Commission has failed to delegate the approval process to another agency, and suffers from a conflation of executive and bureaucratic functions. The Commission and EU agencies may profit from asymmetric information, cause agency losses, or exploit conflicting interests of multiple principals.[32] Agencies can suffer capture by special interests such as multinationals. The Commission and the regulating agency are one and the same.

But on the whole, the EU's legitimacy seems not to be declining but growing, according to Eurobarometers that regularly measure EU public opinion. In 1998, only 35 percent of European citizens said they trusted the Commission; but by May 2004, 54 percent of people said they trusted the Parliament and 47 percent the Commission (trust for the Council was lowest, at 40 percent). In fact, European citizens felt that the EU as a whole was more trustworthy than their own national governments.[33] By the way, low election turnouts do not have to mean a democratic deficit.[34] Take Switzerland, where voter participation is usually even lower than in European Parliament elections.

In sum, the EU is the most democratic of all international organizations reviewed in this book. Of course, there is still much to do; but its transnational democracy comes close to that of federal democracies like Switzerland and the United States. Its agencies might not be less accountable than agencies in national governments: a comparison of merger policies found that EU merger regulators are less accountable and independent than US agencies—but more so than Swiss agencies.[35] And if we take a look at history, the lack of a common European culture is probably a question of time: both Switzerland and the United States integrated their multiple demoi and cultures over time (note that the name "United States" is plural, not singular). A demos is not a fixed quantity, but historically constructed. In the meantime, Europe's very diversity might not be an obstacle but actually a source of democracy.

So the EU is a tough act to follow. How do other regional organizations perform? In the next chapter, we look at one that aspires to become very much like the EU—in Africa.

Notes

1. *International Herald Tribune,* June 29, 2004: 3. On June 3, 1999, in the aftermath of the Kosovo crisis, the leaders of fifteen European countries had decided to make the EU a military power, with command headquarters, staffs, and forces of its own for peacekeeping and peacemaking missions in future crises. "European Union Vows to Become Military Power," *New York Times,* June 4, 1999: A1, A22.

2. Seidman and Gilmour 1986; Sunstein 1990; Rose-Ackerman 1992; Majone 1996: 55; Majone 1998.

3. Kielmannsegg 1996: 47–51; my translation.
4. Sanchez de Cuenca 1997.
5. Zweifel 2002a: 17–68.
6. Sbragia 1992: 170.
7. Hayes-Renshaw and Wallace 1995; Franklin et al. 1996.
8. Weiler et al. 1995: 2.
9. Weiler et al. 1995: 2.
10. Weiler 1991: 189.
11. Hayes-Renshaw and Wallace 1995.
12. Post-Nice, thirty-five new issues are under QMV, but other important areas—such as taxation, social security, international transport, health, education, culture, certain aspects of immigration, border controls, audiovisual services and broadcasting—still require unanimity.
13. Streeck 1997: 658; Held 1987: 289.
14. Scharpf 1997a, 1997c.
15. Vogel 1995; Genschel and Plümper 1997.
16. Rodrick 1996b: 26.
17. Scharpf 1997a.
18. Weiler et al. 1995: 1.
19. Weiler 1997: 502.
20. European Commission 2004.
21. *The Economist,* April 3, 2004: 43.
22. Nugent 1995.
23. Brent 1995: 278.
24. Majone 1998.
25. Weiler 1991; Volcansek 1992; Burley and Mattli 1993.
26. Scharpf 1999: 64.
27. Eichener 1995; Shapiro 1997.
28. Wood and Waterman 1994: 143.
29. Peters 1994.
30. Czada 1996.
31. Héritier 1997b; 1999: 26. This idea is not new. Madison wrote in *The Federalist* that a diverse society is important for democracy. The variety of parties and interests in a large republic makes it less likely that factions "[w]ill have a common motive to invade the rights of the other citizens; . . . where there is consciousness of unjust or dishonorable purposes, communication is always checked by distrust in proportion to the number of whose concurrence is necessary." Madison 1981 [1787]: 22.
32. Schmidt 1998: 171–172. The Nice rules slowed down the Commission's activism. The member states granted the Commission more scope in international trade by moving trade agreements from unanimity to QMV. See also endnote 12 above.
33. http://europa.eu.int/comm/public_opinion/archives/eb/eb61/eb61_first_res _en.pdf.
34. Bollen 1980.
35. Zweifel 2002a, 2003.

8

From the
Organization of African Unity
to the African Union

When the Organization of African Unity was founded in 1963, with headquarters in Ethiopia, it immediately aspired to be a multipurpose organization. Its fundamental aim was self-government and socioeconomic progress throughout Africa. But right at the outset, Africa's political climate prevented the organization from becoming truly broad and strong. More than most other international bodies, the OAU was rooted in the Western-derived institutions of colonial rule and the perceived inferiority of African nations[1] on what many in the West dismissed as the "dark continent." To get Africa's power back, the OAU founders' driving vision was pan-Africanism, the idea that countries on the continent should unite. The vision had originated 150 years before in the United States: in 1816 the American Colonization Society for the Establishment of Free Men of Color was founded to repatriate freed slaves; in 1847 free slaves from the United States founded the West African nation Liberia. But the pan-African movement gathered momentum only toward the end of the nineteenth century. Its proponents called for dismantling the colonial system, especially the artificial state boundaries agreed upon at the 1885 Berlin Congress, which had deemed Africa unable to govern itself without European patronage.

After World War II, the demand for political, economic, and cultural self-determination became a flood that the colonial powers could not dam. March 6, 1957, the day of Ghana's independence, marked a new dawn in Africa.[2] But even after many African states achieved independence, the yoke of colonial rule was still a fresh and painful memory for politicians and people of many African nations. Many newly installed African heads of state were unwilling to sign anything that might impinge on their new and jealously guarded sovereignty. Nonintervention was a prominent principle in the organization's 1963 charter, both in Article 3(2) and Article 8,[3] and the OAU lacked supranational authority from the very start. Rather than a unifier of African nations, it became an intergovernmental old-boys net-work—without teeth.

For a regional organization, the OAU was to be unusually broad in pur-pose and functions. Its charter said that the OAU would "promote the unity and solidarity of the African States, coordinate and intensify their coopera-tion and efforts to achieve a better life for the peoples of Africa, [and] defend their sovereignty, their territorial integrity and independence." It would coordinate medical aid and health education programs, settle dis-putes between its members, and regulate the African arms trade.

But it hardly succeeded; and after the Cold War ended, the money spig-ot from West and East dried up. By the late 1990s the OAU's shortcomings had become obvious. On the initiative of none other than Libya's ruler Muammar Qaddafi, who has much pull with African leaders because he lib-erally dispenses much-needed aid all across Africa, OAU leaders issued the 1999 Sirte Declaration, calling for an African Union. They met several times over the next three years to detail their plans, and in 2002 the AU for-mally came into existence. It now counts fifty-three members (the lone out-sider is Morocco, which refused to join because of the admission of Western Sahara, which it claims as its own territory). Its mandates are many: to integrate the continent in political and socioeconomic matters (it called for the creation of a central development bank), provide a forum for conflict resolution that protects the sovereignty and territorial integrity of African states, remove any remaining vestiges of colonialism, promote a common African position in world affairs, and last but not least, promote democratic principles and institutions, popular participation, and good gov-ernance.[4]

We saw that the EU, the AU's role model, is a carefully crafted mix between intergovernmental safeguards for the sovereignty of member states, and supranational institutions to make and enforce common rules. The Constitutive Act of the AU includes strong language on AU decisions to penetrate the national boundaries of all member states. Its founders sought to give the AU more independence, allow more public participation, and have better overrule and monitoring procedures than the OAU ever did. These features make the AU a more effective, democratic, and autonomous organization—and not just on paper. The AU's own peacekeeping forces now serve throughout the continent, and the AU may be ready to referee its own disputes.[5] When the unpopular Liberian leader Charles Taylor left office, the president of Ghana, John Kofuor, was on hand in the Liberian capital to announce the terms for the dictator's successor—an act of pan-African defiance of national sovereignty that would have never happened in OAU times. But it was the exception to the rule. The framers also gave the AU the mandate "to defend the sovereignty, territorial integrity and independence of its Member States"[6]; interim institutions remained inter-governmental, not supranational, to ease the transition.

It will become clear only with time whether the AU remains mostly stuck in the intergovernmental reality of the OAU, or meets its supranational promise. Still, there are enough differences between OAU and AU to treat them as distinct organizations and rate each of them along the seven dimensions of transnational democracy. At the end of the chapter is a brief case study on AU independence: How did the AU, in one of its first actions, respond to the Madagascar election? The case is symptomatic of the challenges facing the AU and many of its members.

Appointment

We start with the old OAU, whose four main bodies were the Assembly of Heads of State and Government, the Council of Ministers, the General Secretariat, and the Commission of Mediation, Conciliation, and Arbitration. Its original 1963 Charter also provided for three specialized commissions: an Economic and Social Commission; an Educational, Scientific, Cultural, and Health Commission; and a Defense Commission.

As its name implies, the Assembly of Heads of State and Government was a body of African leaders, one from each member state. The OAU's highest organ, it would gather at least once a year; special sessions could be called by a two-thirds majority vote. Nothing guaranteed that the heads of state were democratically elected or legally representative of their constituents—and for most of the OAU's existence, few were. Heads of state also had a deep aversion, understandably, against any loss of sovereignty or power. Among those who wanted a more powerful Assembly less beholden to the agendas of individual states and their rulers was Kwame Nkrumah, pan-Africanist and president of Ghana. Both during the OAU's formation and in its first years, Nkrumah pushed for the Assembly's democracy. But before he could realize his ideas, he was ousted from power in his own country, and other leaders, many of whom saw his stance as a form of neo-colonialism, no longer had to worry about changes in the OAU's power structure.

The main powers that the Assembly held under these leaders were threefold: to discuss any matter "of common concern to Africa," to resolve disputes between members, and to pass resolutions with a two-thirds majority. Though the OAU could alter its Charter with a supermajority too, that was rarely necessary; the document was intentionally ambiguous to leave the leaders leeway to shape the OAU according to their wishes without having to introduce formal changes.[7] The Assembly could appoint and remove OAU officials, including the secretary-general, his assistants (never *hers:* though women produce 80 percent of Africa's food, there were no women in top leadership positions), and members of the Commission of Mediation, Conciliation, and Arbitration. Articles 8 and 20 granted the

Assembly the power to create new bodies and agencies and to modify existing ones.

The Assembly did not do much before or after its meetings; it relied on the Council of Ministers to prepare its agendas and act on its decisions. The Council consisted of the foreign ministers or other senior national officials anointed by the heads of state; the Charter gave no guidelines on how Council delegates were to be selected. The Council was to meet twice a year and pass resolutions by simple majority. But since the Charter left the effect of these resolutions unclear, the Council had no teeth; it was very much an assistant or helpmate and a completely subordinate body to the Assembly of Heads of State, many of whom were autocrats. National ministers acted in their governments' interests, not those of the OAU as a whole. Only the Assembly could take real decisions.[8]

Following the model of the UN, the Charter also created a secretariat with a secretary-general as the organization's legal head appointed by the Assembly. The secretariat reported to the Council of Ministers; its personnel were to be recruited based on skill, but their tasks and the rules on their appointment were left ambiguous, making the OAU suspect of cronyism. The appointments for other OAU bodies—for example, the specialized commissions—were like those for the Council. The Charter left the appointments of these commissions up to the member states,[9] and left their powers and responsibilities vague. On paper, all commissions reported to both Council and Assembly, which held the purse strings. But practically speaking, the commissions fell apart after a few years for lack of Assembly support and lack of coordination. Attendance at meetings was low, and by 1966 most efforts to imbue the commissions with clear powers had failed (although some—for example, the Economic and Social Commission—did work).[10]

If enforced, the new AU's appointment rules will be a major move toward transnational democracy: just like the European Parliament, the new Pan-African Parliament will eventually have members chosen through universal suffrage. (In its first incarnation of March 2004, parliamentarians were still appointed by their national governments.) Even better, at least one member of each five-person national delegation will be a woman.

The Assembly and the Executive Council (the new name for the Council of Ministers), together the key AU decisionmakers, will remain intergovernmental. Like in the OAU, the Assembly will be the ultimate decisionmaking body with the power to make policy; it will appoint officials nominated by member states for new AU bodies like the Court of Justice and the Commission of the African Union. For the Assembly chairman, the appointment rule is still unclear; the AU Constitutive Act says only that chairmen are to be "elected after consultations among the Member States."[11]

The new Court of Justice is more promising. The 2003 protocol on its creation calls for democratic appointment: a secret ballot with a two-thirds majority of Assembly members is needed to appoint justices to the Court.[12] Another AU organ called the Peace and Security Council has been formally approved but not yet set up. Once fully operational, its mandate would be much like that of the UN Security Council (but with a nicer name): to prevent, resolve, or manage conflicts. The Peace and Security Council will have fifteen members elected by the Executive Council from all the regions on the continent.

Participation

The OAU made it clear from the outset that it was run by and for the heads of African states; its Charter began not with the words "We the People" but with "We, the Heads of African State and Government." The organization's focus was not on African people, but African *nations.* It was managed by an elite group of African bureaucrats and politicians most of whom had come to power through coups. While the organization pledged to improve the quality of life of all Africans, those Africans had no voice. This was hardly surprising, as even the few African nations that were committed to democracy had no popular participation to speak of, and suffered from poor voter education and registration, weak election infrastructures, and a general lack of logistics for voting.[13] If member states themselves did not promote or protect civic participation, it was foolhardy to expect support for local participation in an organization made up of them.

In some ways, the OAU did recognize the need for participation. In 1981 in Banjul, Gambia, the Assembly of Heads of State adopted its African Charter on Human and People's Rights,[14] which entered into force in 1986 once the majority of OAU states had ratified it. The Banjul Charter granted rights owed by a state to its people, including the right to participate freely in government. It specifically reserved to "colonized" or "oppressed" peoples the right to free themselves by any means recognized by the international community, and gave all such peoples the right to assistance from Charter states.[15]

A decade later, the OAU went further. Its Harare Declaration, crafted in an intergovernmental conference of ministers in March 1997, committed the organization to "a democratic Africa that seeks to enhance the active participation of all citizens in all institutions—social, economic, political, *et cetera.*"[16] The Banjul and Harare Declarations were noble goals and used all the right words; but as long as many member states had no systems in place to enhance their own popular participation, there was no prayer for real participation in the OAU.

Will the AU overcome these problems? In its Constitutive Act the AU framers stressed the importance of democratic participation; under Article 3(3), the Union will "promote democratic principles and institutions, popular participation and good governance." Already in its second year the AU cosponsored a conference on elections, democracy, and good governance.[17] The new Pan-African Parliament opened in 2004 in Addis Ababa, Ethiopia, with 202 legislators from forty-one national parliaments and well-known gender activist Gertrude Mongella as president.[18] The Parliament is to meet twice a year in South Africa and will eventually be directly elected (the question, of course, is what "eventually" means, since the Constitutive Act gives no timeline). In its 2004 Addis meeting the Assembly also approved the draft statutes for a new Economic, Social, and Cultural Council[19] to give access to civil society groups, and the Executive Council asked the AU Commission to gather broad input from civil society groups—another silver lining for future participation.[20] The new AU Commission intends to enhance participation in a number of ways:[21] it plans to create links to groups in the African diaspora and improve coordination and consultation with African regional organizations like the Economic Community of West African States (ECOWAS) and the Southern African Development Community (SADC), which it calls its "regional pillars."[22] These bodies could give better access to cross-national civil society groups and play a role in humanitarian relief,[23] conflict prevention,[24] and economic development. Better integration of these regional groupings into AU decisionmaking would make for more participation and better policy.

Transparency

After being shrouded in secrecy for decades, in its last days the OAU did at least give lip service to the need for greater transparency. The AU Commission went further: it wrote in its vision for 2004–2007: "Transparency. This is the key principle of good governance which should guide the participation of various organs and be reflected in credible systems of information circulation, communication, and joint analysis of financial reports."[25] The document specifically called for decision drafts to be submitted three days before decisions and for all AU organs to publish their decisions within three days.[26] But the jury is still out on whether transparency will in fact improve under the AU.

Reason-Giving

The OAU's shortcomings in its reason-giving stemmed from the fact that its actions were nonbinding. It drew up and passed many well-intentioned resolutions, including numerous charters on human rights written with only the best intentions, but rarely acted on them, and blatant human rights violations continued throughout the continent. The AU has no formal agenda to improve its reason-giving, though presumably this will be part of the process to improve transparency in the Commission and other AU organs.

Overrule

In the late 1960s, a power struggle arose between the Assembly and the Council when the latter began acting as an almost autonomous body: ministers passed resolutions in the Assembly without support from their heads of state. Eventually the Assembly emerged from the struggle as the dominant decisionmaking body, all-powerful and not checked by any other OAU organ. As a result, the OAU never developed a system of checks and balances in which one branch could overrule another. Its first attempt at overrule procedures came with the Commission of Mediation, Conciliation, and Arbitration. This judicial commission, under Article 19 of the OAU Charter, was to handle disputes between member states in general, much like the UN's International Court of Justice. But the organ lacked key powers, most of all the authority to interpret the Charter and enforce its decisions—it could not even force disputing parties to appear before it.[27]

The AU shows significantly more commitment to checks and balances than ever was present in the OAU. The Court of Justice—if instituted as planned—will give direct legal standing to individuals in some cases and will provide a counterweight to other AU organs and member states. As we saw in Chapter 7, the ability of individuals to bypass their national governments and bring lawsuits directly to a regional court has been a major component of checks and balances in the EU. If the AU allows individual standing too, this will provide a genuine source of overrule. But the actual behavior of the Court remains to be seen.

Monitoring

A big OAU weakness was monitoring; having no outside monitoring agencies or rules made for an old-boys network vulnerable to manipulation by heads of government. A key reason for this was that no OAU organ held clear budget approval powers; although there was a budget for conferences and administration, this major monitoring tool was missing in the OAU from the start.

By contrast, the new Pan-African Parliament does have the power to review the AU's budget. It monitors the harmonization of national laws and their respect for human rights, can call on Executive Council members to discuss policies openly, and provides for far more monitoring of its own activities by civil society groups. (So does the Economic, Social, and Cultural Council.) But there are limits to the Parliament's "club behind the door": although the 2003 protocol that established it set the long-term goal that it be a legislative body, it granted the Parliament only "advisory and consultative powers"[28]—at least until further notice.

Independence

The OAU's lack of independence was perhaps its biggest failure: its founding members constantly meddled in its work. Although the Charter included a proposal for much more independence, many African leaders ensured that such a supranational "union government" would never come into being if it compromised their autonomy.[29] Many rulers of newly formed countries were in no mood to cede even the slightest bit of power to a regional body. They used the principle of *uti possidetis* in Article 3 of the Charter, on the nonviolation of the former colonial boundaries, to get their way.[30]

There was one notable attempt to endow the OAU with some autonomy. The secretariat, charged with carrying out its day-to-day tasks, was to be thoroughly independent of the member states so that it could devote itself to Africa as a whole.[31] But just as with the other OAU organs, the Charter left too many blanks to be filled in. The Assembly refused any real power to the secretary-general, effectively neutering the position.

The AU touts its independence as the polar opposite of the OAU's; it claims that it will not be a tool of African governments. But such a claim is hard to back up when many African rulers are still notoriously authoritarian and not used to sharing power with anyone. Critics of the OAU agree that a major reason for its failure was the nondemocracy of its member states. Without legitimately elected national governments accountable to the people, the AU will not be much more than another social club for its rulers. Its independence will probably be the acid test of the AU's success or failure. Take its response to Madagascar's election as a case in point (see Case 8.1).

Conclusion

Although the AU promises to be clearly more democratic than the OAU (see Table 8.1), it is still too early to know whether it is a genuine breakthrough for transnational democracy. The Pan-African Parliament and the Economic, Social, and Cultural Council both appear to ensure better participation, transparency, and monitoring. The African Court of Justice and the

Case 8.1 The AU Decision on Madagascar

One of the AU's core principles is the spread of democracy. Right at its founding, it saw a chance to translate its commitment into action—and at the same time show the world that it marked a departure from the OAU in its independence and willingness to muscle member states. In Madagascar's 2001 presidential election, opposition leader Marc Ravalomanana claimed to have won, but the government insisted he had carried only 46 percent of the vote, forcing a runoff between him and incumbent president Didier Ratsiraka. A power struggle between Ravalomanana and Ratsiraka divided Madagascar for six months, causing many to fear a civil war. (Imagine what might have happened to the unity of the United States if the 2000 Bush vs. Gore election had been contested not for a few weeks but for half a year!) The OAU had sent election supervisors, who had reported concerns about the fairness of the election; a recount in April 2002 negotiated by the OAU and agreed to by both candidates declared Ravalomanana the winner; Ratsiraka rejected the recount and fled the island in July of that year.

Ravalomanana insisted that he was much more dedicated to democracy than was incumbent Ratsiraka. Such declarations seemed enough to satisfy Western governments. After all, any new leader was a welcome change for the better when his predecessor had come to power after the death of a military leader in 1975, won a 1989 election under suspicious circumstances, and clung to power for an entire generation. Some of the most influential states in the world, including the United States, Japan, Britain, and France (Madagascar's former colonial ruler), recognized Ravalomanana as the new president. The high court of Madagascar agreed: it ruled that Ravalomanana was the legitimate leader.

The AU realized that an unfair election might undermine not only the legitimacy of Madagascar's new government, but also its own credibility. The AU wants to promote democracy, but it also wants the power to enforce decisions—something the OAU always had trouble doing. At least on paper, it had abandoned its predecessor's doctrine of noninterference. The election dispute in Madagascar was a defining moment for the AU to back up its words with action, and to show that it would not be pushed around by any government. So it went to bat against the powerful Western players, and insisted on a new round of elections that were to be "transparent and free and

(continues)

Case 8.1   continued

organized with the assistance of the AU and the United Nations." But because of squabbles among AU member states, it left open whether by "elections" it meant presidential or parliamentary elections. Elections for parliament were held in December 2002, Ravalomanana's party again won a majority, and the AU recognized the new government. In 2003, Ratsiraka was tried in absentia and convicted of embezzlement.

In sharp contrast to its action on Madagascar, the AU did not take any official action on the undemocratic reelection of Zimbabwe's ancient autocrat Robert Mugabe, whose statements that black Zimbabweans should seize white landholdings violently and that "animals in the jungle are better than" homosexuals (in a 1999 Commonwealth summit the seventy-five-year-old ruler described the British cabinet as a "gay organization" and "gay gangsters") have been derided worldwide. In typical form, the OAU old-boys network had managed to recognize this election as legitimate. Why did the AU join in the conspiracy of silence? And what explains its different behaviors—intervention in Madagascar but nonintervention in Zimbabwe? We can only speculate.

Perhaps AU leaders wanted to pick their battles carefully. Perhaps they feared that confronting Mugabe until he would fall from power might take a very long time and waste valuable resources on what could turn out to be a failed regime change. Perhaps they sought to save face: a high-profile failure would be ridiculed by the continent and the world. In its early days, the AU could ill afford any of these risks; as a young organization, it needed as much legitimacy as it could get. The irony was that its lack of courage and independence toward Zimbabwe might have cost the AU some of the very legitimacy it craved.

There is one more possible explanation. Perhaps, and despite its protests to the contrary, the AU is still the same old-boys network as the OAU. In both Zimbabwe and Madagascar, AU leaders chose to back up the incumbent leader—and showed loyalty to their peer. Mugabe had many friends among the AU leaders who were reluctant to antagonize their old hero from the days of anticolonialism. In Zimbabwe, doing nothing was good enough for keeping Mugabe in power; in Madagascar, the AU had to take action when the opposition won the election. This uncomfortable thought leaves a bad taste in one's mouth, and hopefully the AU will prove it wrong by more courageous actions like those that facilitated the democratization of Liberia.

Table 8.1   Transnational Democracy Ratings, OAU and AU

Dimension	OAU	AU
Appointment	−1	−1
Participation	−1	0
Transparency	−1	0
Reason-giving	−1	−1
Overrule	0	0
Monitoring	−1	0
Independence	−1	0
Total rating	−6	−2

African Court on Human and People's Rights—to be unified in the future—likewise look promising as checks and balances against too much power for the Assembly and the Executive Council.

But the independence of these institutions remains unclear. Although the 2004 Addis Ababa meeting reiterated the AU's commitment to independence as laid out in the Constitutive Act and the Commission's strategic vision for 2004–2007,[32] it still looks mainly intergovernmental, and the AU's weak response to antidemocratic moves by rulers like Zimbabwe's longtime dictator Robert Mugabe cast a cloud on its commitment to independence.

This could change within a few years—if the AU's framers and officials capitalize on a unique window of opportunity for reform while the organization is still malleable. They could create clear criteria and rules for appointing AU officials, set up elections for the Pan-African Parliament, and give the Parliament broad monitoring powers over other AU organs. They could give voice to nonstate actors such as African civil society and African citizens, especially women. They could improve transparency by publishing decisions immediately—for example, on the Web or by radio, Africa's best medium for spreading information. They could start giving the public reasons for AU decisions. They could strengthen the overrule powers of the Court of Justice and give individuals standing in the court. They could give budget review powers to an independent or elected body. And most important, they could push aggressively for democracy in all AU member states.

To make real progress toward AU independence, leaders across the continent need to be willing to have the Union function freely. One way they can do this is by having clear-cut rules not hidden beneath bureaucratic mumbo-jumbo. If AU members can learn one thing from the OAU, it is this: no matter how good the intentions of the framers, if an organization leaves too many procedural questions unanswered, it cannot avoid being manipulated. How can the AU avoid this pitfall? Strong precedents are crucial. Insistence that states honor the decisions of its new legislative bodies will give the Union the power to resist member states that want to control it. Though its constitution is still ambiguous, the AU now has the chance to build credibility by making the independence of the Parliament, the Court of Justice, and the Commission a reality. The protocols setting up these bodies have gone some way in this direction, but it will take honest dedication to realize democracy. Without it, the AU runs the risk of being a castle built on sand.

Notes

Elliott Bernstein and Yoram Wurmser contributed research to this chapter.
1. Slomanson 1995: 148.
2. Naldi 1992.
3. Jacobson 1984: 155.
4. Constitutive Act of the AU (2000): Article 3.
5. *New York Times,* August 12, 2003: A8.
6. Constitutive Act of the AU (2000): Article 3(b).
7. Woronoff 1970: 160.
8. Woronoff 1970: 163.
9. OAU Charter (1963): Articles XIX, XX.
10. Asante 1987: 130.
11. Constitutive Act of the AU (2000): Article 6(4).
12. Protocol of the Court of Justice (2003): Article 7.
13. http://www.idea.int/2000df/papers_presented_1.html.
14. OAU Doc. CAB/LEG/67/3 rev.5, reprinted in I.L.M. 58 (1982).
15. Henkin et al. 1993.
16. http://www.bisharat.net/harare97declaration.htm.
17. EX/CL/Dec. 35 (III).
18. Assembly/AU/Dec. 39 (III).
19. Assembly/AU/Dec. 48 (III).
20. EX/CL/Dec. 21 (III).
21. Commission of the African Union 2004a.
22. Commission of the African Union 2004a: 28–29.
23. O'Brien 1999.
24. Armstrong and Rubin 2002.
25. Commission of the African Union 2004b: 37.
26. Commission of the African Union 2004b: 28.
27. Asante 1987: 129.
28. Protocol on Establishing the African Economic Community Relating to the Pan-African Parliament (2001): Article 11.
29. Woronoff 1970: 155.
30. Rich 2000: 18.
31. Woronoff 1970: 187.
32. Assembly/AU/Dec. 33 (III).

9

Other Regional Organizations: NAFTA, NATO, and ASEAN

The African Union is far from the only African regional organization. In 1998 the Economic Community of West African States created guidelines for regional peacekeeping and conflict prevention to go along with its economic goals.[1] Western Africa alone counts at least fifteen other regional organizations.[2] Globally, as many as fifty-nine regional organizations have multiple purposes and functioning secretariats.[3] The Asia Pacific Economic Cooperation, the Arab League, the European Free Trade Agreement, and the customs union of Brazil, Uruguay, and Argentina, known as Mercosur, are only a few examples of this regionalist trend.

The past two decades have seen dramatic moves toward closer ties among neighboring countries. Regional organizations have sprung up in all parts of the globe with all types of purposes and have become important forces in the international system. At the very least, national governments have transferred parts of their sovereignty to them, and some, like the European Union, have become advanced international states. Whether this pooling of sovereignty is permanent or merely a temporary tactical decision makes no difference to the people and organizations affected. As with all organizations discussed so far in this book, the increasing powers makes it essential to see whether they represent the people who live within their boundaries. But while they change more and more people's lives, their transnational democracy is still underexplored.

Regional organizations come in all sizes and have all types of mandates and structures; there are too many organizations to review all of them here. This chapter applies the seven criteria of transnational democracy to three regional organizations with three different purposes: one focusing on trade (NAFTA), one on defense (NATO), and one on multiple purposes (ASEAN).

Regional Trade Organizations: NAFTA

Economic regionalism can be defined simply as preferential trading agreements among a subset of nations,[4] or more broadly as a whole emerging pattern of concentrating trade and investment on regional partners.[5] Neither is new: economics has long driven international treaties and alliances. As far back as the Hanseatic League in medieval Europe, city-states formed a governing structure with trading rights and rules for large parts of northern Europe. Today, nations all over the globe enter regional trade agreements, for obvious reasons: The larger a trading area, the more consumers. Countries can benefit from their economies of scale and/or lower their costs of production if they build partnerships with neighbors. Common markets can make industries and merchants richer and more efficient in the face of global competition. And countries can depend on a steady stream of commodities, products, or services that they themselves do not supply within their borders. This is especially true for products for which demand is inelastic; that is, consumers need these commodities regardless of how much they cost, because substitutes are hard to come by, costly, or missing altogether (oil or gas are good examples).

Miles Kahler makes a distinction between "soft" regionalism, which means regional interactions and transactions of private individuals—investors, traders, or migrating workers, but also Australian tourists in Bali, for example—and "hard" regionalism, meaning through deliberate political and institutional design.[6] Even when we take only the rarer form, hard regionalism, quite a few organizations qualify; one of the largest is NAFTA, which is in fact the largest free trade area worldwide in sheer economic output. In force since January 1994, the agreement has served mainly to eliminate tariffs, to promote fair competition among its three members—Canada, Mexico, and the United States—and to massively boost trade compared to other regional organizations, especially its rival the EU. (In 2004, Costa Rica agreed to join the United States and four other Central American nations in a new regional free trade pact that might eventually expand NAFTA throughout the Western Hemisphere.[7]) NAFTA's other objectives are to increase foreign direct investment and to protect intellectual property rights from technology to software to drug patents. How does it perform in the seven dimensions of transnational democracy?

Appointment

NAFTA's framers deliberately avoided supranational rules. The three member states implement the laws and policies of their agreement through various intergovernmental commissions, including the NAFTA secretariat and the Commission for Labor Cooperation (CLC). The overarching NAFTA body, the Free Trade Commission (FTC), oversees the work of other committees, monitors implementation, and attempts to resolve disputes. It is made up of the trade ministers of the three members, so each commissioner is also a member of his or her national bureaucracy. But the treaty's implementation is left to each member state: a national NAFTA secretariat in each country is headed by a secretary responsible for managing it. NAFTA spells out no specific appointment or removal procedures—neither for cabinet-level representatives on the FTC nor for officials at the national secretariats. Since these appointments are up to the member states, this gives them much leeway in how exactly each wants to honor the agreement.[8]

As we see often in strongly intergovernmental organizations, NAFTA is democratic only as long as its member states are democracies. Ultimately, there is democratic accountability through the election of national politicians in all three countries, but like in any administrative state, there are several degrees of separation between individual voters and officials implementing NAFTA.

Participation

NAFTA opponents have decried the lack of opportunity for civil society organizations to observe and contribute to advisory panels. Its FTC relies heavily on these panels of experts for detailed recommendations on common policies and standards. Not only are NGOs absent from these committees, but they are not invited to their meetings.

In contrast to citizen groups, business and industry organizations have several channels for participation through both advisory committees and dispute settlement mechanisms. Under Chapter 19 and especially Chapter 11, industry can challenge government policies and national court decisions by invoking the NAFTA treaty. In several high-profile cases, such as the *Metalclad Corporation* toxic waste dumping case, business interests prevailed against civil society concerns. Despite backing by public health advocacy groups and even subnational governments (for example, the California state government in the *Methanex* case), other nonstate actors have generally failed to affect NAFTA policies.

The original NAFTA treaty sought to take citizen concerns into consideration by providing for public discussion in the CLC and the Commission for Environmental Cooperation (CEC). But in practice these commissions have been lax if not worse. In its first seven years the CLC received a total of twenty-three complaints—fourteen against Mexico, seven against the United States, and two against Canada[9]—barely three complaints a year. And the International Labor Rights Fund found the CLC's labor agreement to be "wholly inadequate" for the complex issues of cross-border labor regulation. Similarly, environmental groups have attacked the CEC for being a lame duck or serving corporate interests. Environmentalists feel particularly suspicious of the dispute settlement tribunals provided for in Chapter 11.

"In order to prevent the future use of Chapter 11 to undermine domestic environmental laws and regulations," the president of one environmental organization testified to a congressional committee, "and in order to force investment dispute proceedings into full public view, we believe that the U.S. must either renegotiate Chapter 11 or negotiate an interpretive note for its provisions as soon as possible."[10]

To be fair, NAFTA did create two small intergovernmental bodies to spur development along the Mexican-US border: the North American Development Bank and the Border Environment Cooperation Commission (BECC). The BECC in particular has improved access and participation for local communities on both sides of the border. But these limited venues for civil society and local involvement are just not enough.

Transparency

Secrecy has been as much a complaint as exclusivity. In response, NAFTA created various commissions to improve transparency. In addition to the CLC and the CEC, the three NAFTA countries each set up a national administrative office as a point of contact and information for their respective government agencies and for government outsiders on activities of their NAFTA secretariats. The national secretariats also keep some records of panel, tribunal, and commission meetings—both at their offices and online. But this is voluntary and up to each secretariat, and mere record-keeping does not make for transparency, which is an ongoing commitment, not something that is grudgingly complied with. The secrecy is worst in dispute settlement and advisory panels; for instance, one advisory panel held discussions at a secret location in Maryland to avoid the attention of labor and environmental groups.

Reason-Giving

Do officials have to explain the reasons for NAFTA decisions? The NAFTA framers mentioned that panel reports should give reasons but never made it an official commitment. They likely saw reason-giving as an unnecessary burden—a barrier in the path of NAFTA's "smooth and efficient" operation. And since big business often has more resources for lobbying and more seats on the panels, the little reason-giving that does happen has a strong whiff of free market and deregulation ideology.

Overrule

What is interesting is that despite its ambitious goals, NAFTA has created only minor institutions to oversee its operation. How is this possible? The answer is: specificity. Its treaty is thousands of pages long, deals with detailed scenarios in trading goods, services, and intellectual property, and leaves little room for interpretation.[11] As a result of these extremely detailed rules, NAFTA's dispute settlements matter less than settlements in, say, the EU or the WTO, whose broad principles and laws are open to interpretation by the courts and other bodies. Still, NAFTA did create dispute settlement panels under Chapters 11, 19, and 20;[12] they have the power to overturn a national court ruling or a member government action that contradicts NAFTA requirements. A panel ruling is the final word on a case. "The dispute settlement mechanisms of [NAFTA] have worked reasonably well" according to one Canadian observer; "the basic goal of trade dispute settlement . . . is to enforce the agreed-upon rules. By and large, these dispute-settlement mechanisms have done that."[13] But panels are flawed in two ways: largely ad hoc, they rarely set legal precedents; and panelists change from case to case, the same procedural and judicial errors may be repeated, and little or no organizational learning is possible.

National executive branches act as both NAFTA's principals (using it as their agent and keeping an eye on its officials) and its agents (implementing NAFTA and keeping their promises). These mixed roles lead to conflicts of interest and to fuzzy chains of command. There is no meaningful check on NAFTA decisions other than the panels themselves (and of course national elections, held only every few years). Worse, since dispute settlement panelists are chosen by each national bureaucracy, NAFTA actually strengthens the executive branch of each national government at the expense of the national judiciary and legislature. By curtailing each country's freedom to amend its own trade laws, NAFTA ends up weakening even the domestic checks and balances in the member states.

Monitoring

The original NAFTA treaty provides for no independent monitoring agency; the chief monitors are the member states themselves: Mexico, Canada, and the United States. They dictate the actions of their NAFTA delegates, control the budgets of their own secretariats, and manipulate the agreement by withholding, or threatening to withhold, funds necessary for running each secretariat. Affected firms, often armed with substantial lobbying budgets, also monitor NAFTA decisions, as do trade and environmental NGOs, though the latter complain that their monitoring is minimal and has little influence.

In the United States, concerns over this lack of oversight led to a new monitoring committee. In exchange for support of a new trade promotion authority, congressional Democrats and their allies insisted on a congressional oversight group on trade as part of the 2002 trade laws. Composed of members of Congress and their staffs, this oversight body aims to create a legislative counterpoint to the US executive branch. It monitors trade negotiations on new treaties, but also FTC activities. It is yet to be seen whether the oversight group will monitor NAFTA effectively. Much depends on the party that controls Congress; and congressional Republicans generally are less enthusiastic than Democrats about the need for such a group.

Independence

How independent is NAFTA? The short answer is, not very independent of control by the principals (its member states, which are also its agents). NAFTA was formed as a vehicle to facilitate trade between three nations in North America. The few organizations it spawned are composed of members of national bureaucracies that serve directly under their executive branches. Only the dispute panels enjoy some independence, but not much: the member governments, through their NAFTA secretariats, control the list of eligible panelists. Needless to say, funding for the dispute panels is completely government-sponsored. Once chosen, these arbitrators have some autonomy, but their tenure lasts for one case only.

Since there are no public records of negotiations or decisions, NAFTA is vulnerable to capture by bureaucratic or business interests. The real fear among NAFTA opponents is that the agreement has given business an institutionalized advantage over environmentalists and labor. And business has a privileged position in the advisory panels that formulate many of the details of NAFTA implementation. Business interests and government interests often converge, especially when governments have neoliberal economic agendas. To say the obvious: this is not good for independence.

Regional Security Organizations: NATO

Regional security organizations go as far back as economic organizations. Thucydides, the classic Greek writer on politics and history, wrote of the Delian League, a military alliance of city-states in Greece, nearly 2,500 years ago. Switzerland began as a security community of small local cantons or states to protect themselves against the Habsburg Empire's expansion in central Europe in the thirteenth century, and gradually developed into a more centralized country. Today, the best-known and most institutionalized regional security organization is the North Atlantic Treaty Organization.

Military alliances have shaped history, but formal security organizations are less common. The reason why states come together to form alliances in the first place is usually a common threat. What makes states create formal rules and/or institutions to run an alliance? Karl Deutsch in 1957 called these institutionalized alliances "pluralized security communities" and pointed to common values, expectations, and responsiveness to each other that raise them above a mere tactical alliance.[14]

NATO was founded following World War II as a defense pact among twelve states in the North Atlantic region. Originally meant as a bulwark against the socialist Warsaw Pact, the organization after the end of the Cold War came to include several Eastern European countries—the very ones that had once been its enemies. The key provision of the treaty is that "an armed attack against one or more of [the signatories] in Europe or North America shall be considered an attack against them all."

NATO has moved far past operating only within the boundaries of its members. In the 1990s the organization sent forces to the Balkans on several occasions to end conflict and "ensure regional stability." If such moves continue, NATO might not be a regional organization much longer. Already it reaches deep into southeastern Europe and Turkey; in 2003, in its first mission beyond Europe's frontiers, it took formal control of Afghanistan's multinational peacekeeping force; and in 2004 the United States turned to NATO as it sought to reduce its own military presence and vulnerability in Iraq.[15] This territorial expansion reaffirms what has been known for a while: NATO's influence and power are felt far beyond the North Atlantic region.[16] It is growing not only geographically, but in scope too; while its original goal was mutual defense, it has expanded its role to peacekeeping, regional stability and security, deterrence, control of the weapons trade, and disarmament. In many ways, NATO has moved from being a means to achieve collective security to becoming an end in itself.[17] European countries seek membership not only for protection, but also to declare themselves as part of the "West" and its democratic ideals. NATO demands democracy explicitly as a prerequisite for membership. But is the organization itself democratic?

Appointment

The NATO Council, headed by the secretary-general, is responsible for implementing the treaty, but its decisions are not necessarily binding. The Council is further divided into specialized committees and agencies; committees deal with diverse matters, from press service to economics. The secretary-general is elected by the member states, which now all have democratically elected governments. That has not always been the case: during the Cold War, NATO allowed the then-dictatorial regimes of Greece and Turkey to join. But NATO's latest expansion into Eastern Europe has made democracy an explicit precondition for any candidate country that wishes to join, along with civilian control over the military and the resolution of any border disputes with neighbors. Slovakia's "good" election campaign in 1998 was overwhelmingly caused by its desire to become a NATO member. Entrenching democracy in the political cultures of the former communist countries of Eastern Europe was a key rationale for NATO expansion.[18]

NATO's first secretary-general was Lord Ismay, a British general who had been chief of staff to Britain's defense minister in World War II. Though it is not a formal rule, secretaries-general have always been European. But NATO's military direction is left to the Military Committee; its chairman, traditionally a US citizen (the first was Dwight Eisenhower), is selected for a three-year term by the Chiefs of Defense, who are in turn appointed by the member states. There are numerous subordinate committees to the Military Committee, including the Supreme Allied Command Europe (SACEUR), the Supreme Allied Command Atlantic (SACLANT), and the Canada-US Regional Planning Group (CUSRPG). The Military Supreme Headquarters sits in Brussels with subordinate agencies located in Paris, Bonn, and Rome.[19] NATO's secretariat is divided into six divisions: political affairs, defense planning and policy, defense support, infrastructure, logistics and council operations, and scientific affairs.

Participation

All democratic participation in NATO is indirect, through the member states. Since only democratic governments can join NATO, democracy is built in at the member state level. But nonstate actors have no formal avenue for participating in NATO's decisionmaking.

Transparency

NATO publishes a vast amount of information—reports, communiqués, press statements, speeches, and more—through its Office of Information and Press. It also has a number of information centers, libraries, and offices at which records and data are stored. Its website houses much of this information in electronic form. But it keeps much of its deliberations and resolutions secret; the decisionmaking process remains hidden, and only final decisions are made public. In the name of national and international security, it has not only refused to provide potentially sensitive information to the public, but has also asked that states wishing to join NATO pass domestic laws limiting public and individual access to military information. While NATO promotes transparency between governments in areas such as disarmament and control of the arms trade, the organization itself is not fully transparent.

Reason-Giving

Giving or not giving reasons behind decisions is at the discretion of each member state. While media offices have been created to help member state governments publish information on NATO, the organization's formal policy is to let each state make its own decisions about how much information it gives to citizens and the media. NATO has no explicit reason-giving rule of its own.

Overrule

There is no judicial review of NATO decisions; this highlights NATO's nature as a treaty based on an alliance of sovereign states. The consensual decisionmaking structure makes unilateral action difficult, even for the militarily preeminent United States. When NATO intervened in Kosovo to protect ethnic Albanians, each military action required approval by all members. These checks slowed military operations but lent the operation legitimacy throughout the NATO community and beyond.[20] On the other hand, there might have been a downside: NATO's slow military responses may have contributed to US unilateralism after the September 11, 2001, terrorist attacks on New York and Washington, D.C.

Monitoring

While NATO monitors military situations across the globe, the organization itself lacks a proper system of monitoring, let alone by a legislative body accountable to the citizenries of the NATO member states; monitoring duties are left to national legislatures. One might see Russia's and Ukraine's recent cooperation with NATO as a sort of monitoring system: outsiders are observing and giving input about the organization's decisions and actions without being official members. But again, private actors have no formal way of monitoring NATO.

Independence

As with many international organizations to which the United States belongs, a major concern is whether or not NATO is independent of US pressure, or whether it caters to US government interests (and in this case, military interests), either blatantly or covertly. Members of the EU have claimed that the United States manipulated NATO throughout the 1990s in its dealings with Eastern European conflicts. Though there is no evidence that NATO's actions in Yugoslavia were a result of undue US influence, it is widely recognized that the United States initiated and led the operation.[21]

Nevertheless, as the Kosovo example above showed, the United States cannot do whatever it wants with NATO. Take, for example, the deployment of US troops in Germany. The United States has protested that it is unfair to expect a single country to pay for such a large portion of Germany's defense budget, and that Germany should reduce its defense demands given the smaller dues it pays. Yet despite US pressure, NATO has not changed its position. Defense is not based on financial contributions, but on whether the organization sees a need for defense.[22]

NATO's secretary-general and military commanders take their roles very seriously. Regardless of the nations from which they stem, they realize the impact that mutual defense—and its weakness—has, potentially on the entire world. For over half a century, the organization has made valuable contributions to the stability of Western Europe (and increasingly, Eastern Europe) as well as other regions, including North America.

Regional Multipurpose Organizations: ASEAN

While NAFTA and NATO are single-focus, specialized organizations (with NATO beginning to branch out into areas other than defense), other regional organizations began with a single mandate but have grown to take on multiple roles. The Association of Southeast Asian Nations is one example. Founded in 1967 with the mandate to foster economic cooperation among its five original members, ASEAN soon came to serve as a forum for resolving conflicts and promoting peace. Some forty years later, it has ten members and has become Asia's premier regional organization. It has also been a force in creating other Asian regional groups like the ASEAN Free Trade Area (AFTA) and the ASEAN Regional Forum (ARF). The latter has brought together key players in East Asia, such as India and former archenemies Japan and China, in a forum to discuss political and security cooperation. Today, ASEAN is a force to be reckoned with.

Appointment

ASEAN's power structure remains rooted in its intergovernmental origins. Its supreme organ is the Heads of Government, who meet formally every three years and informally as often as once a year. Beneath them, national ministers meet more frequently to set policy on foreign affairs, economics, and finance. The ASEAN secretary-general, whom the foreign ministers appoint to a five-year term, together with a standing committee of national bureaucrats, report to the annual ministerial committee on topics that come up during the year. This permanent committee is the most powerful and prominent of several, including committees on trade and tourism, finance and banking, social development, and budget. On all the permanent committees, subcommittees, and ad hoc committees sit national government officials. The standing committee of national bureaucrats appoints directors nominated by member states, whose economics and foreign ministers charge each committee with follow-up on decisions made at ASEAN meetings. So as in the NAFTA system, action on ASEAN policies is left to the national bureaucracies, and each member has a national ASEAN secretariat as part of its own civil service.

In 1976, ASEAN member states created a regional secretariat too, led by the secretary-general. As the most fully developed ASEAN institution, the secretariat is tasked with coordinating between the committees, proposing policies, and ensuring that decisions are carried out properly. But it has only a few dozen staff members. And not only the secretary-general, but all ASEAN officials (except for the staff of the secretariat and some small ASEAN organizations) are appointed by the member governments. Since some members are dictatorships, this arrangement does not help democratic representation.

Participation

ASEAN has formed or certified many private sector groups from business and tourism, but also from such diverse areas as journalism, women's affairs, trade unionism, and orchid growing. Though they have no legislative powers, these groups bring people from a broader spectrum of ASEAN society into the organization's fold.[23] Throughout the region, community-based organizations (CBOs) have helped city governments tackle water and air pollution problems in slum areas. ASEAN has had a hard time interfacing with these CBOs, because they often deal with people living in illegal conditions and because government agencies cannot work with them. This is unfortunate: cooperation with CBOs is one of the main opportunities for ASEAN to encourage popular participation.[24]

In addition to CBOs, over fifty NGOs have formal affiliations with the ASEAN secretariat. Civil society groups, for instance, fully participated in the 1993 Asian regional human rights meeting.[25] To broaden participation and representation in ASEAN, delegates suggested the creation of a regional parliament (similar to the European Parliament). But no steps were taken to make this parliament a reality.

Transparency

ASEAN publishes summaries of its meetings, key decisions, factual reports, and speeches. But there is no guarantee that all documents are open and easily accessible to the public. Moreover, the consensual decisionmaking structure, known by the Malay word *mufakat,* often hides the real positions of the governments. That said, ASEAN has made an explicit commitment to openness. In a strategic vision statement crafted in 1997, the Heads of Government pledged to build a "vibrant and open" ASEAN society by 2020. The 1998 Hanoi action plan called for greater transparency of government procurement, trade policy, and standards. Responding to the wake-up call of the 1997 Asian financial crisis, ASEAN also designed a surveillance process to exchange information between finance ministries, track international economic trends that could affect ASEAN states, provide early warning systems for looming crises, and recommend actions to avoid them. (The Chinese word for "crisis" means both "danger" and "opportunity"; ASEAN sought to seize the opportunity that came along with the danger.) The result is more transparent policy and record-keeping.

Reason-Giving

ASEAN is not obliged to give reasons for decisions to the public. This is left to the member states, many of which have scant traditions of democracy or of explaining their decisions to anyone.

Overrule

In 1995, ASEAN created dispute settlement rules to resolve economic disagreements between members. Although far from a system of real checks and balances, the rules do provide for the first formal sanctions against member states. Two governments can agree to bring a dispute to a panel chosen by a committee of experts from national economics ministries. The panel reports its findings to the committee, which decides based on a majority vote. States can appeal the ruling; it then goes to the ASEAN economics ministers, who also decide by majority. States must abide by these rulings, or ASEAN (much like the WTO) can authorize the affected member states to retaliate. ASEAN seems to be heading toward more formalized dispute settlement,[26] and the majority-based decisionmaking marks a shift away from the consensus and consultation known as the "ASEAN way."[27] But the mechanism has yet to be tested in more cases.

Monitoring

The ASEAN secretariat checks on policy implementation, and national member secretariats monitor what other member states do; but since ASEAN is mostly intergovernmental, the agents are also the principals, and since there is no regional elected parliament as in the EU, no elected officials monitor key ASEAN organs or their budgets. The lack of monitoring can lead to dangerous moments. When in 1997 Indonesian forest fires caused a regionwide haze with real health risks, ASEAN responded with a regional haze action plan, but since member governments had long avoided a powerful internal monitor, ASEAN lacked the ability to perform crucial monitoring tasks. This forced the member states to turn to outside help: embarrassed, they had to ask the UN Development Programme for assistance.

Independence

The ASEAN members stressed from the outset that they wanted an intergovernmental and not a supranational organization. Reflecting its member states' reluctance to give up their sovereignty, ASEAN long acted through consensus. But this changed in the 1980s and even more so in the 1990s when many Asian countries began to liberalize. Several member states knew that they would need to strengthen ASEAN's supranational institutions if it was to deliver on its mission.

ASEAN built several supranational mechanisms for interpreting rules and resolving disputes, but these institutions are still tiny, having only a few dozen staff and being almost completely dependent on member governments. As long as many member governments are undemocratic, it is unlikely that ASEAN will gain real legal independence.[28] It is no surprise that Thailand, one of the region's democracies, has been a proponent of deeper organizational development, from instituting a regional parliament to policing member states for human rights violations. Just as unsurprising, the more autocratic ASEAN members have opposed both initiatives.

Conclusion

As long as individual states face transnational issues and global organizations remain understaffed, too far removed from the people whose lives they change and eyed with suspicion, regional organizations will continue to proliferate. Even for issues that ultimately the UN could step in to address, states are required to seek a regional solution first.[29] The trend is clear: regional organizations will only become more important in the future. With increased powers but without democratic oversight, this trend could threaten global accountability. The threat is real. As Table 9.1 shows, NAFTA, NATO, and ASEAN all fall short in their transnational democracy and have room for improvement nearly everywhere (ASEAN more so than the other two). But their transnational democracy is on the agenda.

None of the three organizations has clear appointment procedures independent of its members; but the democracy of appointment stands and falls

Table 9.1   Transnational Democracy Ratings, NAFTA, NATO, and ASEAN

Dimension	NAFTA	NATO	ASEAN
Appointment	0	0	−1
Participation	0	−1	0
Transparency	0	0	0
Reason-giving	−1	−1	−1
Overrule	0	0	−1
Monitoring	0	0	0
Independence	−1	0	−1
Total rating	−2	−2	−4

with the regime type of member states. Since ASEAN includes current dictatorships like Myanmar and Vietnam, and former ones like Indonesia, it is the weakest in appointment, and gets a rating of −1 (weak democracy). Neither NAFTA nor NATO have to deal with dictatorships as members, but their appointments are not subject to clear rules or else happen away from the public glare; they both get a rating of 0 (medium democracy).

In participation, none of the three organizations is decisive about giving citizens a voice or empowering them to participate. NATO is the weakest: it offers no avenues for popular participation at all, and so gets a rating of −1 (weak democracy). But NAFTA and ASEAN are not much better; although nonstate actors have formal status in them, they have no voice in rulemaking.

With regard to transparency, all three organizations publish their decisions and keep their publics informed, but all are shrouded in secrecy and hide much of their proceedings from the public. All three get a rating of 0 (medium democracy).

None of the three is obliged to give reasons for decisions; they all leave it to their member states, which is bad enough when all member states are democratic, as in NATO and NAFTA, but disastrous when some members are dictatorial, as in ASEAN. All three get a rating of −1 (weak democracy) in reason-giving.

In terms of overrule, while none of the three feature judicial review, NAFTA has dispute panels (ASEAN will too, but they have yet to be seriously tested), and NATO checks the unilateral actions of its members. ASEAN gets a rating of −1 (weak democracy), while NAFTA and NATO each get a rating of 0 (medium democracy).

None of the three entities has empowered an outside monitor. Since all three are intergovernmental organizations, the member states do some of the monitoring—but they are principals and agents simultaneously, which makes for messy accountability. All three get a rating of 0 (medium democracy) in monitoring.

Finally, in terms of independence, NAFTA and ASEAN are so inter-governmental that they literally depend on member states, and so get a rating of –1 (weak democracy). NATO has shown independence from its chief sponsor, the United States, and gets a rating of 0 (medium democracy).

As long as it remains intergovernmental, an organization cannot be more democratic than its members. Take the Arab League, which met in March 2005 in Algiers to unveil ambitious plans for an Arab common market by 2015 and an Arab parliament modeled on that of the EU. While these goals are admirable, as long as most of its member states are ruled by autocrats like Muammar Qaddafi of Libya (who in an apparent gesture of disdain lit a cigarette at the start of the session), Bashar Assad of Syria (who proposed to house a democratically elected Arab parliament in his dictatorial country), or a monarchy of some 3,000 princes in Saudia Arabia (who are unwilling to yield power), transnational democracy has no prayer at the League itself. According to Imad Hmoud, editor of the Jordanian newspaper *Al-Ghad*, "Everybody knows the final result before they even sit down to talk." Rami Khouri, editor at large of the Lebanese *Daily Star,* agreed: "It's an institution of the 1960s and hasn't changed."[30] But even in the intergovernmental NAFTA, whose members are all democracies and retain ultimate control, the democracy of the organization itself must still be safeguarded lest NAFTA override the democracy of its members. At the same time, NATO (and the EU) show that an organization can promote democratization in potential member states. Perhaps ASEAN's strategic vision for 2020 will begin to promote democratization as well. Transnational democracy on a regional level is within reach, but only time will tell whether all regional organizations will do what it takes to achieve it.

Notes

Yoram Wurmser and Elliott Bernstein provided research for this chapter.
1. O'Brien 1999.
2. Henkin et al. 1993: 1551.
3. O'Brien 2000.
4. Bhagwati 1992.
5. Kahler 1995.
6. Kahler 1995.
7. *New York Times,* January 26, 2004: A6.
8. Pastor 2001: 73.
9. Pastor 2001: 75.
10. Brent Blackwelder, president of Friends of the Earth, testimony to the Senate Subcommittee on International Trade, September 5, 2000.
11. Abbot 2000.
12. NAFTA's Chapters 1, 2, 11, 18, 19, and 20 are dedicated to creating its institutional structure.
13. Davey 1996: 288–289.

14. Deutsch 1957.

15. *New York Times,* August 12, 2003: A9; February 23, 2004: A6.

16. Bennett and Oliver 2002: 260.

17. Alexander Wendt has made this argument: "Even if [NATO's] original design reflected the self-interests of its members, over time they arguably have come to identify with the institution and thus see themselves as a collective identity, valuing NATO as an end in itself rather than just as a means to an end." Wendt 2001: 1033.

18. Kydd 2001: 806.

19. Duignan 2000: 10–12.

20. Though the Kosovo operation may not have had as much legitimacy under international law.

21. Duignan 2000: 134.

22. Golden 1983: 93–115.

23. Irvine 1982: 63.

24. Webster 1995: 53.

25. Abad 2003: 43.

26. Davidson 2002: 149.

27. Kahler 2000: 552.

28. Miles Kahler argues that the choice to legalize an international organization can be viewed both as an instrumental and a strategic choice, meaning that states will give legal authority to a regional organization when it helps them meet national choices and fill functional needs. Kahler 2000.

29. Slomanson 1995: 17.

30. Cited in *New York Times,* March 24, 2005: A12.

10

Global Citizenship?

U nder the heading "Democracy at Risk," scholar-activist David Korten and his colleagues write: "We the people of the world have yielded our sovereign democratic authority power to institutions that are now using their military and police powers in ways that threaten freedom, democracy, and security everywhere."[1] To what extent is this claim valid? In an attempt to give a more differentiated picture, Table 10.1 summarizes the findings from Chapters 3 to 9. Again, the simple rating system gives institutions a rating of +1 where their transnational democracy is strong, 0 where it is medium, and –1 where it is weak.

Again, the ratings are admittedly subjective (based on the literature about each organization, on each organization's stated and informal rules, and on interviews with informed observers). Each indicator carries equal weight, which is of course an oversimplification; in the real world, some dimensions matter more than others. It is conceivable that future transnational democracy scales would give different weights to different dimensions; for courts or central banks like the International Criminal Court or the European Central Bank, independence might matter more than participation, while for executive bodies like the UN Security Council or the European Commission, reason-giving is more important than independence. Although both ratings and weightings are rough and could surely be refined, they give us at least an impression of the relative democratic strengths and weaknesses—in other words, the democratic surpluses and democratic deficits—of the international organizations reviewed in this book. And perhaps these indicators will do more than merely permit comparison; they might allow policymakers to pick and emulate best practices from each institution (and/or avoid the worst ones). Who knows, they might even help improve bureaucratic democracy in other settings—national or organizational—where legitimacy cannot be based on elections. They wouldn't be the first: another systematic analysis compared various multilateral agencies, multinational firms, and NGOs on four criteria of "internal stakeholder accountability" (member control, appointment procedures, compliance mechanisms, and evaluation processes) and four criteria of "external accountability" (stakeholder consultation, compliance mechanisms, corporate social responsibility, and access to information). It is possible to compare and evaluate a wide variety of organizations along the same set of criteria.[2]

Building on my findings, this final chapter offers some recommendations for improving transnational democracy, but also explores a phenomenon that Michael Wolff first dreamed about in the eighteenth century and that may soon become reality, given recent trends in globalization and international law: a global citizenry. Democracy cannot exist where citizens do not have rights and liberties—this is true by definition. And if we look at women's rights, we must ask: Is global citizenship within reach? (See Case 10.1.)

But first, some ratings and rankings. The average transnational democracy score is positive (a democratic surplus) in only two cases: the European Union, with a cumulative transnational democracy rating of +4, and on its heels the new International Criminal Court, with a rating of +3. All other organizations show a negative score (a democratic deficit) of between –1 (the World Bank) and –6 (the Organization of African Unity). The OAU finishes last and shows the most severe democratic deficit, one point behind the UN.

Are younger international organizations more democratic than older ones? In other words, is there a trend over time toward more transnational democracy? That would be wonderful, but unfortunately the findings refute such a trend. True, the newest organization, the ICC, is ranked second; but the relatively old EU is ranked first, while the relatively new NAFTA is ranked fourth and the new AU only seventh. The lesson from this is that we cannot lean back; international organizations will not democratize if left to their own devices. Those committed to democracy, inside and outside each institution, must actively work to bring it about.

Based on these rankings, and putting aside the realities of institutional rigidity and path-dependency (the phenomenon that all organizations tend to find themselves on a particular track they cannot get off, save in an organizational crisis),[3] we could imagine, at least in theory, the perfectly democratic international institution. It would borrow the features from those organizations that perform best in each dimension.

But back to reality. Which organization performs best? For appointment, only the EU gets the top rating of +1. (Other organizations should emulate one not scored here: the International Labour Organization. As we saw in Case 3.1., the ILO is the oldest organization still in existence today, but one of the most democratic ones—largely because of its tripartite appointment and decisionmaking rules.) In participation, two organizations—the ICC and the EU—get the top score, a rating of +1, for their

Table 10.1 Transnational Democracy Ratings, Summary

Dimension	Global Organizations		Functional Organizations				Regional Organizations				
	UN	ICC	World Bank	IMF	WTO	EU	OAU	AU	NAFTA	NATO	ASEAN
Appointment	−1	0	0	−1	0	+1	−1	−1	0	0	−1
Participation	−1	+1	0	0	−1	+1	−1	0	0	−1	0
Transparency	0	0	0	0	−1	0	−1	0	0	0	0
Reason-giving	0	+1	+1	−1	0	+1	−1	−1	−1	−1	−1
Overrule	−1	0	−1	−1	+1	+1	0	0	0	0	−1
Monitoring	−1	0	0	0	−1	+1	−1	0	0	0	0
Independence	−1	+1	−1	0	0	−1	−1	0	−1	0	−1
Total rating	−5	+3	−1	−3	−2	+4	−6	−2	−2	−2	−4
Ranking	10	2	3	8	4	1	11	7	4	4	9

Notes: Ratings for the UN are based on the Security Council. Ratings for the EU are based on its biotechnology policy.

efforts to involve nonstate actors. In transparency, none gets a rating of +1, so there is no strong role model in this area. But in reason-giving, three get a rating of +1: the ICC, the EU, and the World Bank, for their efforts to explain decisions clearly and proactively to the public. In overrule, the WTO and the EU both get the top mark, a rating of +1; only these two have fully functioning judicial review and checks and balances. In monitoring, only the EU gets a positive score, a rating of +1, for letting its legislature and outside actors watch over it. And in independence, the ICC alone achieves a rating of +1; it still lacks a meaningful track record, but at least its rules are clearly designed to keep it from being the servant of any (state or nonstate) actor.

But to build transnational democracy, we somehow have to expand the term "the people"[4]—for example, by conceiving of a global citizen. Again, without global citizens, there is no transnational democracy.

Global Citizenship?

Globalization has two faces. One is the tearing down of national borders and the opening of every land to global trade. It is the twenty-four-hour rhythm of the global stock exchanges, the declining sovereignty of states, and the unification of diverse cultures. In the view of German social philosopher Oskar Negt, it is the "third Copernican revolution," in which human beings revolve around the center of the capitalist universe, the sun of global capital.[5] But there is another face of globalization. It is the rise of global, human standards, and ultimately of humans as agents of change, each with a voice, and all in charge of their own future. It is civil society actors tearing down the Berlin Wall or ending apartheid in South Africa. It is "globalization from below."[6]

Against this background, technology can have two faces as well. It can deepen the digital divide, the gulf between rich and poor, or a uniformity of cultures in which everybody wears jeans and listens to the same pop stars, like Madonna and Britney Spears; or it can give a voice and political and economic empowerment to millions of people in developing countries. One example is the villages in the Hin Heup district, a remote region of Laos that has neither electricity nor telephone connections. A prototype personal computer built by the US-Lao Jhai Foundation can be powered by a car battery charged with bicycle cranks, and needs no connection to the electricity grid. Wireless Internet cards link each Jhai computer to a solar-powered hilltop relay station that passes the signals on to a computer in town, joining the Lao phone system with the Internet. The Linux-based software running the computers was "localized" into Lao by a group of expatriates in the United States.[7] Initiatives like this one can give people everywhere a voice and a chance to be part of the global community. "Anyone with a modem is potentially a global pamphleteer," as one activist put it. "Electrons [are] more fascinating than elections."[8] (Given globalization's two faces, the Internet can of course also deepen people's exposure to and dependence on Western-style consumption and materialism.)

For much of the twentieth century, such initiatives were not possible, because the interests of human beings were drowned out by geopolitical agendas or ideological warfare. A struggle between two ideologies, communism versus capitalism, dominated the century. Communism centralized all power in the state; capitalism put all power in the market; neither focused on the human being. The UN and the Bretton Woods system were founded by leading states, not by the human community. And remember, most third world states, comprising some 80 percent of the human population, did not even exist yet as independent entities.[9]

Late in the century, a fundamental transformation occurred. All over the world, there were signs of an emerging global civil society. The 1972 Stockholm Conference on the Human Environment was originally conceived as a traditional intergovernmental forum, but militant grassroots and environmental activists crashed the meeting, made their presence felt so vividly that the media could not ignore them, and became the real news.[10] Stockholm was only the beginning. With the fall of the Berlin Wall and the end of the Cold War, human issues long suppressed by ideology could become top priorities. A flurry of UN world summits held in the 1990s helped create global standards for the conduct of states vis-à-vis their people, and these standards were widely publicized: on children (1990 in New York), sustainable development (1992 in Rio), population (1994 in Cairo), human rights (1995 in Vienna), social issues (1995 in Copenhagen), and women's rights (1996 in Beijing), to highlight just the most prominent gatherings. Take Rio, for example: the 1992 UN Conference on Environment and Development inspired initiatives in over 3,000 communities around the world to create their own local "Agenda 21" as expressions of "The People's Earth Declaration."

These developments have led to a reshaping of what it means to be human and what is possible for human beings. "We have evolved from family, to tribe, to community, to a world of nations. And now we have passed into a new time in which this world of nations has developed into a world of people—a community. What else is it but a global neighborhood?" asked Shridath Ramphal, cochairman of the Commission on Global Governance:

> I was involved in the major UN Conferences in Rio, Cairo, Beijing and Istanbul. What was the dominant factor in these gatherings? It wasn't that they were all great assemblies of governments. It was that they were great occasions on which anything good that emerged did so because of the

non-governmental organizations (NGOs). Civil society, NGOs, the people, are now forcing governments to make compromises and agreements based on human values, both on the national and global level.[11]

International negotiations used to happen in "clubs" of government ministers in secret, but colorful demonstrators chanting slogans are much more telegenic than officials in gray suits discussing arcane technical issues.[12] "Contested issue networks" emerged that made use of their brainpower, the Internet, and global media to drag issues that have winners and losers—like trade, labor, poverty, or the environment—into broad daylight and focus world attention on them.[13] This phenomenon has been called "complex multilateralism,"[14] which goes beyond complex interdependence, a concept that still centered around the nation-state as primary actor in international relations.[15] Complex multilateralism is concerned less with efficient relations among states or efficient management of the global economy, and more with understanding how nonelites can participate with multilateral institutions in global governance.[16]

Three types of transnational networks are increasingly visible in international politics: economic actors and firms; networks of experts whose professional ties and shared causal ideas aim to influence policy;[17] and "transnational advocacy networks" of activists motivated by principled ideas of values.[18] The last work through a "boomerang effect": for example, Nepalese activists might reach out to international allies, who then bring pressure on the Nepalese government to change its domestic practices.[19] Fired up by a sense of mission and unconstrained by canons of reasoning, transnational advocacy networks can frame issues in black-and-white terms, dividing the world into "bad guys" and "good guys."[20]

In campaigning on an issue, global activists create a causal story about who bears responsibility or guilt.[21] Some causal stories work better than others. Activists have convinced many people in many countries that the World Bank bears responsibility for the human and environmental impact of projects it directly funds, but holding the IMF responsible for hunger or food riots in the developing world has been harder because the causal chain is longer, more complex, and less visible, and because the IMF and governments keep the exact content of their negotiations to themselves. For transnational advocacy to be successful, there are at least three conditions: actors have to spread compelling messages; networks have to be dense, with many actors, strong connections among groups, and reliable information flows; and target actors (be they multinationals, governments, or international organizations) have to be sensitive to incentives, sanctions, or moral pressure.

Some groups go beyond advocacy. An international group of eco-enforcers called WildAid has taken matters into its own hands and does the dirty work individual governments cannot do to protect endangered species. From Cambodia to Thailand to Russia, WildAid rangers hunt down poachers to keep them from killing endangered species—Siberian tigers, elephants, turtles, snakes, or monkeys. They work along the entire food chain of the illegal wildlife market: as rangers in the jungle; as urban detective squads in Bangkok or Phnom Penh; as job trainers in villages adjacent to the jungle, helping convert poachers into mushroom farmers; or as media advertisers, driving down demand—for example, through television spots across Asia in which mega-stars like Jackie Chan denounce the use of endangered wildlife for food or medicine.[22] Such eco-enforcers and other action-oriented groups fill a gap left by global deregulation.

One potentially huge group in this global civil society is a long-standing silent majority—the world's women. All over the world, from parliamentarians in Iran to mothers in Ecuador to sex workers in Nigeria who organize to refuse customers unless they use condoms, women are beginning to make their voices heard. Increasingly, women are becoming global citizens who know that human rights include women's rights and who insist that their marginalization must stop.

World Parliament?

In Hugo Grotius's view, the law of nations was supposed to reflect the will of peoples. Who—or what body—represents the global citizenry? The short answer is: nobody. This is not for lack of designs. Early in the twentieth century, the League of Nations commission at the Versailles Peace Conference received a proposal: "At least once in four years, an extraordinary meeting of the Body of Delegates shall be held which shall include representatives of national parliaments, and other bodies representative of public opinion."[23] The proposal was never adopted, but might be worth reconsidering today. Richard Falk and Andrew Strauss have proposed a similar global parliament, even one without extensive powers, whose authority would come directly from the global citizenry. Unlike UN delegates today, members of such a world parliament would not be bound by the interests of their respective nations, but would vote based on their own worldview, political orientation, and interests. Setting up such a global assembly would not even have to depend on ratification by states; instead, a coalition of civil society, media, business, and receptive nation-states could articulate a simple treaty for a global parliament that would represent world public opinion.[24]

This boldly optimistic vision is not widely shared, to say the least. Some argue that there is no evidence that national identities are changing in a manner that would make global representative democracy feasible anytime soon. There is scant evidence of a strong sense of community at the global level today, or that one could soon develop.[25] And absent such a

Case 10.1 The Beijing Women's Summit and Female Genital Mutilation

Rani is an unlikely leader. From the lowly washermen's caste, scorned by the Brahmins who have long dominated her village, she is illiterate, thirty years old, and pregnant. But now Rani has been elected to the panchayat, the village governing council, and proclaims defiantly: "I am the boss."

Rani lives in India, largely a rural nation. Hers is one of 500,000 villages populated by more than 600 million people—about one in every ten people on the planet. In the broadest representative base anywhere in the world, some 3.4 million local elected representatives run panchayats that affect hundreds of millions of people. Not long ago, and for centuries, virtually all panchayat leaders had been elderly men, but in the mid-1990s India passed a new law. Now one-third of all panchayat leaders must be women, which has led to the unprecedented fact that in every election, more than 1.1 million women are elected to panchayat leader positions.

The problem is, women like Rani have never known how to lead or manage, or how to run a meeting. In fact, few of them ever lift their gaze above ground when they talk to someone. Many of them are Muslims and wear the customary veil that shields them from the public. And if this is not enough, many of these women leaders have powerful enemies. Alam Singh, a Brahmin farmer who used to rule Rani's village, said angrily: "She is stupid. She is illiterate. She doesn't listen to anybody." A peer of Singh's did not leave it at angry outbursts. When a woman in his village ran to unseat him as incumbent panchayat leader, he openly threatened to kill her if she won. She won; he killed her. But then her daughter decided to run for her mother's seat. She won; he did not dare touch her anymore.

But men still dominate the political life of most nations; laws and traditions in many countries discriminate in their favor. Often men can own land and use that land as collateral to get credit while women cannot; often men are the only government representatives while women are not. But women bear the children, educate them, and feed them; in Africa, for example, women produce 80 percent of the food.

Women have gained much wider participation in political processes in recent years. Ever since June 1946, when the new UN set up its Commission on the Status of Women to explore how the legal equality women had obtained could become real de facto equality, the UN has served as a venue for discussing women's status, rights, health, education, and economic empowerment. Many conventions on the rights of women followed—for example, the 1949

(continues)

Convention for the Suppression of the Traffic in Persons and the Exploitation of the Prostitution of Others by the General Assembly; the ILO's Convention Concerning Equal Remuneration for Men and Women Workers for Work of Equal Value that same year; the 1950 Convention on the Political Rights of Women; and the 1957 International Convention on the Nationality of Married Women, which gave women the right to choose their nationality upon marriage. The 1960s witnessed more UN resolutions: the 1960 Convention Concerning Discrimination in Respect to Employment and Occupation; the 1962 Convention on Consent to Marriage, Minimum Age for Marriage, and Registration of Marriage; and the 1967 Convention on the Elimination of All Forms of Discrimination Against Women. The UN declared 1975 as International Women's Year and created UNIFEM at that same time.[a] Over the next two decades, it held meetings on issues relevant to women in Mexico City, Copenhagen, Nairobi, Vienna, and Cairo. At the 1993 World Conference on Human Rights in Vienna, thirty-three women from twenty-five countries testified before three judges and an international audience about their own experiences or the ones they had witnessed, and their testimonies reached a global audience through the media. But it took an Organization of American States meeting in 1994 to define the term "violence against women" as "any act or conduct, based on gender, which causes death or physical, sexual or psychological harm or suffering to women, whether in the public or private sphere."[b] The meeting adopted the Inter-American Convention on the Prevention, Punishment, and Eradication of Violence Against Women, a first in an official intergovernmental forum.

A breakthrough came the next year, in September 1995, when representatives from 189 participating governments, some 2,100 nongovernmental organizations, many intergovernmental organizations, the Commission on the Status of Women, and over 50,000 women and men met in Beijing for the fourth UN Conference on Women since 1975, informally known as the Beijing Women's Summit. For countless rural women in China itself, the summit marked the first time they had ever heard of their own inalienable rights. It resulted in an action platform that focused on twelve critical policy areas: poverty, education and training, health, violence, armed conflict, economics, decisionmaking, institutional mechanisms, human rights, media, environment, and the girl-child. This may sound like an obvious laundry list, but none of the twelve areas can be taken for granted. Take violence against women, which as late as the 1970s was still not on the agenda of international human rights-groups or even a priority of the women's movement.[c] Scholars estimate that 60–100 million women in the world are "missing" as a

(continues)

result of the most extreme forms of violence against female infants, children, and adults. But the main normative legal code on women's rights, the Convention on the Elimination of All Forms of Discrimination Against Women, does not even mention, let alone ban, violence against women. The thirty articles establish detailed and comprehensive norms on women's equality and opportunity. Yet they contain not a single word about rape, domestic or sexual abuse, female genital mutilation, or any other instance of violence against women (although one article calls on governments to suppress traffic in women and exploitation of prostitution).[d]

Was the Beijing Women's Summit a launching pad for global citizenship? Yes and no. The summit exemplified global citizenship ideals, but had no legal authority to enforce them. Its main accomplishment was that it raised central human rights issues higher on the international agenda, and led more than a hundred countries and most UN organizations to implement formal commitments they had made at Beijing. Violence against women was one of them, became a major topic, and was declared a fundamental human rights violation. Paragraph 232(h) of the action platform specifically called for an end to female genital mutilation (FGM) "wherever it exists, and the support of efforts among non-governmental and community organizations and religious institutions to eliminate such practices." Paragraph 93 acknowledged the widespread practice of FGM. Paragraph 232(g) called for urgent government action "to combat and eliminate violence against women, which is a human rights violation, resulting from harmful traditional or customary practices, cultural prejudices and extremism."[e] With such statements the Beijing Women's Summit prompted specific legislation, coalitions, and educational programs to abolish FGM.

A joint declaration by the WHO, UNICEF, and the UNFPA in 1997 minced no words about what FGM is: "Female genital mutilation comprises all procedures involving partial or total removal of the external female genitalia or other injury to the female genital organs whether for cultural or other non-therapeutic reasons."[f] FGM is a long-standing cultural tradition prevalent in twenty-eight African countries, and to a lesser extent in Middle Eastern and Asian countries. Due to growing global migration, it is also spreading to Europe, Canada, Australia, and the United States. The World Bank estimates that 80–114 million girls and women have undergone FGM. The global health burden of such violence against women, as measured by healthy years of life lost, is comparable to the burden of AIDS, tuberculosis, cancer, and cardiovascular disease—each of which is

(continues)

already high on the world agenda.[g] Usually midwives and traditional birth attendants perform the procedure on girls in unsanitary conditions, with pieces of glass, dirty scalpels, or razor blades, without anesthesia as their female relatives hold them down; it is accompanied by severe pain and extreme loss of blood, which can lead to hemorrhage and possibly death. Long-term complications include infections, urinary tract problems, obstructed menstrual flow, prolonged labor, cysts, abscesses, stenosis of the artificial opening to the vagina, sexual dysfunction, and psychological trauma.

Justifications for practicing FGM vary from culture to culture. Some teach women that the Quran declares the practice necessary, some that their genitalia are dirty and can cause health problems, others that men find circumcised women more appealing. Young women are often reluctant to refuse FGM, be it for fear of being ostracized by their community or because they see in it a ritual of female pride, depending on their point of view.

Many African nations have passed legislation banning FGM since 1995, including Burkina Faso, Côte d'Ivoire, Senegal, Tanzania, Togo, Kenya, Ghana, Somalia, Djibouti, the Central African Republic, and Egypt. Penalties range from six months to life in prison, and some countries also impose monetary fines. Other countries have proposed laws but are waiting for them to be passed. (While FGM is also practiced in many parts of Europe, mostly by immigrants from Africa, legislation covering it explicitly exists in only three European countries: Sweden, Norway, and the United Kingdom. The rest of Europe has general bodily injury laws that cover FGM without mentioning it.) But saying that a traditional practice is illegal does not put an end to it. In 1999, European and US aid organizations offered military and economic assistance to countries that passed laws against FGM. The desire for economic aid led many countries to pass anti-FGM legislation, regardless of whether or not they meant to actually enforce these laws. Studies show that educational programs to change perceptions of FGM at the grassroots level have been more successful.[h] Paragraph 277 of the action platform called for "the development of policies and programs, giving priority to formal and informal education programs that support girls."[i] Now some sixty-six African NGOs in over twenty African countries work to eradicate FGM. In March 1997 the WHO's Africa office launched an action plan to end FGM in that region. Media coverage also proved a useful tool: in 1998 the Gambia government authorized certain NGOs to air information about FGM, and broadcasters began speaking out on their programs. Studies have shown that increased media exposure has led to increases in negative perceptions of FGM. Li'emet Fitsum, a woman from Mere Miti, a village in northern

(continues)

Ethiopia's Tigray region, said that she had decided against having her two youngest daughters undergo the practice because of information she heard on the radio and in her women's group.

Programs to change attitudes on FGM have often been creative. In Sudan, small financial grants were given to midwives and traditional birth practitioners to discourage them from performing FGM. In Kenya, the Maendeleo Ya Wanawake Organization developed a program called "circumcise with words," an alternative ritual for the coming-of-age ceremony. After undergoing a week-long class teaching them sex education, family planning, and the harmful effects of FGM, girls are tested on the information and given a certificate. They then participate in a traditional coming-of-age ceremony with symbolic gift-giving, dancing, food, and other festivities. The ritual allows them to live in their cultural tradition without being physically harmed. In only five years, from the program's inception in 1996 to 2001, FGM, which had existed for probably thousands of years, decreased in Kenya from 50 percent to 38 percent; in the Reproductive, Educative, and Community Health Program (REACH) in Uganda, it helped decrease FGM by 36 percent.

Notes: Mithulina Chatterjee, Liubov Grechen, Shanka Tawarie, and Melissa Yan, together with The Hunger Project, contributed research for this case study.

a. Gorman 2001: 256–262.

b. The convention was adopted by acclamation at the twenty-fourth regular session of the General Assembly of the OAS on June 9, 1994, in Belem de Pará, Brazil.

c. Convention on the Elimination of All Forms of Discrimination Against Women, adopted and opened for signature, ratification, and accession by UN General Assembly Resolution 34/180 of December 18, 1979; entered into force on September 3, 1981.

d. Keck and Sikkink 1998: 166.

e. http://www.who.int/dsa/cat98/fgmbook.htm.

f. There are four different types of FGM: "Type 1—Excision of the prepuce, with or without excision of part or all of the clitoris. Type 2—Excision of the clitoris with partial or total excision of the labia minora. Type 3—Excision of part or all of the external genitalia and stitching/ narrowing of the vaginal opening (infibulation). Type 4—Unclassified: includes pricking, piercing, or incising of the clitoris and/or labia; stretching of the clitoris and/or labia; cauterization by burning of the clitoris and surrounding tissue; scraping of tissues surrounding the vaginal orifice (angurya cuts) or cutting of the vagina (gishiri cuts); introduction of corrosive substances or herbs into the vagina to cause bleeding or for the purposes of tightening or narrowing it; and any procedure that falls under the definition of female genital mutilation given above." http://www.who.int/dsa/cat98/fgmbook.htm.

g. Heise, Pitanguy, and Germain 1994: 17.

h. http://www.unicef.org/programme/gpp/new/beijing5/violence.htm.

i. http://www.who.int/dsa/cat98/fgmbook.htm.

community feeling, the creation of a global parliament, even if technically feasible, makes little normative sense.[26]

But even without a global parliament, world public opinion could serve as the ultimate sanction for international law—for example, by excluding states from public goods if they defect from agreements that benefit the global community, or if they behave badly in some other way.[27] In extreme cases, the UN could ban nations from membership if they fail to meet minimum requirements of democracy and human rights (much as do the EU and NATO, which already use working definitions of democracy and human rights as conditions for membership). But since the UN Charter does not mandate democracy as an explicit criterion for membership, this is a long shot. Meanwhile, insistence on democratic governance at the national level is perhaps the best strategy for ultimately achieving transnational democratic governance.[28] After all, the problems we face now in building democracy in international organizations may well mirror the problems democratizers faced—and successfully addressed—in setting up the modern nation-state.[29]

Be that as it may, one thing is clear: transnational democracy is not a luxury but a matter of life and death. The world is sitting on a powder keg. By 2050, six out of ten humans (59.1 percent of the world population) will live in Asia, two in Africa, and one in Latin America; less than one will live in Europe, North America, and Oceania combined.[30] India alone will have 1.5 billion people, even ahead of China's 1.4 billion. The overwhelming majority of these people will be fifteen years old or younger. They will be poor, young, and feeling left out of the global game if income inequality increases further (already today the richest 20 percent of humanity own some 86 percent of the wealth). Unless international organizations become democratic and represent the interests of all human beings, we will pay a hefty price. It might cost us our future.

Notes

1. Korten, Perlas, and Shiva 2002: 4.
2. Kovach, Nelligan, and Burall, 2003.
3. Take the curious layout of the QWERTY keyboard on a computer as just one example of path-dependency, and ask yourself why it came to be designed this way. Certainly not on grounds of efficiency.
4. Wendt 1994.
5. *Die Zeit,* December 2001: 41–42.
6. Falk 1993: 39–50.
7. *The Economist,* September 28, 2002: 89.
8. "If Medium Is the Message, the Message Is the Web," *New York Times,* November 20, 1995: A1; "Brave New Cyberworld," *Washington Post,* August 29, 1997: A19.
9. Culpeper 2002.
10. Falk 1998: 321.

11. Interview, *World Goodwill Newsletter* 1996 (no. 4): 2–4.
12. For a review of NGOs and their contribution to transnational standards of democracy, see also Heins 2002.
13. Keohane and Nye 2001a.
14. O'Brien et al. 2000: 5.
15. Keohane and Nye 1977.
16. O'Brien et al. 2000: 207.
17. Haas 1989: 377–404.
18. Keck and Sikkink 1998: 1.
19. Keck and Sikkink 1998: 36.
20. Peterson 1992.
21. Stone 1989: 281–300.
22. *New York Times Magazine,* August 4, 2002: 24–29.
23. Miller 1928, vol. 1: 274.
24. Falk and Strauss 2000, 2001.
25. Nye 2001.
26. Norris 2000.
27. Boyle 1985.
28. Bienen, Rittberger, and Wagner 1998: 304.
29. Weinstock 2001.
30. United Nations Population Division 1998.

Acronyms

AEC	Atomic Energy Commission
AFTA	ASEAN Free Trade Area
AIDS	acquired immunodeficiency syndrome
APEC	Asia Pacific Economic Cooperation
ARDE	Annual Review of Development Effectiveness (of the IFC/ World Bank)
ARF	ASEAN Regional Forum
AROE	Annual Review of Operations Evaluation (of the IFC/World Bank)
ASEAN	Association of Southeast Asian Nations
AU	African Union
BECC	Border Environment Cooperation Commission (of NAFTA)
BEUC	Bureau of Consumers' Unions (of the EU)
BIS	Bank for International Settlements
CAS	Country Assistance Strategy (of the World Bank)
CBO	community-based organization
CEC	Commission for Environmental Cooperation (of NAFTA)
CEN	Comité Européen de Normalisation (European Standardization Committee, of the EU)
CFI	Court of First Instance
CLC	Commission for Labor Cooperation (of NAFTA)
CODE	Committee on Development Effectiveness (of the World Bank)
CSCE	Conference on Security and Cooperation in Europe
CUSRPG	Canada-US Regional Planning Group (of NATO)
DNA	deoxyribonucleic acid
DPI	Department of Public Information (of the UN General Assembly)
ECJ	European Court of Justice

ECOSOC	Economic and Social Council (of the UN)
ECOWAS	Economic Community of West African States
ECSC	European Coal and Steel Community
ESAF	Extended Structural Adjustment Facility (of the IMF)
EU	European Union
EVO	Evaluation Office (of the IMF)
FAO	Food and Agriculture Organization
FGM	female genital mutilation
FTC	Free Trade Commission (of NAFTA)
GATS	General Agreement on Trade in Services
GATT	General Agreement on Tariffs and Trade
GMO	genetically modified organism
HIPC	Highly Indebted Poor Countries
HIV	human immunodeficiency virus
HNP	health, nutrition, and population
IAEA	International Atomic Energy Agency
IBRD	International Bank for Reconstruction and Development
ICC	International Criminal Court
ICJ	International Court of Justice
ICR	Implementation Completion Report (of the World Bank)
ICRC	International Committee of the Red Cross
ICW	International Council of Women
IDA	International Development Association
IFAD	International Fund for Agricultural Development
IFC	International Finance Corporation
IGO	international governmental organization
ILO	International Labour Organization
IMF	International Monetary Fund
INGO	international nongovernmental organization
ISA	International Seabed Authority
IT	information technology
ITO	International Trade Organization
ITU	International Telecommunications Union
MFN	most-favored nation
MIA	Multilateral Investment Agreement
MIGA	Multilateral Investment Guarantee Agency
MINURCA	United Nations Mission in the Central African Republic
MINURSO	United Nations Mission for the Referendum in Western Sahara
MIPONUH	United Nations Civilian Police Mission in Haiti
MONUA	United Nations Observer Mission in Angola
MSCA	member state competent authority
NAFTA	North American Free Trade Agreement

NATO	North Atlantic Treaty Organization
NGO	nongovernmental organization
OAS	Organization of American States
OAU	Organization of African Unity
PCIJ	Permanent Court of International Justice
PLO	Palestinian Liberation Organization
PPA	Project Performance Assessment (of the IFC/World Bank)
PRGF	Poverty Reduction and Growth Facility (of the IMF)
PRSP	Poverty Reduction Strategy Paper (of the World Bank)
QMV	qualified majority voting
REACH	Reproductive, Educative, and Community Health Program (Uganda)
SACEUR	Supreme Allied Command Europe (of NATO)
SACLANT	Supreme Allied Command Atlantic (of NATO)
SADC	Southern African Development Community
SAF	Structural Adjustment Facility (of the IMF)
SARS	severe acute respiratory syndrome
TRIPs	trade-related intellectual property rights
UN	United Nations
UNCED	United Nations Conference on Environment and Development
UNDOF	United Nations Disengagement Observer Force
UNDP	United Nations Development Programme
UNEP	United Nations Environment Programme
UNESCO	United Nations Educational, Scientific, and Cultural Organization
UNFICYP	United Nations Peacekeeping Force in Cyprus
UNFPA	United Nations Population Fund
UNHCR	United Nations High Commissioner for Refugees
UNICEF	United Nations Children's Fund
UNIFEM	United Nations Development Fund for Women
UNIFIL	United Nations Interim Force in Lebanon
UNIKO	United Nations Iraq-Kuwait Observation Mission
UNMOGIP	United Nations Military Observer Group in India and Pakistan
UNRRA	United Nations Relief and Rehabilitation Administration
UNSCOM	United Nations Special Commission on Iraq
UNTSO	United Nations Truce Supervision Organization
UPU	Universal Postal Union
WFP	World Food Programme
WHO	World Health Organization
WIPO	World Intellectual Property Organization
WTO	World Trade Organization

References

Abad, M. C. 2003. "The Association of Southeast Asian Nations: Challenges and Responses." In Michael Wesley (ed.), *The Regional Organizations of the Asian-Pacific: Exploring Institutional Change.* London: Palgrave Macmillan.

Abangwu, George C. 1975. "Systems Approach to Regional Integration in West Africa." *Journal of Common Market Studies* 13(1–2): 133.

Abbot, Frederick. 2000. "NAFTA and the Legalization of World Politics: A Case Study." *International Organization* 54(3): 519–547.

Abbott, Kenneth W., and Duncan Snidal. 1998. "Why States Act Through Formal International Organizations." *Journal of Conflict Resolution* 42(1) (February): 3–32.

Ackerman, Bruce. 1995. *Is NAFTA Constitutional?* Cambridge: Harvard University Press.

Aksu, Esref, and Joseph A. Camilleri. 2002. *Democratizing Global Governance.* Houndmills: Palgrave Macmillan.

Allott, Philip. 1990. *Eunomia.* Oxford: Oxford University Press.

Alvarez, Jose E. 1996. "Judging the Security Council." *American Journal of International Law* 90(1) (January): 1–39.

Amin, Samir. 1997. *Capitalism in the Age of Globalization.* London: Zed Press.

Ammann, Daniel. 1999. "Gentechnik an Lebensmitteln." Zurich: Schweizerische Arbeitzgruppe Gentechnologie (SAG)/Swiss Workgroup Biotechnology.

Anderson, Benedict. 1983. *Imagined Communities.* London: Verso.

Archibugi, Daniele. 1993. "The Reform of the UN and Cosmopolitan Democracy." *Journal of Peace Research* 30(3): 301–315.

Archibugi, Daniele, David Held, and Martin Köhler (eds.). 1998. *Reimagining Political Community: Studies in Cosmopolitan Democracy.* Stanford: Stanford University Press.

Armstrong, Andrea, and Barnett Rubin. 2002. "Conference Summary: Policy Approaches to Regional Conflict Formations." New York: Center on International Cooperation, New York University.

Asante, S. K. B. 1987. "The Role of the Organization of African Unity in Promoting Peace, Development and Regional Security in Africa." In Emmanuel Hansen (ed.), *Africa: Perspectives on Peace and Development.* London: United Nations University/Zed Books.

Baldwin, David (ed.). 1993. *Neorealism and Neoliberalism: The Contemporary Debate.* New York: Columbia University Press.

Banks, Jeffrey S., and Barry R. Weingast. 1992. "The Political Control of Bureaucracies Under Asymmetric Information." *American Journal of Political Science* 36(2) (May): 509–524.

Barber, Benjamin. 1984. *Strong Democracy: Participatory Politics for a New Age.* Berkeley: University of California Press.

———. 1996. *Jihad vs. McWorld: How Globalism and Tribalism Are Reshaping the World.* New York: Ballantine Books.

Barnaby, Frank (ed.). 1991. *Building a More Democratic UN: Proceedings of the First International Conference on a More Democratic UN.* London: Frank Cass.

Barnett, Michael N., and Martha Finnemore. 1999. "The Politics, Power, and Pathologies of International Organizations." *International Organization* 53(4) (Autumn): 699–732.

Barro, Robert J., and David B. Gordon. 1983. "Rules, Discretion, and Reputation in a Model of Monetary Policy." *Journal of Monetary Economics* 12: 101–121.

Beattie, Alan. 2002. "IMF Seeks to Draw Lessons from Turmoil in Argentina." *Financial Times,* January 1.

Bederman, David J. 1992. "Book Review." *American Journal of International Law* 86(2) (April): 411.

Beetham, David. 1998. "Human Rights as a Model for Cosmopolitan Democracy." In Daniele Archibugi, David Held, and Martin Köhler (eds.), *Reimagining Political Community: Studies in Cosmopolitan Democracy.* Stanford: Stanford University Press.

Behn, Robert. 2001. *Accountability.* Washington, D.C.: Brookings Institution.

Belous, Richard, and Jonathan Lemco. 1995. *NAFTA as a Model of Development: The Benefits and Costs of Merging High- and Low-Wage Areas.* Albany: State University of New York Press.

Bendor, Jonathan. 1988. "Formal Models of Bureaucracy." *British Journal of Political Science* 18(3) (July): 353–395.

Bennett, A. LeRoy, and James K. Oliver. 2002. *International Organizations: Principles and Issues.* Upper Saddle River, N.J.: Prentice Hall.

Bentham, Jeremy. 1838–1843. *The Works of Jeremy Bentham.* 11 vols. Edited by John Bowring. Edinburgh: William Tait.

———. 1838–1843. "Plan of Parliamentary Reform." In John Bowring (ed.), *The Works of Jeremy Bentham.* Edinburgh: William Tait.

———. 1930. "Theory of Legislation." Cited in Robert Luce, *Legislative Principles.* Boston: Houghton Mifflin.

Bhagwati, Jagdish. 1988. *Regionalism.* Cambridge: MIT Press.

———. 1992. "Regionalism and Multilateralism: An Overview." Paper presented to a World Bank conference, Washington, D.C., April 2–3.

———. "Patents and the Poor." *Financial Times,* September 16, 2002. Available at http://www.southcentre.org/info/southbulletin/bulletin43/bulletin43.pdf.

Bhagwati, Jagdish, and Petros Mavroidis. 2002. "Why the Byrd Amendment Must Be Buried." *Financial Times,* November 21.

Bienen, Derk, Voker Rittberger, and Wolfgang Wagner. 1998. "Democracy in the United Nations System: Cosmopolitan and Communitarian Principles." In Daniele Archibugi, David Held, and Martin Köhler (eds.), *Reimagining Political Community: Studies in Cosmopolitan Democracy.* Stanford: Stanford University Press.

Bignami, Francesca, and Steve Charnovitz. 2001. "Transatlantic Civil Society Dialogues." In Mark A. Pollack and Gregory C. Shaffer (eds.), *Transatlantic Governance in the Global Economy.* Lanham: Rowman and Littlefield.

Blanton, Shannon Lindsey. 2000. "Promoting Human Rights and Democracy in the Developing World: U.S. Rhetoric Versus U.S. Arms Exports." *American Journal of Political Science* 44(1): 123–131.

Blustein, Paul. 2001. "Critics Get World Bank to Ease Disclosure Policy." *Washington Post,* September 6.

Bogdanor, Vernon, and Geoffrey Woodcock. 1991. "The European Community and Sovereignty." *Parliamentary Affairs* 44(4): 481–492.

Bohman, James. 1999. "International Regimes and Democratic Governance: Political Equality and Influence in Global Institutions." *International Affairs* 75(3): 499–513.

Bollen, Kenneth A. 1980. "Issues in the Comparative Measurement of Political Democracy." *American Sociological Review* 45(4): 370–390.

Boutros-Ghali, Boutros. 1996. *An Agenda for Democratization.* New York: United Nations.

Boyle, Francis A. 1985. *World Politics and International Law.* Durham, N.C.: Duke University Press.

Bradlow, Daniel D. 1993. "The Case for a World Bank Ombudsman." *Hearings on Appropriations for International Financial Institutions: Banking, Finance, and Monetary Policy.* US House of Representatives. Washington, D.C., May.

Brent, Richard. 1995. "The Binding of Leviathan: The Changing Role of the European Commission in Competition Cases." *International and Comparative Law Quarterly* 44(2): 255–279.

Brink, Lindsey. 1999. *The US Antidumping Law: Rhetoric Versus Reality.* Trade Policy Analysis no. 7. Washington, D.C.: Cato Institute, August.

British Medical Association. 1999. "The Impact of Genetic Modification on Agriculture, Food, and Health." Interim statement. London: British Medical Association, Board of Science and Education, May.

Brown, L. David, and Jonathan Fox. 1998. *The Struggle for Accountability: The World Bank, NGOs, and Grassroots Movements.* Cambridge: MIT Press.

Brown, Laura Ferris. 1993. "Arbitration Institutions in International Commercial Arbitration." In Laura Ferris Brown (ed.), *The International Arbitration Kit: A Compilation of Basic and Frequently Requested Documents.* New York: American Arbitration Association.

Brown, Paul. 1999. "World Bank Pushes Chad Pipeline." *The Guardian,* October 11.

Buchanan, Allen, and Robert O. Keohane. 2004. "The Preentive Use of Force: A Cosmopolitan Institutional Proposal." *Ethics and International Affairs* 18(1).

Bull, Hedley. 1977. *The Anarchical Society.* New York: Columbia University Press.

Bulmer, Simon. 1994. "Institutions and Policy Change in the European Communities: The Case of Merger Control." *Public Administration* 72(3): 423–444.

Burley, Anne-Marie. 1993. "Regulating the World: Multilateralism, International Law, and the Projection of the New Deal Regulatory State." In John Gerard Ruggie (ed.), *Multilateralism Matters: The Theory and Praxis of an Institutional Form.* New York: Columbia University Press.

Burley, Anne-Marie, and Walter Mattli. 1993. "Europe Before the Court: A Political Theory of Legal Integration." *International Organization* 47(1): 41–76.

Calhoun, John C. 1963 [1848]. *Disquisition on Government.* New York: P. Smith.
Calomiris, Charles W. 2000a. "The IMF Needs More Than a New Boss." *Wall Street Journal,* March 2.
————. 2000b. "When Will Economics Guide IMF and World Bank Reforms?" Statement before the US Senate Committee on Foreign Relations, May 23.
Cardoso, Fernando H. 1973. "Associated Dependent Development." In Alfred Stepan (ed.), *Authoritarian Brazil.* New Haven: Yale University Press.
Carlsson, Ingvar. 1995. "The U.N. at 50: A Time to Reform." *Foreign Policy* 100 (25th anniversary issue) (Autumn): 3–18.
Caron, David D. 1993. "The Legitimacy of the Authority of the Security Council." *American Journal of International Law* 87(4) (October): 552–588.
Cary, William L. 1974. "Federalism and Corporate Law: Reflections on Delaware." *Yale Law Review* 83(4): 663–705.
Childers, Erskine, with Brian Urquhart. 1994. *Renewing the United Nations System.* Uppsala, Sweden: Dag Hammarskjöld Foundation.
Christiansen, Thomas. 1997. "Tensions of European Governance: Politicized Bureaucracy and Multiple Accountability in the European Commission." *Journal of European Public Policy* 4(2) (March): 73–90.
Clark, Elizabeth Spiro. 2002. "International Standards and Democratization: Certain Trends." In Edward R. McMahon and Thomas A. P. Sinclair (eds.), *Democratic Institution Performance: Research and Policy Perspectives.* Westport: Praeger.
Coffey, Peter, Colin Dodds, Enrique Lazcano, and Robert Riley. 1999. *NAFTA: Past, Present, and Future.* Boston: Kluwer Academic.
Commission of the African Union. 2004a. *The Strategic Plan of the Commission of the African Union.* Vol. 1, *Vision and Mission of the African Union.* Addis Ababa.
————. 2004b. *The Strategic Plan of the Commission of the African Union.* Vol. 2, *The 2004–2007 Strategic Framework of the Commission of the African Union.* Addis Ababa.
Commission of the European Communities. 1998. Efficiency and Accountability of Standardisation Under the New Approach, DG III, Com (98) 291 Final, May 13.
Commission on Global Governance. 1995. *Our Global Neighborhood: The Report of the Commission on Global Governance.* Oxford: Oxford University Press.
Conybeare, John A. 1980. "International Organization and the Theory of Property Rights." *International Organization* 34(2): 307–334.
Cooper, Robert. 2000. *The Post-Modern State and the World Order.* London: Demos.
Couloumbis, Theodore A., and James H. Wolfe. 1990. *Introduction to International Relations: Power and Justice.* Englewood Cliffs, N.J.: Prentice-Hall International.
Covey, Jane. 1998. "Critical Cooperation? Influencing the World Bank Through Policy Dialogue and Operational Cooperation." In Jonathan A. Fox and L. David Brown (eds.), *The Struggle for Accountability: The World Bank, NGOs, and Grassroots Movements.* Cambridge: MIT Press.
Cowhey, Peter. 1990. "The International Telecommunications Regime: The Political Roots of Regimes for High Technology." *International Organization* 44(2) (Spring): 169–200.
Cox, Robert. 1987. *Production, Power, and World Order.* New York: Columbia University Press.
Crawford, James, and Susan Marks. 1998. "The Global Democracy Deficit: An

Essay in International Law and Its Limits." In Daniele Archibugi, David Held, and Martin Köhler (eds.), *Reimagining Political Community.* Stanford: Stanford University Press.

Cronin, Thomas E. 1989. *Direct Democracy. The Politics of Initiative, Referendum, and Recall.* Cambridge: Harvard University Press.

Crooks, Ed. 2002. "The Odd Couple of Global Finance." *Financial Times,* July 5.

Culpeper, Roy. 2002. "Unbalanced Representation and Global Inequity." Paper presented to the Friedrich-Ebert-Stiftung conference "Global Governance and Financing for Development," Berlin, February 7–9.

Czada, Roland. 1996. "Vertretung und Verhandlung: Aspekte Politischer Konfliktregelung in Mehrebensystemen" [Representation and Deliberation: Aspects of Political Conflict Resolution in Multiple-Level Systems]. In Arthur Benz and Wolfgang Seibel (eds.), *Theorieentwicklungen in der Politikwissenschaft* [Theory Developments in Political Science]. Baden-Baden: Nomos.

Czempiel, Ernst-Otto. 1999. *Kluge Macht: Aussenpolitik für das 21 Jahrhundert* [Prudent Power: Foreign Policy for the 21st Century]. Munich: Beck.

Dahl, Robert A. 1956. *A Preface to Democratic Theory.* Chicago: Chicago University Press.

———. 1971. *Polyarchy: Participation and Opposition.* New Haven: Yale University Press.

———. 1999. "Can International Organizations Be Democratic? A Skeptic's View." In Ian Shapiro and Casiano Hacker-Cordon (eds.), *Democracy's Edges.* Cambridge: Cambridge University Press.

D'Amato, Anthony (ed.). 1994. *International Law Anthology.* Cincinnati: Anderson.

Dashwood, Alan. 1996. "The Limits of European Community Powers." *European Law Review* 21(1): 113–128.

Davey, William. 1996. *Pine and Swine: Canada–United States Trade Dispute Settlement—The FTA Experience and NAFTA Prospectus.* Ottawa: Center for Trade Policy and Law.

Davidson, Paul J. 2002. *ASEAN: The Evolving Legal Framework for Economic Cooperation.* Singapore: Time Academic Press.

Day, Gerald W. 1988. *Genoa's Response to Byzantium, 1155–1204: Commercial Expansion and Factionalism in a Medieval City.* Urbana: University of Illinois Press.

Dehousse, Renaud. 1995. "Constitutional Reform in the European Community: Are There Alternatives to the Majority Avenue?" In Jack Hayward (ed.), *The Crisis of Representation in Europe.* London: Frank Cass.

———. 1997. "Regulation by Networks in the European Community: The Role of European Agencies." *Journal of European Public Policy* 4(2) (June): 246–261.

Dehousse, Renaud, Christian Joerges, Giandomenico Majone, Francis Snyder, and Michelle Everson. 1992. "Europe After 1992: New Regulatory Strategies." EUI Working Paper, LAW 92/31.

DePalma, Anthony. 2001. "NAFTA'S Powerful Little Secret: Obscure Tribunals Settle Disputes, but Go Too Far, Critics Say." *New York Times,* March 11.

De Roover, Raymond. 1948. *Money, Banking, and Credit in Mediæval Bruges: Italian Merchant-Bankers, Lombards, and Money-Changers.* Cambridge: Mediæval Academy of America.

———. 1966. "The Organization of Trade." In *Cambridge Economic History of Europe.* Vol. 3. Cambridge: Cambridge University Press.

Deutsch, Karl W. 1957. *Political Community and the North Atlantic Area.* Princeton: Princeton University Press.

Dixit, Avinash. 1996. *The Making of Economic Policy: A Transaction-Cost Perspective.* Cambridge: MIT Press.

Docksey, Christopher, and Karen Williams. 1994. "The Commission and the Execution of Community Policy." In G. Edwards and D. Spence (eds.), *The European Commission.* London: Longman.

Doerfler, Walter, et al. 1997. "Integration of Foreign DNA and Its Consequences in Mammalian Systems." *Trends in Biotechnology* 15(8) (August): 297–301.

Dollinger, Philippe. 1970. *The German Hansa.* Stanford: Stanford University Press.

Dornbusch, Rüdiger. 2000. "Reply to Stiglitz." *New Republic,* May 29.

Dos Santos, Theotonio. 1970. "The Structure of Dependency." *American Economic Review* 60 (May): 231–236.

Doyle, Michael. 1992. "An International Liberal Community." In Graham Allison and Gregory F. Treverton (eds.), *Rethinking America's Security.* New York: W. W. Norton.

Downs, Anthony. 1957. *An Economic Theory of Democracy.* New York: Harper and Brothers.

Drucker, Peter F. 1997. "The Global Economy and the Nation-State." *Foreign Affairs* 76(5): 159–171.

Duignan, Peter. 2000. *NATO: Its Past, Present, and Future.* Stanford: Hoover Institution Press.

Dunn, John. 1999. "Situating Democratic Political Accountability." In Bernard Manin, Adam Przeworski, and Susan Stokes (eds.), *Democracy, Accountability, and Representation.* Oxford: Cambridge University Press.

Earnshaw, David, and David Judge. 1995. "Early Days: The European Parliament Co-decision and the European Union Legislative Process Post-Maastricht." *Journal of European Public Policy* 2(4) (December): 624–649.

Easton, David. 1965. *The Political System.* New York: Knopf.

Eichener, Volker. 1995. "Die Rückwirkungen der Europäischen Integration auf Nationale Politikmuster" [The Reverse Effects of European Integration on National Policy Patterns]. In Markus Jachtenfuchs and Beate Kohler-Koch (eds.), *Europäische Integration* [European Integration]. Opladen: Leske und Buderich.

———. 1997. "Effective European Problem-Solving: Lessons from the Regulation of Occupational Safety and Environmental Protection." *Journal of European Public Policy* 4(4) (December): 591–608.

Eijffinger, Sylvester C. W., and Jakob de Haan. 1996. "The Political Economy of Central-Bank Independence." *Princeton Studies in International Economics* 19: 1–82.

Einhorn, Jessica. 2001. "Notes for Trilateral Commission Meeting." London.

Eiras, Ana I., and Gerald P. O'Driscoll. "U.S. Policy Toward Latin America: Lessons from Argentina." Paper no. 798. Washington, D.C.: Center for International Trade and Economics (CITE), Heritage Foundation, January.

Epstein, David, and Sharon O'Halloran. 1999. *Delegating Powers: A Transaction Cost Politics Approach to Policy Making Under Separate Powers.* Cambridge: Cambridge University Press.

Eskridge, William N., Jr., and John Ferejohn. 1992. "The Article I, Section 7 Game." *Georgetown Law Review* 80(3): 565–582.

European Commission. 2004. "Summary of the Agreement on the Constitutional Treaty." Provisional document. Brussels, June 28.

Evans, Peter B., Harold K. Jacobson, and Robert D. Putnam. 1993. *Double-Edged*

Diplomacy: International Bargaining and Domestic Politics. Berkeley: University of California Press.

Ewen, Stanley W. B., and Arpad Puztai. 1999. "The Health Risks of Genetically Modified Foods." *The Lancet* 354(9179): 684–689.

Fagan, John B. 2000. "Assessing the Safety and Nutritional Quality of Genetically Engineered Foods." Manuscript/Web report. Available at http://www.netlink.de/gen/jfassess.htm.

Falk, Richard. 1993. "The Making of Global Citizenship." In Jeremy Brecher, John Brown Childs, and Jill Cutler (eds.), *Global Visions: Beyond the New World Order.* Boston: South End Press.

———. 1998. "Global Civil Society: Perspectives, Initiatives, Movements." *Oxford Development Studies* 26(1): 99–110.

Falk, Richard, and Andrew Strauss. 2000. "On the Creation of a Global People's Assembly: Legitimacy and the Power of Popular Sovereignty." *Stanford Journal of International Law* 36 (Summer): 191–220.

———. 2001. "Toward Global Parliament." *Foreign Affairs* 80–81 (January–February): 212–220.

Finer, Herman. 1940–1941. "Administrative Responsibility in Democratic Government." *Public Administration Review* 1 (Summer): 335–350.

Finnemore, Martha. 1996. *National Interests in International Society.* Ithaca: Cornell University Press.

Fiorina, Morris P. 1985. "Group Concentration and the Delegation of Legislative Authority." In Roger Noll (ed.), *Regulatory Policy and the Social Sciences.* Berkeley: University of California Press.

Fox, Jonathan A. 2000. "The World Bank Inspection Panel: Lessons from the First Five Years." *Global Governance* 6(3) (July–September): 279–318.

Francis, David. 2000. "ECOMOG: A New Security Agenda in World Politics." In *Africa at the Millennium: An Agenda for Mature Development.* New York: Palgrave.

Franck, Thomas M. 1990. *The Power of Legitimacy Among Nations.* Oxford: Oxford University Press.

———. 1992a. "Editorial Comment: The 'Powers of Appreciation'—Who Is the Ultimate Guardian of UN Legality?" *American Journal of International Law* 86(3) (July): 519–523.

———. 1992b. "The Emerging Right to Democratic Governance." *American Journal of International Law* 86(1) (January): 46–91.

———. 1995. *Fairness in International Law and Institutions.* Oxford: Clarendon Press.

———. 1998. *Fairness in International Law and Institutions.* Oxford: Clarendon Press.

Frank, André Gunder. 1966. "The Development of Underdevelopment." *Monthly Review* no. 18 (September): 17–31.

Franklin, Mark, Cees van der Eijk, and Michael Marsh. 1996. "Conclusions: The Electoral Connection and the Democratic Deficit." In Cees van der Eijk and Mark Franklin (eds.), *Choosing Europe? The European Electorate and National Politics in the Face of Union.* Ann Arbor: University of Michigan Press.

Frey, Bruno S. 1984. "The Public Choice View of International Political Economy." *International Organization* 38(1): 199–223.

Friedman, Benjamin M. 2002. "Globalization: Stiglitz's Case." *New York Review of Books,* August 15. Available at http://www.nybooks.com/articles/15630.

Friedman, Thomas. 2000. *The Lexus and the Olive Tree.* New York: Farrar, Strauss, and Giroux.

———. 2002. "India, Pakistan, and G.E." *New York Times,* August 11.

Gambari, Ibrahim A. 1996. "The Role of Regional and Global Organizations." In Edmond J. Keller and Donald Rothchild (eds.), *Africa in the New International Order: Rethinking State Sovereignty and Regional Security.* Boulder: Lynne Rienner.

Garrett, Geoffrey. 1998. *Partisan Politics in the Global Economy.* Cambridge: Cambridge University Press.

Gasiokwu, Martin. 1998. *Ecowas: Problems of Citizenship and Free Movement.* Jos, Nigeria: Mono Expressions.

Gatsios, Konstantine, and Paul Seabright. 1989. "Regulation in the European Community." *Oxford Review of Economic Policy* 5(2): 37–60.

Genschel, Philipp, and Thomas Plümper. 1997. "Regulatory Competition and International Co-operation." *Journal of European Public Policy* 4(4) (December): 626–642.

Gershman, J. 1996. "Making the World Bank More Accountable: Activism in the North." *NACLA Report on the Americas* 29(6) (May–June): 22–23.

Gilligan, Michael J. 1997. *Empowering Exporters: Reciprocity, Delegation, and Collective Action in American Trade Policy.* Ann Arbor: University of Michigan Press.

Gilpin, Robert. 1987. *The Political Economy of International Relations.* Princeton: Princeton University Press.

Golden, James R. 1983. *The Dynamics of Change in NATO.* New York: Praeger.

Goldstein, Judith, Miles Kahler, Robert O. Keohane, and Anne-Marie Slaughter. 2000. "Introduction: Legalization and World Politics." *International Organization* 54(3) (Summer): 385–399.

Goldstein, Leslie Friedman. 1997. "State Resistance to Authority in Federal Unions: The Early United States (1790–1860) and the European Community (1958–94)." *Studies in American Political Development* 11 (Spring): 149–189.

Gorman, Robert F. 2001. *Great Debates at the United Nations: An Encyclopedia of Fifty Key Issues, 1945–2000.* Westport: Greenwood Press.

Grant, Ruth W., and Robert O. Keohane. 2005. "Accountability and Abuses of Power in World Politics." *American Political Science Review* 99(1) (February): 1–15.

Great Britain. 1919. *The Covenant of the League of Nations with a Commentary Thereon; Presented to Parliament by Command of His Majesty, June 1919 (Cmd. 151).* Miscellaneous no. 3. London: His Majesty's Stationery Office.

Greif, Avner, Paul Milgrom, and Barry Weingast. 1994. "Coordination, Commitment, and Enforcement: The Case of the Merchant Guild." *Journal of Political Economy* 102(4): 745–776.

Grindle, Merilee S. 2000. "Ready or Not: The Developing World and Globalization." In Joseph S. Nye and John D. Donahue (eds.), *Governance in a Globalizing World.* Washington, D.C.: Brookings Institution.

Grotius, Hugo. 1913–1925 [1646]. *De Jure Belli ac Pacis Libri Tres* [On the Law of War and Peace]. Edited by Francis W. Kelsey. Classics of International Law no. 3. Oxford: Clarendon Press.

Guéhenno, Jean-Marie. 1995. *The End of the Nation-State.* Minneapolis: University of Minnesota Press.

Haas, Ernst. 1958. *The Uniting of Europe: Political, Social, and Economic Forces, 1950–1957.* Stanford: Stanford University Press.

———. 1964. *Beyond the Nation-State: Functionalism and International Organization.* Stanford: Stanford University Press.

————. 1990. *When Knowledge Is Power.* Berkeley: University of California Press.

Haas, Peter. 1989. "Do Regimes Matter? Epistemic Communities and Mediterranean Pollution Control." *International Organization* 43(3) (Summer): 377–404.

Hall, Peter A., and Robert J. Franzese Jr. 1998. "Central Bank Independence, Wage Bargaining, and EMU." *International Organization* 52(3) (Summer): 505–536.

Hanke, Steve H. 2000. "Abolish the IMF." *Forbes,* April 17. Available at http://www.forbes.com/columnists/global/2000/0417/0308034a.html.

Hardin, Russell. 2000. "Democratic Epistemology and Accountability." *Social Philosophy and Policy* 17(1): 110–126.

Hartley, Trevor C. 1988. *The Foundations of European Community Law: An Introduction to the Constitutional and Administrative Law of the European Community.* 2nd ed. Oxford: Clarendon Press.

Hayes-Renshaw, Fiona, and Helen Wallace. 1995. "Executive Power in the European Union: The Functions and Limits of the Council of Ministers." *Journal of European Public Policy* 2(4) (December): 559–582.

Hegeland, Hans, and Ingvar Mattson. 1996. "To Have a Voice in the Matter: A Comparative Study of the Swedish and Danish European Committees." *Journal for Legislative Studies* 2(3) (Autumn): 198–215.

Heins, Volker. 2002. *Weltbürger und Lokalpatrioten: Eine Einführung in das Thema Nichtregierungsorganisationen* [World Citizens and Local Patriots: An Introduction to the Topic of Nongovernmental Organizations]. Opladen: Leske + Budrich.

Heise, Lori L., with Jacqueline Pitanguy and Adrienne Germain. 1994. *Violence Against Women: The Hidden Health Burden.* World Bank Discussion Paper no. 255. Washington, D.C.: International Bank for Reconstruction and Development.

Held, David. 1987. *Models of Democracy.* Cambridge: Polity Press.

————. 1996. *Models of Democracy.* 2nd ed. Stanford: Stanford University Press.

————. 1998. "Democracy and Globalization." In Daniele Archibugi, David Held, and Martin Köhler (eds.), *Reimagining Political Community.* Stanford: Stanford University Press.

Helliwell, John. 1998. *How Much Do National Borders Matter?* Washington, D.C.: Brookings Institution.

Henkin, Louis, Richard Crawford Pugh, Oscar Schachter, and Hans Smit. 1993. *International Law: Cases and Materials.* 3rd ed. St. Paul, Minn.: West.

Héritier, Adrienne. 1997a. "Market-Making Policy in Europe: Its Impact on Member-State Policies—The Case of Road Haulage in Britain, the Netherlands, Germany, and Italy." *Journal of European Public Policy* 4(2): 539–555.

————. 1997b. "Policy-Making by Subterfuge: Interest Accommodation, Innovation, and Substitute Democratic Legitimation in Europe—Perspectives from Distinctive Policy Areas." *Journal of European Public Policy* 4(2) (June): 171–189.

————. 1999. *Policy-Making and Diversity in Europe: Escape from Deadlock.* Cambridge: Cambridge University Press.

Hertz, Noreena. 2001. *The Silent Takeover: Global Capitalism and the Death of Democracy.* London: William Heinemann.

Higgins, Rosalyn. 1963. *The Development of International Law Through the Political Organs of the United Nations.* London: Oxford University Press.

Hilferding, Rudolf. 1981. *Finance Capital.* London: Routledge and Kegan Paul.

Hobbes, Thomas. 1651 [1982]. *Leviathan.* London: Penguin Classics.

Hormats, Robert D. 1987. *Reforming the International Monetary System: From Roosevelt to Reagan.* New York: Foreign Policy Association.

Horn, Murray. 1995. *The Political Economy of Public Administration.* Cambridge: Cambridge University Press.

Huffschmid, Jörg. 2000. "Demokratisierung, Stabilisierung, und Entwicklung: Ein Reformszenario für IWF und Weltbank" [Democratization, Stabilization, and Development: A Reform Scenario for IMF and World Bank]. *Blätter für Deutsche und Internationale Politik* [Pages for German and International Politics] 45(11) (November): 1345–1354.

Hull, Robert. 1993. "Lobbying Brussels: A View from Within." In Sonia Mazey and Jeremy Richardson (eds.), *Lobbying in the European Community.* Oxford: Oxford University Press.

Huntington, Samuel P. 1991. *The Third Wave: Democratization in the Late Twentieth Century.* Norman: University of Oklahoma Press.

———. 1999. "The Lonely Superpower." *Foreign Affairs* 78(2) (March–April): 36.

Hurrell, Andrew. 1990. "Kant and the Kantian Paradigm in International Relations." *Review of International Studies* 16(3): 183–205.

Hurrell, Andrew, and Ngaire Woods. 1995. "Globalisation and Inequality." *Millennium* 24(3): 447–470.

Inkeles, Alex. 1990. "Introduction." *Studies in Comparative International Development* 25(1): 3–6.

International Monetary Fund. 2000a. "Executive Board Report to the IMFC on the Establishment of the Independent Evaluation Office (EVO) and Its Terms of Reference." September 12. Available at http://www.imf.org.

———. 2000b. "Making the IMF's Independent Evaluation Office (EVO) Operational: A Background Paper." Washington, D.C.: International Monetary Fund, August.

———. 2002. Public Information Notice no. 02/26. Washington, D.C., March 8. Available at http://www.imf.org/external/np/sec/pn/2002/pn0226.htm.

Irvine, Roger. 1982. "The Formative Years of ASEAN: 1967–1975." In Alison Broinowski (ed.), *Understanding ASEAN.* London: Macmillan.

Iversen, Torben. 1998. "Wage Bargaining and Central Bank Independence." *International Organization* 52(3) (Summer): 469–504.

Jackson, John H. 2000. "Dispute Settlement and a New Round." In Jeffrey J. Schott (ed.), *The WTO After Seattle.* Washington, D.C.: Institute for International Economics.

Jackson, Karl, Paribatra Sukhumbhand, and Soedjati Djiwandono. 1986. *ASEAN in Regional and Global Context.* Berkeley: Institute of East Asian Studies, University of California.

Jacobson, Harold K. 1979. *Networks of Interdependence: International Organizations and the Global Political System.* New York: Alfred A. Knopf.

Janis, Mark W. 1984. "Jeremy Bentham and the Fashioning of 'International Law.'" *American Journal of International Law* 78: 405.

Jessup, Philip C. 1948. *A Modern Law of Nations.* New York: Macmillan.

Kahler, Miles. 1995. "A World of Blocs: Facts and Factoids." *World Policy Journal* 12(1) (Spring): 19–27.

———. 2000. "Legalization as Strategy: The Asia-Pacific Case." *International Organization* 54(3) (Summer): 552.

Kahler, Miles, and David Lake. 2000. "Globalization and Governance." In Miles Kahler and David Lake (eds.), *Governance in a Global Economy: Political Authority in Transition.* Princeton: Princeton University Press.

Kant, Immanuel. 1983 [1795]. *Perpetual Peace*. Rev. ed. Edited by T. Humphrey. Indianapolis: Hackett.

Kawai, Masahiro, Richard Newfarmer, and Sergio Schmukler. 2001. "Crisis and Contagion in East Asia: Nine Lessons." Washington, D.C.: World Bank, February.

Keck, Margaret E., and Kathryn Sikkink. 1998. *Activists Beyond Borders: Advocacy Networks in International Politics*. Ithaca: Cornell University Press.

Keohane, Robert O. 1984. *After Hegemony*. Princeton: Princeton University Press.

Keohane, Robert O., and Helen V. Milner (eds.). 1996. *Internationalization and Domestic Politics*. New York: Cambridge University Press.

Keohane, Robert O., and Joseph S. Nye Jr. 1974. "Transgovermental Relations and World Politics." *World Politics* 27(1) (October): 39–72.

———. 1977. *Power and Interdependence*. 1st ed. Boston: Addison-Wesley.

———. 2000a. "Globalization: What's New? What's Not? (And So What?)" *Foreign Policy* 118 (Spring): 104–119.

———. 2000b. Introduction to Joseph S. Nye and John D. Donahue (eds.), *Governance in a Globalizing World*. Washington, D.C.: Brookings Institution.

———. 2001a. "Democracy, Accountability, and Global Governance." Paper prepared for the University of California Institute on Global Conflict and Cooperation conference "Globalization and Governance," La Jolla, March 23–24. Rev. June 27.

———. 2001b. *Power and Interdependence*. 3rd ed. Boston: Addison-Wesley.

Khor, Martin. 1999. "Foreign Investment Policy, the Multilateral Agreement on Investment, and Development Issues." Paper contributed to *UNDP Human Development Report 1999*. New York: United Nations.

———. 2000. "Globalization and the South: Some Critical Issues." Discussion Paper no. 147. Geneva: UNCTAD, April.

Kielmannsegg, Peter Graf. 1996. "Integration und Demokratie" [Integration and Democracy]. In Markus Jachtenfuchs/Beate Kohler-Koch (eds.), *Europäische Integration* [European Integration]. Opladen: Leske und Buderich.

Kiewiet, D. Roderick, and Mathew McCubbins. 1991. *The Logic of Delegation: Congressional Parties and the Appropriations Process*. Chicago: University of Chicago Press.

Kindleberger, Charles. 1973. *The World in Depression, 1929–1939*. Berkeley: University of California Press.

King, Alexander, and Bertrand Schneider. 1991. *The First Global Revolution: A Report of the Council of Rome*. New York: Pantheon.

Kissinger, Henry. 2001. *Does America Need a Foreign Policy? Toward a Diplomacy for the 21st Century*. New York: Simon and Schuster.

Knight, W. Andy. 2000. *A Changing United Nations: Multilateral Evolution and the Quest for Global Governance*. London: Palgrave.

Kobrin, Stephen. 1998. "The MAI and the Clash of Globalization." *Foreign Policy* 112 (Fall): 97–109.

Kooiman, J. 1993. "Findings, Speculations, and Recommendations." In J. Kooiman (ed.), *Modern Governance*. London: Sage.

Koremenos, Barbara, Charles Lipson, and Duncan Snidal. 2001. "The Rational Design of International Institutions" and "Rational Design: Looking Back to Move Forward." *International Organization* 55(4) (Autumn): 761–799, 1051–1082.

Korey, William. 1989. "Raphael Lemkin: The Unofficial Man." *Midstream* (June–July): 45–48.

Korten, David C. 1995. *When Corporations Rule the World.* New York: Kumarian Press.

———. 1998. *Globalizing Civil Society.* New York: Seven Stories Press.

Korten, David C., Nicanor Perlas, and Vandana Shiva. 2002. "Global Civil Society: The Path Ahead." People-Centered Development Forum discussion paper. Available at http://www.pcdf.org/civilsociety/path.htm.

Kovach, Hetty, Caroline Nelligan, and Simon Burall. 2003. *Power Without Accountability?* London: One World Trust.

Krasner, Stephen D. 1983. *International Regimes.* Ithaca: Cornell University Press.

Krey, August C. 1923. "The International State of the Middle Ages: Some Reasons for Its Failure." *American Historical Review* 28: 1–7.

Krueger, Anne O. 1974. "The Political Economy of the Rent-Seeking Society." *American Economic Review* 64 (June): 291–303.

———. 2001a. "International Financial Architecture for 2002: A New Approach to Sovereign Debt Restructuring." Washington, D.C.: International Monetary Fund, November.

———. 2001b. "A New Approach to Sovereign Debt Restructuring." Washington, D.C.: International Monetary Fund, April.

Krueger, Hilmar C. 1932. "The Commercial Relations Between Genoa and Northwest Africa in the Twelfth Century." PhD diss., University of Wisconsin–Madison.

———. 1933. "Genoese Trade with Northwest Africa in the Twelfth Century." *Speculum* 8 (July): 377–395.

Krugman, Paul, and Maurice Obstfeld. 1994. *International Economics: Theory and Policy.* 3rd ed. New York: HarperCollins.

Kydd, Andrew. 2001. "Trust Building, Trust Breaking: The Dilemma of NATO Enlargement." *International Organization* 55(4) (Autumn): 801–828.

Laffont, Jean, and Jean Tirole. 1993. *A Theory of Incentives in Procurement and Regulation.* Cambridge: MIT Press.

Lane, Timothy, and Steven Phillips. 2002. "Moral Hazard: Does IMF Financing Encourage Imprudence by Borrowers and Lenders?" Washington, D.C.: International Monetary Fund, March.

Laver, Michael, and Kenneth A. Shepsle. 1997. "Government Accountability in Parliamentary Democracy." Mimeo.

League of Nations. 1924. *Procès-Verbal of the 5th Session of the Council.*

Leibfried, Stephan. 1992. "Towards a European Welfare State?" In Walter R. Heinz (ed.), *Status Passages and the Life Course.* Vol. 3, *Institutions and Gatekeeping in the Life Course.* Weinheim: Deutscher Studien Verlag.

Leibfried, Stephan, and Paul Pierson. 1995. *European Social Policy: Between Fragmentation and Integration.* Washington, D.C.: Brookings Institution.

Lenin, V. I. 1939. *Imperialism: The Highest Stage of Capitalism. A Popular Outline.* New York: International.

Lessig, Lawrence. 1999. *Code and Other Laws of Cyberspace.* New York: Basic Books.

Levins, Richard A. 2000. "Farmers and Agribusiness: Partners or Competitors?" In Michael C. Stumo (ed.), *A Food and Agriculture Policy for the 21st Century.* Lincoln, Nebr.: Organization for Competitive Markets.

Libby, Ronald T. 1992. *Protecting Markets: US Policy and the World Grain Trade.* Ithaca: Cornell University Press.

Lijphart, Arend. 1984. *Democracies: Patterns of Majorities and Consensus Government in Twenty-one Countries.* New Haven: Yale University Press.

Linklater, Andrew. 1998. "Citizenship and Sovereignty in the Post-Westphalian European State." In Daniele Archibugi, David Held, and Martin Köhler (eds.), *Reimagining Political Community: Studies in Cosmopolitan Democracy.* Stanford: Stanford University Press.

Linz, Juan. 1984. "Democracy: Presidential or Parliamentary—Does It Make a Difference?" New Haven: Yale University. Manuscript.

Lipset, Seymour Martin. 1960. *Political Man.* Garden City, N.Y.: Doubleday.

Lopez, Robert Sabatino. 1943. "European Merchants in the Medieval Indies: The Evidence of Commercial Documents." *Journal of Economic History* 3 (November): 164–184.

Lowi, Theodore. 1969. *The End of Liberalism: The Second Republic of the United States.* New York: W. W. Norton.

Luck, Edward. 2003. *Reforming the United Nations: Lessons from a History in Progress.* International Relations Studies and the UN, Occasional Paper no. 1. New Haven: Academic Council on the United Nations System.

Lukas, Aaron. 2000. "WTO Report Card III: Globalization and Developing Countries." Washington, D.C.: Cato Institute, June.

Lupia, Arthur, and Matthew D. McCubbins. 1994. "Learning from Oversight: Fire Alarms and Police Patrols Reconstructed." *Journal of Law, Economics, and Organization* 10(1) (April): 96–125.

Macho-Stadler, Inés, and J. David Pérez-Castrillo. 2001. *An Introduction to the Economics of Information: Incentives and Contracts.* Oxford: Oxford University Press.

Madison, James. 1981 [1787]. "The Federalist no. 10." In R. E. Fairfield (ed.), *The Federalist Papers,* 2nd ed. (from the 1787 original texts by Alexander Hamilton, James Madison, and John Jay). Baltimore: Johns Hopkins University Press.

Maier, Lothar. 1993. "Institutional Consumer Representation in the European Community." *Journal of Consumer Policy* 16(3–4): 355–374.

Majone, Giandomenico. 1996. *Regulating Europe.* London: Routledge.

———. 1997a. "Europe's 'Democratic Deficit': The Question of Standards." Paper presented at the Cost A7 conference "Integration and Enlargement: Implications for Rule-Setting and Regulation." London, December 12–13.

———. 1997b. "From the Positive to the Regulatory State: Causes and Consequences of Changes in the Mode of Governance." Working Paper no. 93. Madrid: Instituto Juan March de Estudios e Investigaciones.

———. 1997c. "The New European Agencies: Regulation by Information." *Journal of European Public Policy* 4(2) (June): 262–275.

———. 1998. "The Regulatory State and Its Legitimacy Problems." Vienna: Institut für Höhere Studien (HIS).

Manin, Bernard. 1994. "Checks, Balances, and Boundaries: The Separation of Powers in the Constitutional Debate of 1787." In Biancamaria Fontana (ed.), *The Invention of the Modern Republic.* Cambridge: Cambridge University Press.

Manin, Bernard, Adam Przeworski, and Susan Stokes. 1999. *Democracy, Accountability, and Representation.* Oxford: Cambridge University Press.

Mann, Catherine L., and Sarah Cleeland Knight. 2000. "Electronic Commerce in the WTO." In Jeffrey J. Schott (ed.), *The WTO After Seattle.* Washington, D.C.: Institute for International Economics.

Martin, D. Guy. 1989. *African Regional Integration: Lessons from the West and Central African Experiences.* Lagos: Nigerian Institute of International Affairs.

Martin, Lisa L. 1992. *Coercive Cooperation: Explaining Multilateral Economic Sanctions.* Princeton: Princeton University Press.

———. 2000. *Democratic Commitments: Legislatures and International Cooperation.* Princeton: Princeton University Press.

Mattli, Walter. 2001. "Private Justice in a Global Economy: From Litigation to Arbitration." *International Organization* 55(4) (Autumn): 918–940.

Mazey, Sonia, and Jeremy Richardson. 1993. "Environmental Groups and the EC: Challenges and Opportunities." In David Judge (ed.), *A Green Dimension for the European Community: Political Issues and Processes.* London: Frank Cass.

McConnell, Grant. 1966. *Private Power and American Democracy.* New York: Knopf.

McCubbins, Matthew D., Roger G. Noll, and Barry R. Weingast. 1987. "Administrative Procedures as Instruments of Political Control." *Journal of Law, Economics, and Organization* 3(2) (Fall): 243–287.

McCubbins, Matthew D., and Thomas Schwartz. 1984. "Police Patrols vs. Fire Alarms." *American Journal of Political Science* 28(1) (February): 165–179.

McDougal, Myres, and Harold Lasswell. 1969. "The Identification and Appraisal of Diverse Systems of Public Order." In Leo Gross (ed.), *International Law in the Twentieth Century.* New York: ASIL and Appleton-Century-Crofts.

McMahon, Edward R., and Thomas A. P. Sinclair (eds.). 2002. *Democratic Institution Performance: Research and Policy Perspectives.* Westport: Praeger.

McNamara, Robert S., and James G. Blight. 2001. *Wilson's Ghost: Reducing the Risk of Conflict, Killing, and Catastrophe in the 21st Century.* New York: PublicAffairs.

Means, Gordon P. 1995. "ASEAN Policy Responses to North American and European Trading Agreements." *New Challenges for ASEAN.* Vancouver: University of British Columbia Press.

Meier, Gerald, and Dudley Seers. 1984. *Pioneers in Development.* New York: Oxford University Press.

Meyer, John W., and Michael T. Hannan (eds.). 1979. *National Development and the World System.* Chicago: University of Chicago Press.

Mill, John Stuart. 1874. "Thoughts on Parliamentary Reform." In *Dissertations and Discussions,* vol. 4. New York: Henry Holt.

Miller, David Hunter. 1928. *The Drafting of the Covenant.* 2 vols. New York: G. P. Putnam.

Milner, Helen V. 1988. *Resisting Protectionism: Global Industries and the Politics of International Trade.* Princeton: Princeton University Press.

Minford, Patrick. 1995. "Time-Inconsistency, Democracy, and Optimal Contingent Rules." *Oxford Economic Papers* 47(2) (April): 192–210.

Mitchell, Ronald B., and Patricia M. Keilbach. 2001. "Situation Structure and Institutional Design: Reciprocity, Coercion, and Exchange." *International Organization* 55(4) (Autumn): 891–917.

Mitrany, David. 1946. *A Working Peace System.* 4th ed. London: National Peace Council.

Moe, Terry M. 1985. "The Politicized Presidency." In John Chubb and Paul E. Peterson (eds.), *New Directions in American Politics.* Washington, D.C.: Brookings Institution.

Moffitt, Michael. 1983. *The World's Money: International Banking from Bretton Woods to the Brink of Insolvency.* New York: Simon and Schuster.

Moravcsik, Andrew. 2004. "Is There a 'Democratic Deficit' in World Politics? A Framework for Analysis." *Government and Opposition* 39(2) (April): 336–362.

Morgenthau, Hans. 1971. "Emergent Problems in United States Foreign Policy." In Karl Deutsch and Stanley Hoffmann (eds.), *The Relevance of International Law.* Garden City, N.Y.: Doubleday.

Mosley, Layna. 2000. "Room to Move: International Financial Markets and National Welfare States." *International Organization* 54(4) (Autumn): 737–774.

Murphy, Craig N. 1994. *International Organization and Industrial Change: Global Governance Since 1850.* Cambridge: Polity Press.

Naldi, G (ed.). 1992. *Documents of the Organization of African Unity.* London: Mansell.

Navia, Patricio, and Thomas D. Zweifel. 2003. "Democracy Saves Children: Regimes and Infant Mortality Post–Cold War." *Journal of Democracy* 14(3) (July): 1–28.

Ndiaye, Babacar. 1992. "International Cooperation to Promote Democracy and Human Rights: Principles and Programmes." *International Commission of Jurists Review* 49(23): 25–29.

Neunreither, Karl-Heinz. 1994. "The Democratic Deficit of the European Union: Towards Closer Cooperation Between the European Parliament and the National Parliaments." *Government and Opposition* 29(3): 299–314.

Neven, Damien, Robin Nuttall, and Paul Seabright. 1993. *Mergers in Daylight: The Economics and Politics of European Merger Control.* London: Centre for Economic Policy Research.

Newcombe, Hanna. 1991. "Democratic Representation in the UN General Assembly." In Frank Barnaby (ed.), *Building a More Democratic UN: Proceedings of the First International Conference on a More Democratic UN.* London: Frank Cass.

Nicholas, H. G. 1975. *United Nations as a Political Institution.* Oxford: Oxford University Press.

Nielson, Daniel, and Michael Tierney. 2001. "Principals and Interests: Agency Theory and Multilateral Development Bank Lending Since 1980." Unpublished paper.

Noll, Roger G. 1989. "Economic Perspectives on the Politics of Regulation." In R. Schmalensee and R. D. Willing, *Handbook of Industrial Organization,* vol. 11. Amsterdam: Elsevier Science.

Norris, Pippa. 2000. "Global Governance and Cosmopolitan Citizens." In Joseph S. Nye and John D. Donahue (eds.), *Governance in a Globalizing World.* Washington, D.C.: Brookings Institution.

North, Douglass C. 1990. *Institutions, Institutional Change and Economic Performance.* Cambridge: Cambridge University Press.

Nugent, Neill. 1994. *The Government and Politics of the European Union.* 3rd ed. Durham, N.C.: Duke University Press.

———. 1995. "The Leadership Capacity of the European Commission." *Journal of European Public Policy* 2(4) (December): 603–623.

Nussbaum, Arthur. 1954. *A Concise History of the Law of Nations.* Rev. ed. New York: Macmillan.

Nye, Joseph S., Jr. 2001. "Globalization's Democratic Deficit: How to Make International Institutions More Accountable." *Foreign Affairs* 80(4) (July–August): 2–6.

———. 2002. *The Paradox of American Power: Why the World's Only Superpower Can't Go It Alone.* Oxford: Oxford University Press.

Nye, Joseph S., and John D. Donahue (eds.). 2000. *Governance in a Globalizing World.* Washington, D.C.: Brookings Institution.

O'Brien, David. 1999. "Regional Burden-Sharing for Humanitarian Action." Discussion paper. New York: Center on International Cooperation, New York University.

———. 2000. "A Geographically-Based Introduction to Regional Intergovernmental Organizations." Discussion paper. New York: Center on International Cooperation, New York University.

O'Brien, Richard. 1992. *Global Financial Integration: The End of Geography.* New York: Council on Foreign Relations Press.

O'Brien, Robert, Anne Marie Goetz, Jan Aart Scholte, and Marc Williams. 2000. *Contesting Global Governance: Multilateral Economic Institutions and Global Social Movements.* Cambridge: Cambridge University Press.

O'Connell, Daniel Patrick. 1970. *International Law.* 2nd ed., vol. 1. London: Stevens.

Ohmae, Kenichi. 1990. *The Borderless World. Power and Strategy in an Interlinked Economy.* New York: Harper.

Oppenheim, Lassa F. L. 1912. *International Law: A Treatise.* Vol. 1, *Peace.* Vol. 2, *War and Neutrality.* 2nd ed. London: Longmans Green.

———. 1921. *The Future of International Law.* Oxford: Clarendon Press.

Ortega Carcelén, Martin C. 1991. "La Reforma de la Carta de Naciones Unidas: Algunas Propuestas Institucionales" [The Reform of the United Nations Charter: Some Institutional Proposals]. *Revista Española de Derecho Internacional* 43.

Palmeter, David, and Petros C. Mavroidis. 1998. "The WTO Legal System: Sources of Law." *American Journal of International Law* 92(3) (July): 398–413.

Pastor, Robert. 2001. *Toward a North American Community.* Washington, D.C.: Institute for International Economics.

Persson, Torsten, Gérard Roland, and Guido Tabellini. 1996. "Separation of Powers and Accountability: Towards a Formal Approach to Comparative Politics." Discussion Paper no. 1475. London: Centre for Economic Policy Research, September.

Peters, B. Guy. 1994. "Agenda-Setting in the European Community." *Journal of European Public Policy* 1(1): 9–26.

Peterson, John. 1995. "Decision-Making in the European Union: Towards a Framework for Analysis." *Journal of European Public Policy* 2(1) (March): 69–93.

Peterson, M. J. 1992. "Whalers, Cetologists, Environmentalists, and the International Management of Whaling." *International Organization* 46 (Winter): 149–158.

Pettifor, Ann. 2002. "Resolving International Debt Crises: The Jubilee Framework for International Insolvency." London: New Economics Foundation, January.

Pitkin, Hanna F. 1967. *The Concept of Representation.* Berkeley: University of California Press.

Plamenatz, John. 1973. *Democracy and Illusion.* London: Longman.

Polak, Jacques J. 1998. "IMF Study Group Report: Transparency and Evaluation: Report and Recommendations by a Special Study Group Convened by the Center of Concern." Washington, D.C.: Center of Concern, April.

Pollack, Mark A. 1997. "Representing Diffuse Interests in EC Policy-Making." *Journal of European Public Policy* 4(4) (December): 572–590.

Pollack, Mark A., and Gregory C. Shaffer (eds.). 2001. *Transatlantic Governance in the Global Economy.* Lanham: Rowman and Littlefield.

Popper, Karl R. 1987. "Zur Theorie der Demokratie" [On the Theory of Democracy]. *Der Spiegel* 32(3) (August): 54–55.

Prahalad, C. K., and Kenneth Lieberthal. 1998. "The End of Corporate Imperialism." *Harvard Business Review* (July–August): 69–79.

Przeworski, Adam. 1991. *Democracy and the Market.* Cambridge: Cambridge University Press.

Pufendorf, Samuel. 1927 [1682]. *De Officio Hominis et Civis Juxta Legem Naturalem Libri Duo* [On the Duty of Man and Citizen Linked (with) Natural Law]. 2 vols. (vol 1: text of 1682 ed.; vol 2: translation of 1688 ed. by Frank Gardner Moore). New York: Oxford University Press.

———. 1931 [1660]. *Elementorum Jurisprudentiae Universalis Libri Duo.* 2 vols. (vol 1: text of 1672 ed.; vol. 2: translation of 1672 ed. by W. A. Oldfather). Oxford: Clarendon Press.

———. 1935 [1672]. *De Jure Naturae et Gentium Libri Octo* [On the Law of Nature and Peoples]. 2 vols. (vol. 1: text of 1688 ed.; vol 2: translation of 1688 ed. by C. H. and W. A. Oldfather). Oxford: Clarendon Press.

Putnam, Robert D. 1988. "Diplomacy and Domestic Politics: The Logic of Two-Level Games." *International Organization* 42(3) (Summer): 427–460.

Ratner, Steven R., and Jason S. Abrams. 2001. *Accountability for Human Rights Atrocities in International Law: Beyond the Nuremberg Legacy.* 2nd ed. Oxford: Oxford University Press.

Raustiala, Kal. 1997. "The 'Participatory Revolution' in International Environmental Law." *Harvard Environmental Law Review* 21(2): 537–586.

Rawls, John. 1993. *Political Liberalism.* New York: Columbia University Press.

Reinalda, Bob. 2001. "Decision Making Within International Organizations: An Overview of Approaches and Case Studies." Paper prepared for the European Consortium for Political Research (ECPR), Grenoble, France, April 6–11.

Reinicke, Wolfgang H. 1998. *Global Public Policy: Governing Without Government.* Washington, D.C.: Brookings Institution.

———. 1999–2000. "The Other World Wide Web: Global Public Policy Networks." *Foreign Policy* no. 117 (Winter): 44–57.

Reisman, Michael. 1990. "Sovereignty and Human Rights in Contemporary International Law." *American Journal of International Law* 84: 867.

———. 1993. "The Constitutional Crisis in the United Nations." *American Journal of International Law* 87: 83–99.

Rhodes, R. A. W. 1997. *Understanding Governance: Policy Networks, Governance, Reflexivity, and Accountability.* Buckingham, UK: Open University Press.

Rich, Bruce. 1990. "The Emperor's New Clothes: The World Bank and Environmental Reform." *World Policy Journal* 7(2) (Spring): 305–330.

———. 1994. *Mortgaging the Earth: The World Bank, Environmental Impoverishment, and the Crisis of Development.* Boston: Beacon Press.

Rich, Paul. 2000. "The Peripheralization of Africa in Global Politics." In Sagarika Dutt and Bakut Tswah Bakut (eds.), *Africa at the Millennium: An Agenda for Mature Development.* New York: Palgrave.

Ritchie, Mark, Suzanne Wisniewski, and Sophia Murphy. 2000. "Dumping as a Structural Feature of US Agriculture: Can WTO Rules Solve the Problem?" Minneapolis: Institute for Agriculture and Trade Policy.

Roberts, Alasdair. 2004. "A Partial Revolution: The Diplomatic Ethos and Transparency in Intergovernmental Organizations." *Public Administration Review* 64(4) (July–August): 410–424.

Rodrik, Dani. 1996a. "Understanding Economic Policy Reform." *Journal of*

Economic Literature 34 (March): 9–41.

———. 1996b. "Why Do More Open Economies Have Bigger Governments?" Working Paper no. 5537. Cambridge, Mass.: National Bureau of Economic Research.

———. 1997. *Has Globalization Gone Too Far?* Washington, D.C.: Institute for International Economics.

———. 1999. "The New Global Economy and Developing Countries: Making Openness Work." ODC Policy Essay no. 24. Washington, D.C.: Overseas Development Council.

———. 2001. "The Global Governance of Trade as If Development Really Mattered." Background paper. New York: United Nations Development Programme, October.

Rogowski. Ronald. 1989. *Commerce and Coalitions: How Trade Affects Domestic Political Alignments.* Princeton: Princeton University Press.

Rose-Ackerman, Susan. 1992. *Rethinking the Progressive Agenda: The Reform of the American Regulatory State.* New York: Free Press.

Rosenau, James N. 1998. "Governance and Democracy in a Globalizing World." In Daniele Archibugi, David Held, and Martin Köhler (eds.), *Reimagining Political Community: Studies in Cosmopolitan Democracy.* Stanford: Stanford University Press.

Rosenau, James N., and Ernst-Otto Czempiel. 1992. *Governance Without Government: Order and Change in World Politics.* Cambridge: Cambridge University Press.

Ross, George. 1995. "Assessing the Delors Era and Social Policy." In Stephan Leibfried and Paul Pierson (eds.), *European Social Policy: Between Fragmentation and Integration.* Washington, D.C.: Brookings Institution.

Rousseau, Jean-Jacques. 1905–1912. *Œuvres Complètes* [Complete Works]. Paris: Librairie Hachette.

Rowat, Malcolm. 1997. *Competition Policy and Mercosur.* Washington, D.C.: World Bank.

Ruggie, John G. 1983. "Continuity and Transformation in the World Polity: Toward a Neorealist Synthesis." *World Politics* 35 (January): 261–285.

———. 1993. "Territoriality and Beyond: Problematizing Modernity in International Relations." *International Organization* 47(1) (Winter): 139–174.

———. (ed.). 1993. *Multilateralism Matters.* New York: Columbia University Press.

Russett, Bruce, and John Oneal. 2001. *Triangulating Peace: Democracy, Interdependence, and International Organizations.* New York: W. W. Norton.

Sachs, Jeffrey. 1995. "Do We Need an International Lender of Last Resort?" Frank D. Graham Lecture, Princeton University, April 20.

Sachs, Jeffrey, and Andrew M. Warner. 1995. "Economic Reform and the Process of Global Integration." Papers on Economic Activity no. 1. Washington, D.C.: Brookings Institution.

Sanchez de Cuenca, Ignacio. 1997. "The Democratic Dilemmas of the European Union." Manuscript.

Sbragia, Alberta M. (ed.). 1992. *Euro-Politics: Institutions and Policy-Making in the New European Community.* Washington, D.C.: Brookings Institution.

Scharpf, Fritz W. 1988. "The Joint-Decision Trap: Lessons from German Federalism and European Integration." *Public Administration* 66(3): 239–278.

———. 1997a. "Economic Integration, Democracy, and the Welfare State." *Journal of European Public Policy* 4(2) (March): 219–242.

————. 1997b. *Games Real Actors Play: Actor-Centered Institutionalism in Policy Research.* Boulder: Westview.

————. 1997c. "Introduction: The Problem-Solving Capacity of Multi-Level Governance." *Journal of European Public Policy* 4(4) (December): 520–538.

————. 1999. *Governing in Europe: Effective and Democratic?* Oxford: Oxford University Press.

Schiffer, Walter. 1954. *The Legal Community of Mankind.* New York: Columbia University Press.

Schmidt, Susanne. 1998. "Commission Activism: Subsuming Telecommunications and Electricity Under European Competition Law." *Journal of European Public Policy* 5(1) (March): 169–184.

Schott, Jeffrey J., and Jayashree Watal. 2000. "Decision-Making in the WTO." Washington, D.C.: Institute for International Economics, March.

Schultze, Charles L. 1968. *The Politics and Economics of Public Spending.* Washington, D.C.: Brookings Institution.

Schumpeter, Joseph S. 1976 [1942]. *Capitalism, Socialism, and Democracy.* New York: Harper Torchbook.

Scott, Nancy F. 1994. "Early Twentieth Century Feminism in Political Context: A Comparative Look at Germany and the United States." In Caroline Daley and Melanie Nolan (eds.), *Suffrage and Beyond: International Feminist Perspectives.* New York: New York University Press.

Seabright, Paul. 1996. "Accountability and Decentralization in Government: An Incomplete Contracts Model." *European Economic Review* 40(1): 61–89.

Seidman, Harold, and Robert Gilmour. 1986. *Politics, Position, and Power.* 4th ed. New York: Oxford University Press.

Sen, Amartya. 1999. *Development as Freedom.* New York: Knopf.

Shapiro, Martin. 1988. *Who Guards the Guardians? Judicial Control of Administration.* Athens: University of Georgia Press.

————. 1992. "The Giving-Reasons Requirement." Paper read at the University of Chicago Legal Forum.

————. 1997. "The Problems of Independent Agencies in the United States and the European Union." *Journal of European Public Policy* 4(2) (June): 276–291.

Shaw, Martin. 1997. "The State of Globalization: Towards a Theory of State Transformation." *Review of International Political Economy* 4(3): 472–496.

Shepsle, Kenneth A., and Barry R. Weingast. 1987. "The Institutional Foundations of Committee Power." *American Political Science Review* 81(3): 85–104.

Shiller, Robert. 2000. *Irrational Exuberance.* Princeton: Princeton University Press.

Sieghart, Paul. 1985. *The Lawful Rights of Mankind: An Introduction to the International Legal Code of Human Rights.* Oxford: Oxford University Press.

Simmons, Beth A. 2000. "The Legalization of International Monetary Affairs." *International Organization* 54(3) (Summer): 573–602.

Simon, Herbert A. 1996. *The Sciences of the Artificial.* 3rd ed. Cambridge: MIT Press.

Singer, Peter. 2002. *The Ethics of Globalization.* New Haven: Yale University Press.

Slaughter, Anne-Marie. 2000. "Governing the Global Economy Through Governance Networks." In Michael Byers (ed.), *The Role of Law in International Politics: Essays in International Relations and International Law.* Oxford: Oxford University Press.

Slomanson, William R. 1995. *Fundamental Perspectives on International Law.* Saint Paul, Minn.: West.

Staudt, Kathleen (ed.). 1997. *Women, International Development, and Politics: The Bureaucratic Mire.* Philadelphia: Temple University Press.

Stein, Eric. 2001. "International Integration and Democracy: No Love at First Sight." *American Journal of International Law* 95(3) (July): 489–534.

Stephan, Paul B. 1996–1997. "Accountability and International Lawmaking: Rules, Rents, and Legitimacy." *Northwestern University School of Law Journal of International Law and Business* 17(2–3) (Winter–Spring): 681.

———. 1999. "Legitimacy, Accountability, Authority, and Freedom in the New Global Order." *University of Colorado Law Review* 70(4) (Fall): 1089–1594.

Stiglitz, Joseph E. 1999. "On Liberty, the Right to Know, and Public Discourse: The Role of Transparency in Public Life." Oxford Amnesty Lecture, January 27.

———. 2000. "The Insider: What I Learned at the World Economic Crisis." *New Republic,* April 17 and April 24.

———. 2002a. *Globalization and Its Discontents.* New York: W. W. Norton.

———. 2002b. "A Second Chance for Brazil and the IMF." *New York Times,* August 13. Available at http://www.globalpolicy.org/socecon/bwi-wto/imf/2002/0813stiglitz.htm.

Stokes, B. 1990. "Reinventing the Bank." *National Journal* 25(38) (September): 232–2236.

Stone, Deborah A. 1989. "Causal Stories and the Formation of Policy Agendas." *Political Science Quarterly* 104(2): 281–300.

Stone, Julius. 1954. *Legal Controls of International Conflict.* New York: Rinehart.

Strange, Susan. 1994. "Wake Up, Krasner! The World Has Changed." *Review of International Political Economy* 21(2): 209–219.

———. 1996. *The Retreat of the State: The Diffusion of Power in the World Economy.* Cambridge: Cambridge University Press.

Streeck, Wolfgang. 1996. "Neo-Voluntarism: A New European Social Policy Regime?" In G. Marks, F. W. Scharpf, P. C. Schmitter, and W. Streeck (eds.), *Governance in the European Union.* London: Sage.

———. 1997. "Industrial Citizenship Under Regime Competition: The Case of the European Works Councils." *Journal of European Public Policy* 4(4) (December): 643–664.

Streeck, Wolfgang, and Philippe C. Schmitter. 1991. "From National Corporatism to Transnational Pluralism: Organized Interests in the Single European Market." *Politics and Society* 19(2): 133–164.

Strong, Maurice. 1989. "Ending Hunger Through Sustainable Development." Third Arturo Tanco Memorial Lecture, Tokyo, April.

Sunstein, Cass R. 1990. *After the Rights Revolution: Reconceiving the Regulatory State.* Cambridge: Harvard University Press.

Sutherland, S. L. 1993. "Independent Review Agencies and Accountability: Should Democracy Be on Autopilot?" *Optimum* 24(2): 23–40.

Tannenwald, Nina. 1999. "The Nuclear Taboo: The United States and the Normative Basis of Nuclear Non-Use." *International Organization* 53(3) (Summer): 433–468.

Tanzi, Vito. 1997. "The Changing Role of the State in the Economy: A Historical Perspective." Draft seminar paper presented at the OECD-ESAF seminar "Decentralization, Intergovernmental Fiscal Relations, and Macroeconomic Governance," Brasília, Brazil, May 30.

Thomas, George, John Meyer, Francisco Ramirez, and John Boli (eds.). 1987. *Institutional Structure: Constituting State, Society, and Individual.* Newbury Park, Calif.: Sage.

Thompson, Janna. 1998. "Community Identity and World Citizenship." In Daniele Archibugi, David Held, and Martin Köhler (eds.), *Reimagining Political Community: Studies in Cosmopolitan Democracy.* Stanford: Stanford University Press.

Tinbergen, Jan. 1965. *International Economic Integration.* 2nd ed. Amsterdam: Elsevier.

Trachtman, Joel P. 1996. "The Theory of the Firm and the Theory of International Economic Organization: Toward Comparative Institutional Analysis." Unpublished manuscript.

Tsebelis, George, and Geofffrey Garrett. 2001. "The Institutional Foundations of Intergovernmentalism and Supranationalism in the European Union." *International Organization* 55(2) (Spring): 357–390.

United Nations. 1995. "Secretary-General Reflects on Global Prospect for United Nations." Address to annual meeting of the World Economic Forum, Davos, January.

United Nations Association of the USA. 2002. *A Global Agenda: Issues Before the 56th General Assembly of the United Nations.* Edited by Diana Ayton-Shenker and John Tessitore. Lanham: Rowman and Littlefield.

United Nations Population Division. 1998. *Briefing Packet: 1998 Revision of World Population Prospects.* New York.

US Senate. 1919. *Addresses of President Wilson . . . on His Western Tour, September 4 to September 25, 1919, on the League of Nations, Treaty of Peace with Germany.* 66th Congress, 1st session.

van der Krol, A. R., P. E. Lenting, J. Veenstra, I. M. van der Meer, R. E. Koes, A. G. M. Gerats, J. N. M. Mol, and A. R. Stuitje. 1988. "An Anti-Sense Chalcone Synthase Gene in Transgenic Plants Inhibits Flower Pigmentation." *Nature* 333: 866–869.

Vaubel, Roland. 1995. *The Centralization of Western Europe.* Hobart Paper no. 127. London: Institute of Economic Affairs.

Victor, David G. 1998. "The Operation and Effectiveness of the Montreal Protocol's Noncompliance Procedure." In David G. Victor, Kal Raustiala, and Eugene B. Skolnikoff (eds.), *The Implementation and Effectiveness of International Environmental Commitments.* Cambridge: MIT Press.

Vogel, David. 1995. *Trading Up: Consumer and Environmental Regulation in a Global Economy.* Cambridge: Harvard University Press.

Volcansek, Mary L. 1992. "The European Court of Justice: Supranational Policy-Making." *West European Politics* 15(3): 109–121.

Walker, R. B. J. 1990. "Sovereignty, Identity, Community." In R. B. J. Walker and S. Mendlovitz (eds.), *Contending Sovereignties.* Boulder: Lynne Rienner.

Wallach, Lori. 1999. *Whose Trade Organization? Corporate Globalization and the Erosion of Democracy.* Washington, D.C.: Public Citizen.

Wallach, Lori, and Michelle Sforza. 1999. *The WTO: Five Years of Reasons to Resist Corporate Globalization.* New York: Seven Stories Press.

Wallerstein, Immanuel. 1974. *The Modern World-System: Capitalist Agriculture and the Origins of the European World-Economy in the Sixteenth Century.* New York: Academic Press.

———. 1980. *The Modern World-System II: Mercantilism and the Consolidation of the European World-Economy, 1600–1750.* New York: Academic Press.

Waltz, Kenneth N. 1979. *Theory of International Politics.* Reading, Mass.: Addison-Wesley.

Warren, Charles. 1991. "Legislative and Judicial Attacks on the Supreme Court of the United States—A History of the Twenty-Fifth Section of the Judiciary Act." *American Law Review* 47.

Washington Office on Africa. 1997 "Africans Must Have Voice in Economic Policy Making." Available at http://www.africanews.org/specials/19970611-feat1.html.

Weber, Eugen Joseph. 1976. *Peasants into Frenchmen: The Modernization of Rural France, 1870–1914.* Stanford: Stanford University Press.

Weber, Max. 1946. "Bureaucracy." In Hans H. Gerth and C. Wright Mills (eds.), *From Max Weber: Essays in Sociology.* Oxford: Oxford University Press.

Webster, Douglas. 1995. "Managing the Environment in ASEAN: The Case of Extended Urban Regions." In Amitav Acharga and Richard Stubbs (eds.), *New Challenges for ASEAN: Emerging Policy Issues.* Vancouver: University of British Columbia Press.

Wehr, Elizabeth. 1986. "Congress Clears $576 Billion Spending Measure." *Congressional Quarterly Weekly Report* 43: 1863.

Weiler, Joseph H. H. 1991. "Problems of Legitimacy in Post-1992 Europe." *Aussenwirtschaft* 46(3–4): 411–437.

———. 1992. "After Maastricht: Community Legitimacy in Post-1992 Europe." In William James Adams (ed.), *Singular Europe: Economy and Polity of the European Community After 1992.* Ann Arbor: University of Michigan Press.

———. 1997. "To Be a European Citizen: Eros and Civilization." *Journal of European Public Policy* 4(4) (December): 495–519.

———. 1999. *The Constitution of Europe.* Cambridge: Cambridge University Press.

Weiler, Joseph H. H., Ulrich Haltern, and Franz Mayer. 1995. "European Democracy and Its Critique." *West European Politics* 18(3): 4–39.

Weinstein, Michael M., and Steve Charnovitz. 2001. "The Greening of the WTO." *Foreign Affairs* 80(6) (November–December): 147–156.

Weinstock, Daniel M. 2001. "Prospects for Transnational Citizenship and Democracy." *Ethics & International Affairs* 15(2): 53–66.

Weintraub, Sidney. 1997. *NAFTA at Three: A Progressive Report.* Washington, D.C.: Center for Strategic and International Studies.

Weiss, Linda 1998. *The Myth of the Powerless State.* Ithaca: Cornell University Press.

Wendt, Alexander. 1992. "Anarchy Is What States Make of It: The Social Construction of Power Politics." *International Organization* 46(2): 391–425.

———. 1994. "Collective Identity Formation and the International State." *American Political Science Review* 88(2) (June): 384–396.

———. 2001. "Driving with the Rearview Mirror: On the Rational Science of Institutional Design." *International Organization* 55(4) (Autumn): 1019–1049.

Whitworth, Sandra. 1994. *Feminism and International Relations: Toward a Political Economy of Gender in Interstate and Nongovernmental Institutions.* Basingstoke: Macmillan Press.

Wildavsky, Aaron. 1964. *The Politics of the Budgetary Process.* Boston: Little, Brown.

Williams, Shirley. 1991. "Sovereignty and Accountability in the European Community." In Robert O. Keohane and Stanley Hoffmann (eds.), *The New European Community.* Boulder: Westview.

Williamson, John. 1990. *Latin American Adjustment: How Much Has Happened?* Washington, D.C.: Institute for International Economics, Washington D.C.

Williamson, Oliver E. 1985. *The Economic Institutions of Capitalism.* New York: Free Press.

Wincott, Daniel. 1995. "The Role of Law or the Rule of the Court of Justice? An 'Institutional' Account of Judicial Politics in the European Community." *Journal of European Public Policy* 2(4) (December): 583–602.

Winslow, Anne (ed.). 1995. *Women, Politics, and the United Nations.* Westport: Greenwood.

Wohlforth, William C. 1999. "The Stability of a Unipolar World." *International Security* 24(1) (Summer): 5–41.

Wolff, Christian. 1934 [1764]. *Jus Gentium Methodo Scientifica Pertractatum* [The Law of Peoples Through the Scientific Method, a Tractate]. 2 vols. (vol. 1: text of 1764 ed.; vol. 2: translation of 1764 ed. by Joseph H. Drake). Oxford: Clarendon Press.

Wood, B. Dan, and Richard Waterman. 1994. *Bureaucratic Dynamics: The Role of Bureaucracy in a Democracy.* Boulder: Westview.

Wood, Robert Chapman, and Gary Hamel. 2002. "The World Bank's Innovation Market." *Harvard Business Review* 80(11) (November): 104–111.

Woods, Ngaire. 2003. "Unelected Government: Making the IMF and the World Bank More Accountable." *International Affairs* 21(2): 9–12.

Woods, Ngaire, and Amrita Narlikar. 2001. "Governance and the Limits of Accountability: The WTO, the IMF, and the World Bank." *International Social Science Journal* 170 (November): 569–583.

World Bank. 1997. "Health, Nutrition, and Population." Sector strategy paper. Washington, D.C.

———. 1999. "World Bank Approves Controversial Proposal to Change Inspection Panel." Washington, D.C.: Bank Information Center, and Center for International Environmental Law, April 21. Available at http://www.ciel.org.

———. 2002. "The Role and Effect of Development Assistance: Lessons from the World Bank Experience." Washington, D.C., March. Available at http://econom.worldbank.org.

World Trade Organization. 2001. "WTO Policy Issues for Parliamentarians: A Guide to Current Trade Issues for Legislators." Geneva, May.

Woronoff, Jon. 1970. *Organizing African Unity.* Metuchen, N.J.: Scarecrow Press.

Young, Alasdair R. 1995. "Participation and Policymaking in the European Community: Mediating Contending Interests." Paper presented at the biannual conference of the European Community Studies Association, Charleston, S.C., May 11–14.

Zimmermann, Michael. 1933. "La Crise de l'Organisation Internationale à la Fin du Moyen Âge" [The Crisis of International Organization at the End of the Middle Ages]. Recueil des Cours, Académie de Droit International [Course Collection, Academy of International Law] 44(2).

Ziring, Lawrence, Robert E. Riggs, and Jack C. Plano. 1994. *The United Nations: International Organization and World Politics.* 2nd ed. Belmont, Calif.: Wadsworth.

Zurn, Michael. 2000. "Democratic Governance Beyond the Nation State: The EU and Other International Institutions." *European Journal of International Relations* 6(2) (June): 182–183.

Zweifel, Thomas D. 2002a. *Democratic Deficit? Institutions and Regulation in the European Union, Switzerland, and the United States.* Lanham: Lexington Books/Rowman and Littlefield.

———. 2002b. ". . . Who Is Innocent Cast the First Stone: The EU's Democratic Deficit in Comparison." *Journal of European Public Policy* 9(5) (October): 812–840.

———. 2003. "Best and Worst Practices in European, US, and Swiss Merger Regulation." *Journal of Common Market Studies* 41(3) (June): 541–566.

Zweifel, Thomas D., and Patricio Navia. 2000. "Democracy, Dictatorship, and Infant Mortality." *Journal of Democracy* 11(2) (April): 99–114.

Index

About the Book

D o international organizations represent the interests of the global citizenry? Or are they merely vehicles for the agendas of powerful nations and multinational corporations? Thomas D. Zweifel explores this increasingly contentious issue, deftly blending history, theory, and case studies.

Zweifel's analysis covers both regional organizations (e.g., the EU, NAFTA, NATO, the AU) and such global institutions as the United Nations, the World Bank, and the World Trade Organization. With international organizations becoming perhaps the most appropriate—if not the only—forum for tackling myriad transnational challenges, his study of how these organizations function is central to understanding international relations.

Thomas D. Zweifel, CEO of Swiss Consulting Group, is also adjunct professor at Columbia University's School of International and Public Affairs. His recent publications include *Democratic Deficit? Institutions and Regulation in the European Union, Switzerland, and the United States* and *Culture Clash: Managing the Global High-Performance Team.*